Runaway College Costs

Runaway College Costs

How College Governing Boards Fail to Protect Their Students

James V. Koch and Richard J. Cebula

Johns Hopkins University Press | Baltimore

Printed in the United States of America on acid-free paper
9 8 7 6 5 4 3 2 1

Johns Hopkins University Press
2715 North Charles Street
Baltimore, Maryland 21218-4363
www.press.jhu.edu

Library of Congress Cataloging-in-Publication Data

Names: Koch, James V., 1942- author. | Cebula, Richard J., author.
Title: Runaway college costs : How college governing boards fail to protect their students / James V. Koch and Richard J. Cebula.
Description: Baltimore : Johns Hopkins University Press, 2020. | Includes bibliographical references and index.
Identifiers: LCCN 2019057273 | ISBN 9781421438887 (hardcover) | ISBN 9781421438894 (ebook)
Subjects: LCSH: Public universities and colleges—United States—Finance. | Public universities and colleges—United States—Administration. | College trustees—United States. | College costs—United States. | Tuition—United States. | Education, Higher—Economic aspects—United States. | Higher education and state—United States.
Classification: LCC LB2342 .K59 2020 | DDC 378.3/8—dc23
LC record available at https://lccn.loc.gov/2019057273

A catalog record for this book is available from the British Library.

Special discounts are available for bulk purchases of this book. For more information, please contact Special Sales at specialsales@press.jhu.edu.

Johns Hopkins University Press uses environmentally friendly book materials, including recycled text paper that is composed of at least 30 percent post-consumer waste, whenever possible.

Contents

Preface

As economists, each of us has written a dozen or more books. This volume, however, is one that we felt we *had* to write before matters spin irretrievably out of control in American public colleges and universities. In this book, we illuminate the complicity of American colleges and universities and their governing boards in fatefully modifying or destroying the American Dream.

Historically, public institutions of higher education have functioned as springboards of opportunity enabling individuals to move upward in American society, their progress limited only by their own ambition and talent. Individuals such as Henry Kissinger and Colin Powell graduated from City College in New York City, while on the other coast, Steve Wozniak and Daniel Kahneman are products of the University of California, Berkeley. Historically black colleges and universities generated Martin Luther King Jr. and Oprah Winfrey.

Public colleges and universities consistently opened doors, provided opportunities, and enabled individuals to rise above often challenging circumstances. The result was a vibrant, opportunity-oriented society that was the envy of the world.

Alas, times have changed. Public higher education has evolved into an engine that accentuates rather than reduces social and economic inequality. Student bodies have increasingly become stratified on the basis of income, because public university governing bodies have often failed to act as fiduciaries protecting the interests of the public and students.

Indeed, it appears that 99 percent of all administrative proposals to increase tuition fees are approved unanimously by public college governing boards in the thrall of presidents and senior administrators. Boards incentivize their presidents to increase enrollment, bring in more gifts and research funding, and improve their institution's ratings. Access, affordability, income mobility, student debt, and student learning are seldom included as essential evaluative criteria. Presidents and institutions behave accordingly.

Meanwhile, between 1999–2000 and 2017–18, the average number of hours a typical nonsupervisory worker had to labor in order to pay average annual tuition and fees at a four-year public institution increased from 224 to 446. One can almost see the ideal of American social mobility evaporating into the ether.

But all is not lost. Concerted action, especially at the state level, can steady the higher education ship. We discuss the available possibilities in detail, knowing well that our prescriptions likely will inspire opposition from the higher education establishment. However, the stakes are enormous. We are dealing with the future viability of American society.

Acknowledgments

James V. Koch

This book could not have come to fruition without the support and cooperation of many individuals and organizations. They cannot all be thanked, but among the most influential individuals have been Donna Koch, John Broderick, Jeff Tanner, Helen Dragas, Don Zimmerman, James Toscano, Rich DeMillo, Pat Callan, Dave Harnage, and Ziniya Zahedi. I have been blessed with a series of productive mentors, including Jim Fisher, David Sweet, Sam Braden, Eleanor McMahon, Bob Bell, John Worthen, George Dragas, Dick Barry, and Arthur Diamonstein. Over the years, I tested many ideas with them and benefited from their energy and guidance.

Richard J. Cebula

I am grateful for the loving patience of my wife, Gigi, and for the companionship of Lilly and Angel; my loving children, Christie, Ken, and David; and my loving grandsons, Jeffrey, Richard, Ryan, and Zach. I am also grateful for the mentorship afforded me by John Klein, Rich Vedder, Jim Buchanan, Gordon Tullock, and Jim Barth.

Jointly, we would like to acknowledge Greg Britton, Charles Dibble, and Hilary Jacqmin of Johns Hopkins University Press, the skillful editing of Heidi Fritschel, and the continuing support of the Strome College of Business at Old Dominion University.

Mistakes, errors, and omissions remain our responsibility.

Runaway College Costs

1 Their Answer Is Always Yes
Higher Education Cost Inflation and Governing Boards

Public opinion of higher education is at an all-time low.

Jeffrey Selingo, *Washington Post,* July 17, 2017

Public faith in higher education has waned in recent years. As Jeffrey Selingo of the *Washington Post* and Arizona State University aptly phrased it, "Americans love higher education, just not their universities."[1] Colleges and universities are thought by many to be out of touch with job markets, not particularly well managed, bloated with administrators, burdened with an antiquated system of faculty tenure, too expensive, and perhaps hothouses for indoctrination by either leftists or capitalists.[2]

The 2019 college admissions scandal generated a wave of negative media coverage for universities, not least because the list of alleged malefactors included prominent flagship state universities and elite private institutions. The revelations unleashed a torrent of outrage directed at many institutions of higher education, and the decline in confidence in higher education was perceptible and unambiguous. A *Washington Post* op-ed intoned, "College admissions are corrupt because universities are."[3] Even institutions not believed to be involved in the events quickly crouched into defensive public relations positions to ward off new critics.

The fall in esteem of public higher education has been reflected in other ways as well. A 2017 Gallup poll reported that only 2 percent of Republicans and 5 percent of Democrats believed colleges were training students to think for themselves.[4] A *Consumer Reports* survey revealed that 45 percent of college graduates who left college with student debt say that college was not worth the cost.[5] Meanwhile, even before COVID-19, Moody's predicted that a wave of institutions will be forced to close their doors.[6]

At the same time, paying for a public college education has become increasingly difficult for many families. In January 2000, the median hourly wage paid to a typical production or nonsupervisory worker in the United States was $13.95, while the average tuition and fee charge at a four-year public college or university was $3,360. Fast-forward to January 2018. The median hourly wage for this representative worker had risen to $22.34, but the average tuition and fee charge had vaulted upward to $9,980. For a typical employee in 1999–2000, covering the cost of average tuition and fees took 244.4 hours of work; by January 2018, covering this cost required 446.7 hours of work—an 82.3 percent increase (fig. 1.1).[7] Little imagination is required to visualize the prospect of college attendance gradually disappearing into the mist for many students and their families.

The College Board tells us that in the twenty-five-year period between 1992–93 and 2017–18, the average advertised sum of tuition and fees per full-time equivalent (FTE) student rose 328.3 percent (145.7 percent in inflation-adjusted terms).[8] This is an important factor explaining why student debt spiraled upward to $1.46 trillion by the fourth quarter of 2018—an amazing 461 percent higher than in the first quarter of 2004.[9] Net student debt rose by $79 billion in 2018 alone.[10] Rising inflation-adjusted prices and increasing student debt at least partially explain why headcount undergraduate enrollment in America's colleges and universities fell eight years in a row (2011–18).[11]

In early 2017, relying upon a seminal National Bureau of Economic Research study, the *New York Times* published eye-opening data relating to the college graduating classes of 2013. The *Times* article reported the share of college students who came from the top 1 percent of the nation's household income distribution and the share from the bottom 60 percent of the household income distribution.[12] At the University of Michigan, Ann Arbor, for example, 9.3 percent of undergraduate students came from households in the top one percent of the income distribution, while only 16.5 percent came from the entire bottom 60 percent of the income distribution. At the University of Virginia, those shares were 8.5 percent and 15.0 percent, respectively.

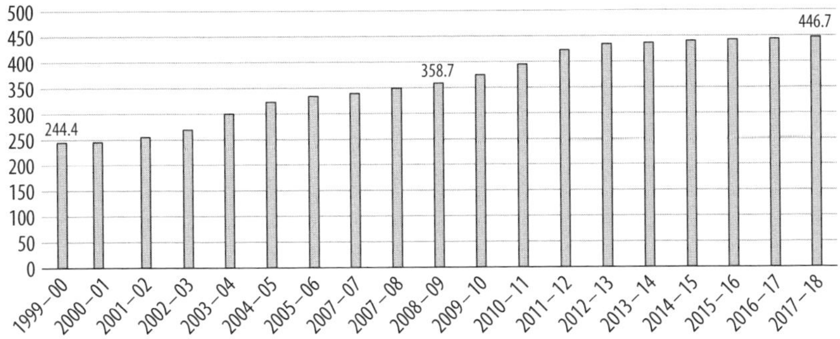

Figure 1.1. Number of Hours of Work Required for a Typical Manufacturing or Nonsupervisory Worker to Pay Average Four-Year Public In-State Tuition and Fees, 1999–2000 to 2017–18. *Sources:* US Bureau of Labor Statistics, "Employment, Hours, and Earnings from the Current Employment Statistics Survey (National)," Series CES0500000008, https://data.bls.gov/timeseries/CES0500000008, for wage rates; College Board, *Trends in College Pricing 2018* (New York: College Board, 2018), https://research.collegeboard.org/pdf/trends-college-pricing-2018-full-report.pdf, for tuition and fees.

Nor has this development been restricted to flagship institutions. At Christopher Newport University in Virginia, only 18.1 percent of undergraduates came from the lower 60 percent of the income distribution, while at New Hampshire's Keene State College, it was only 21.3 percent. The *Times* concluded that only one-half of one percent of children from the bottom one-fifth of the income distribution attended what the *Times* termed an "elite college."

Would that cost and access were the only issues confronting the boards that govern higher education institutions. More than a few campuses have had to deal with major scandals concerning intercollegiate athletics, admissions, financial aid, academic chicanery, a variety of sexual aggressions, malfeasances, and administrative or board attempts to ignore problems that did not go away. Prominent public flagship universities such as Maryland, Michigan State, Ohio State, Penn State, and the University of North Carolina at Chapel Hill were ensnared in these episodes. The academic reputations of these institutions suffered in the process, but the general standing and perceived legitimacy of higher education were injured as well.[13] Many in the media and those roaming legislative halls began to ask, "What else is happening on campuses that we don't know about?"

Additional examples would not be difficult to provide, but it will suffice for us to observe that the circumstances just described are not good omens for higher education. When comparably adverse situations arise in other large public realms (consider law enforcement or military veterans' affairs), they usually generate agitated calls for investigations and strident demands for improvement. Outside of higher education, most citizens, when confronted with subpar or confusing performance in a public service, demand to know why performance has faltered and who is or was in charge. In non-university environments, it is not unusual to find agency heads and CEOs called on the carpet and either admonished or dismissed when scandals arise. Public interest advocates or aggressive stockholders occasionally succeed in cashiering board members.

Interestingly, little of this fervor has been displayed in American higher education. As the *Wall Street Journal* headlined late 2018, "When Scandals Hit Campus, College Boards Rarely Get Hurt."[14] The public has demanded relatively little accountability of either governing boards or their members when outrages have surfaced. On rare occasions, one or two board members have resigned, but typically it has been as if the governing boards bore no responsibility for what occurred. This is remarkable in light of the seriousness of these situations. In the case of Michigan State, the university is going to pay out more than $500 million to sexual abuse victims.[15]

It is clear that the negative circumstances noted here have not contained the seeds of revolution; campuses have remained surprisingly pacific. The United States is not France, and both students and faculty are largely quiescent. No cars have been burned in the streets, and no mass strikes have been called. A few campuses have experienced violent, though unrelated, demonstrations (witness those in and around the University of Virginia), but there has been remarkably little reaction to close-to-home issues such as college costs, student debt, and student access to higher education. Campus pots may heat up, but the contents seldom come to a boil.

> College and university governance "refers to the distribution of authority and functions among the units within a larger entity, the modes of communication and control among them, and the conduct of relationships between the entity and the surrounding environment. When that entity is a contemporary US university, the conventional building blocks for governance within the university are its trustees, the executive administration, the faculty, and other groupings and units, such as student government and alumni. The traditional discussion of the basic internal and external relationships of a private university focuses on the ways boards of trustees, presidents, and numerous other actors discharge their institutional responsibilities. In the case of a public university or multi-campus university system, however, account must be made of the ties to executive and legislative branches of state government and, typically, to a higher education coordinating agency."
>
> Emil Ricci, "College and University Governance in the United States: An Historical Survey," New Foundations (1999), https://www.newfoundations.com/History/HEGovernance.html.

One reason for the pallid response to misdeeds in public higher education is that it is not entirely clear to many who is really in charge on the typical American public college or university campus. Is it the state legislature, the institution's governing board, its president, or even the faculty, who praise the notion of "shared governance"? In whose office does the proverbial rubber truly meet the road on a public university campus? Where does "the buck stop?" It is apparent that this is a mystery to many.

The reality is that either by law or by custom, authority is distributed around public college and university campuses. A variety of checks and balances exist on campuses that bear resemblance to those contained in the Constitution of the United States. Further, even when one constituency enjoys ultimate authority in an arena, it often delegates this authority to another party. For example, governing boards may possess the ultimate authority to decide which textbooks are used on a campus, but they have long since delegated this authority to campuses and therein to the faculty.

In most states, constitutions or legislatures delegate substantial authority to college and university governing boards. The members of these boards are variously known as trustees, regents, governors, visitors, curators, directors, supervisors, fellows, and overseers. Whatever their titles, however, these board members have substantial fiduciary legal responsibilities for the campuses. In nearly every instance, they must vote to approve institutional budgets and tuition and fee charges. In general, in public higher education, administrators may propose, but boards ultimately dispose, where budgets and tuition and fees are concerned.

Consider the case of the University of South Carolina (USC). Between 1998–99 and 2017–18 the advertised, annual sticker-price tuition and fees for in-state undergraduates on the flagship Columbia campus rose 235.5 percent (123.7 percent in real terms).[16] Nineteen years in a row, USC's Board of Trustees approved a succession of tuition and fee increases that generated these rising student expenses. In its defense, the board had to contend with declining state financial support (down 27.2 percent per FTE in real terms between 1991–92 and 2016–17). Nevertheless, the tuition and fee increases approved by the USC trustees more than compensated for these funding cuts. Over this time frame, USC's revenues from the sum of its state support plus its net tuition[17] and fee collections—its inflation-adjusted revenues per FTE student—rose 26.0 percent.[18] That is, USC had more 26 percent more dollars to spend per FTE student at the end of this twenty-five-year period than it had when it began, even after the effects of price inflation were taken into account. Hence, it can be argued that USC's trustees overreacted with tuition and fee increases to USC's state funding cuts.

Did USC use this additional funding support to improve the quality of education at the university? Perhaps, but the ratio of administrative costs to instructional costs increased from 0.13 to 0.17 on the Columbia campus between 2009 and 2016, and its student-to-faculty ratio edged upward from 17:1 to 18:1 during the same period.[19] Regardless, evidence concerning the quality of education is not easy to identify at USC or at most other public campuses—if one insists that actual measures of output (rather than the mere quantity of inputs) constitute the standard. Institutions of higher education tend to substitute input measures such as faculty salaries and class sizes for output measures such as the ability of students and graduates to think critically, earn incomes, and function as citizens. In such a world, "more is better" even if it has not been demonstrated that additional resources generate improved outputs. Indeed, only a few governing states and governing boards have focused attention on evaluating outputs rather than measuring inputs.

As we will see in the next section of this chapter, the University of South Carolina's situation has been widely imitated in American public higher education. The escalation of tuition and fees by amounts that exceed state funding reductions has become increasingly commonplace. *Nota bene*, however, that virtually every one of these increases was approved (or occasionally modified) by a governing board based upon the recommendations of campus administrators.

Why do we observe this repetitive cost-increasing behavior by governing board members? It surely isn't that they do not care. A resounding majority of public university board members are committed to their task. Instead, it is fair to observe that board members become convinced, even if slowly or reluctantly, that they are doing the right thing when they vote for tuition and fee increases that vastly exceed changes in either the Consumer Price Index or median household incomes. This is a dynamic that deserves much more attention, and we will provide that increased attention in the remainder of this book.

What might be an understandable assessment by a governing board of the need for a large tuition and fee increase in a single year, however, can become problematic for students and families when undertaken repeatedly over several decades. Increasing proportions of undergraduate students and their families can no longer pay the swelling costs of public higher education unless they assume significant debt. The notion that it is possible for students to pay for their college expenses by means of summer employment and modest on-campus jobs has become nothing more than a quaint parental memory. Traditional means of paying for college have gradually disappeared under the waves of college cost increases.

We fear that these inflationary developments in higher education bode ill for society and, if not countered, will lead to increasing anomie, social division, and ultimately disruption. Much is said today about the disappearance of the American Dream, which was vigorously articulated in the

Declaration of Independence by assertions such as "all men are created equal" and each individual has the right to "life, liberty and the pursuit of happiness."[20] While practical discussions on the meaning of these statements are understandably complex, we believe that adverse trends in American public higher education during this century are central to the perception of many that the American Dream is the process of dissipating. Further, inside higher education, we argue that governing boards bear significant (although certainly not sole) responsibility for this development.

Our aims in this book are to highlight the problematic nature of governing board membership and decisions, identify the structures and dynamics that generate these decisions, and discuss the ways in which we might remedy this situation. We do not argue that governing boards bear exclusive responsibility for current public higher education deficiencies. Rather, we argue that governing boards and their members have larger-than-usually-acknowledged culpability in this regard because several of today's adverse trends could not have occurred without their explicit or implicit approval.

For example, is the typical public college governing board member aware that college student bodies have become increasingly stratified by income, or that the typical production worker had to work almost twice as many hours in 2017 to pay typical undergraduate state college tuition and fees as she did in 2000? Based primarily upon one of the authors' experience in evaluating more than fifty college presidents, we believe the answer is usually no.

Fortunately, it is less the case that governing board members do not want to know relevant information and more that they do not know what they do not know. Jeffrey Selingo of the *Washington Post* observed, "Public university governing boards oversee multi-billion-dollar operations. They should start acting like it."[21] Therefore, one of the first steps to improving the situation involves making governing board members much more familiar with the circumstances of their institution's primary customers (students) and with how their institution's admissions, pricing, and financial aid policies affect those students. In academic lingo, we're talking about a course that might be entitled "Board Members 101."

It is fortuitous that most of the processes and dynamics that have produced the current problems can also be remedied by amending and tweaking those same processes and dynamics. Public university governing boards need not be destroyed; however, the definition of their responsibilities and duties, the processes by which their members are selected, the nature of members' preparation for their duties, and the ways in which those members carry out their responsibilities must change.

A Mini-Case Study: The State of Minnesota

Minnesota, population 5.58 million in 2017,[22] is a Midwestern state with a long tradition of progressive politics. The home of the Democratic-Farmer-Labor Party and liberal stalwarts such as Orville Freeman, Eugene McCarthy, Walter Mondale, Hubert Humphrey, and Paul Wellstone, Minnesota has voted for the national Democratic presidential candidate in every election since 1976. In a typical national election, voter turnout in Minnesota is approximately 15 percentage points higher than in the United States as a whole.

Minnesota ranks second among the states in terms of the percentage of its population that has earned an associate degree or higher, and among its adults aged twenty-five or older, only 4 percent have not graduated from high school.[23] It certainly cannot be claimed either that the state does not care about education or that its citizens neglect their civic responsibilities.

It is intriguing, therefore, that Minnesota has come to exemplify two major problems in higher education finance today. First, for several decades, in fits and starts, the Minnesota legislature gradually has disinvested in public higher education. The state's appropriations for public higher education, after being adjusted for price inflation and the number of FTE students in Minnesota's public institutions of higher education, fell from $8,765 per FTE student in the 1991-92 fiscal year to only $6,675 in the 2016-17 fiscal year—a 31.2 percent decline.[24] These values are expressed in constant 2017 dollars.[25]

Second, predictably, state funding reductions have prompted tuition increases. Between the 1991-92 and 2016-17 academic years, the State Higher

Education Executive Officers Association (SHEEO) reports that net real per full-time undergraduate student tuition and fees at Minnesota's average public institution rose from $3,476 to $8,625. This is a 148.1 percent increase.

But what does *net* mean here? From total tuition and fee revenue, SHEEO subtracts the grants institutions make to their own students. In other words, net real undergraduate student tuition and fees per FTE student is the tuition and fee revenue realized by institutions after they deduct the grants they have made to their own students.

From these two revenue sources—state appropriations and tuition and fee collections—SHEEO reports that Minnesota's public institutions of higher education had $15,300 per student to spend in the 2017 fiscal year. This sum is over $3,000 more than the $12,232 per student these institutions had available in 1991-92. In other words, the typical institution was 25.9 percent financially better off—on an inflation-adjusted, per student basis—in 2016-17 than it was in 1991-92.

Of course, any per-student measurement depends upon the number of students being counted. Headcount enrollment in Minnesota's public institutions of higher education topped out in 2010 and by 2017 had fallen by 11.7 percent. Plausibly, rising tuition and prices in a new era of falling inflation-adjusted median household incomes had something to do with the enrollment decline. FRED, the Federal Reserve Bank's data depository, reports that while real median household income in Minnesota rose an impressive 35.3 percent between 1992 and 2000, it subsequently fell 7.7 percent between 2000 and 2017.[26] The public institutions of higher education in Minnesota appear to have been slow to recognize the implications of this new financial world for enrollments. It is a world in which students and households have a diminished capacity to tolerate persistent tuition and fee increases.

Nevertheless, the Board of Regents of the University of Minnesota and the Board of Trustees of the Minnesota State Colleges and Universities (which also governs the state's community colleges and vocational-technical programs) have repeatedly approved significant tuition and fee increases since the turn of the century. The *Chronicle of Higher Education* currently reports tuition and fee charges for individual institutions going back to the 1998-1999 academic year. In the case of the state's flagship University of Minnesota campus in the Twin Cities, the *Chronicle* reports that inflation-adjusted "sticker price" tuition and fees for in-state undergraduates rose 115.1 percent between the 1998-99 and 2016-17 academic years. Meanwhile, at a representative regional state university, Minnesota State University Moorhead (MSUM), the comparable increase was a more modest but still substantial 89.0 percent in real terms.[27] Moreover, it is noteworthy that these increases are in excess of the increase in the Consumer Price Index.

SHEEO data for the financial aid provided by Minnesota to its public college and university students begin in 1999-2000. Between 1999-2000 and 2016-17, price-adjusted total public financial aid to students at Minnesota's institutions of higher education increased by 76.6 percent (more than $52 million),[28] which helped parry the financial blow of the tuition and fee increases. But this largesse was dwarfed by the absolute size of the tuition and fees Minnesota's in-state students were obligated to pay. In 2016-17, this state financial aid amounted to $632 per FTE public college student in inflation-adjusted terms, a paltry sum when compared with the same year's average inflation-adjusted real tuition and fee sticker price of $14,386 at the flagship campus or the $8,117 at MSUM.

The financial plight of Minnesota's students did not impress either the state's on-campus leadership or the members of its public university governing boards. Consider the headlined 2018 complaint of Minnesota's public colleges and universities that "tuition freezes aren't working." Anne Blackhurst, president of Minnesota State University Moorhead, opined that "Freezing tuition, even when the Legislature replaces that with the allocation, really removes one of our most important tools in accomplishing our other objectives."[29]

President Blackhurst's observation prompts an obvious and significant question: Not working for whom? The apparent answer is: not working for faculty, administrator, and staff constituencies. Any freeze in tuition and fees would have been welcomed by students, who faced rising real prices coupled with inadequate financial aid and declining household real incomes. Theirs was not the perspective adopted by presidents and board members, however. In this arena, Minnesota's progressive tradition seems to have taken a back seat.

It should be emphasized that the problems and challenges just identified are national in scope. Similar scenarios have played out in all but a few states. Let's provide some detail.

Adopting a Broader Empirical View

The reasons why tuition and fees have far outpaced growth in both the Consumer Price Index and median household income are numerous and cannot be attributed to a single factor. Stingy governors and legislators, sometimes misguided federal student financial aid policies, administrative bloat, mission creep, ratings competitions, the provision and maintenance of superfluous campus amenities, and governing board behavior all explain some portion of the picture. These causal factors were explored recently in *The Impoverishment of the American College Student*,[30] and we will do so further in this volume.

The focus of this book, however, is on the peculiar roles that four-year public college and university governing boards have played in tuition and fee price inflation. In all but a few states, governing boards have approved every tuition and fee increase that has been implemented, and they usually have done so unanimously. Yes, on occasion, there has been some student grumbling accompanied by hand-wringing by presidents and governing board members. Nevertheless, the tuition and fee Leviathan has ultimately chugged forward. Tuition and fee increases that far exceed growth in prices and incomes have been implemented. It has then been up to students to figure out how to pay these rising costs. Variously, they have not started college at all, or dropped out of school, or moved to part-time status, or transferred to other institutions, or increased their out-of-class work schedules, or gone into debt.

It is fair to say that the interests of students have been trumped by those of institutional constituencies. In all but five states, since 1992–93, governing boards have ultimately opted to raise even more tuition and fee revenue than has been required to counteract the effects of state funding reductions. This is a bold statement that requires concrete evidence.

Data on the real state appropriations per FTE student received by public institutions of higher education in the United States and twelve selected states in 1992-93, 2009-10, and 2017-18 supply this evidence (fig. 1.2). The data come from the highly regarded annual report of the State Higher Education Executive Officers Association (SHEEO). The appropriations data have been adjusted using the SHEEO indexes in three ways. First, appropriations are shown in constant dollars—that is, the numbers have been adjusted for inflation over the years, and hence one year is directly comparable with another in terms of the dollar magnitudes. Second, they have been adjusted for state cost-of-living differences. For instance, on average, it is about 38 percent more expensive to live in California than in Florida, and these numbers recognize that a dollar does not go as far in some states as in others.[31] Third, the data in figure 1.2 have been adjusted for levels of instruction. It usually is more expensive to educate graduate students than undergraduate students, and more expensive to educate chemistry majors than sociology majors, and these data reflect these differences.

Taxpayer support for public higher education declined on a per FTE student basis between 1992-93 and 2017-18, but especially during the years surrounding the Great Recession years of 2008-10. Nationally, between 1992-93 and 2009-10 real appropriations per FTE student to public colleges and universities fell by $1,590 per FTE student—20.13 percent. Subsequently, funding for higher education in most states recovered smartly but not sufficiently to counteract the negative long-term trend.

Public institutions of higher education reacted predictably to reductions in state support. They usually increased tuition and fees by whopping amounts, especially in the years surrounding the Great Recession. Moreover, the tuition and fee increases were typically substantially more than required to counteract state funding cuts. Public colleges and universities actually increased their per-student revenues during this period. In 1992-93, the typical institution in the typical state had $10,140 to spend per FTE student, and in 2017-18 it had $14,135 (fig. 1.3). This reflects a 41.17 percent increase.

One of the first analysts to pay attention to the impact of rapidly rising tuition and fees on students and parents and to consider alternative ways they might pay these mounting costs was the Brookings Institution's Arthur Hauptman. His 1990 book *The Tuition Dilemma: Assessing New Ways to Pay for College* was an eye-opener for many individuals.

It is vitally important to understand is that the tuition and fee revenues being reported in figures 1.2 and 1.3 are *net* revenues: these are the tuition and fee revenues realized by institutions after deducting the grants they have made to their own students. Loans are not deducted because they must be repaid. Thus, we have not penalized institutions for the magnitude of their own tuition discounting practices.

There are several lessons to be drawn from these data. First, a representative state college or university in a typical state had substantially more real spending power per FTE student in 2017–18 than it had in 1992–93. Indeed, as we will see in greater detail in chapter 4, SHEEO data show that in only one of the fifty states (Missouri) did the typical state college or university end this twenty-five-year period worse off financially on a price-adjusted FTE basis. This is a financial reality that colleges and universities (and their governing boards) tend to downplay or ignore as they plead their cases for additional public and private support. Whereas they may well deserve additional public and private financial support, it is not true that they have been reduced to poverty over the past quarter century.

Second, insofar as higher education is concerned, significant financial differences exist among the states. North Dakota, a state whose financial picture improved dramatically over this period because of oil fracking and related activities, witnessed an 89.3 percent increase in its real spendable dollars per FTE student. In neighboring Iowa, however, the increase was less than 1 percent, and in Missouri it was negative. Yet over these twenty-five years, approximately one-third of states increased their real financial contributions per FTE student to public higher education. Illinois, for example, increased its inflation-adjusted support by $6,157 per FTE student. Iowa, however, was the slacker in this regard and cut its real financial support to public higher education by $4,534 per FTE student.

Third, public funding of institutions of higher education responded strongly once the Great Recession was in the rearview mirror. Between 2009-10 and 2016-17, only one state (Missouri) experienced a decline in the inflation-adjusted total revenue per FTE student available to its public college and universities.

Fourth, the net revenues available to public colleges and universities are cyclical and are usually sensitive to economic conditions and state tax collections. This reality underlines the need to make funding and tuition and fee comparisons over long periods of time. A strength of the 1992-93 to 2017-18 study period we use here is that it contains one major stock market correction, the deepest economic recession since the Great Depression, and the longest economic expansion since World War II. Although it is always possible to argue that one should have examined a different time span, this one is by no means cherry-picked.

The Remainder of This Book

Many Americans might be inclined to regard public higher education governance issues as so much "inside baseball"—interesting to those involved but essentially irrelevant to everyone else. Alas, this is not the case. In chapter 2, we outline in detail how current policies have turned public higher education into a force that too often promotes economic inequality rather than providing opportunities to the less fortunate. Governing boards, knowledgeably or not, have presided over this development.

In chapter 3, we summarize the different ways the governance of four-year public higher education in the United States is organized and examine the mechanisms by which individuals gain membership on these governing boards. For example, does it make any difference whether a board member has been elected rather than appointed by a governor?

We also will take a more detailed look in chapter 4 at the connections between governing board structures and real tuition and fee increases. In this regard, we pose a series of questions. Are cost increases sensitive to the presence of statewide governing boards? Does it make any difference

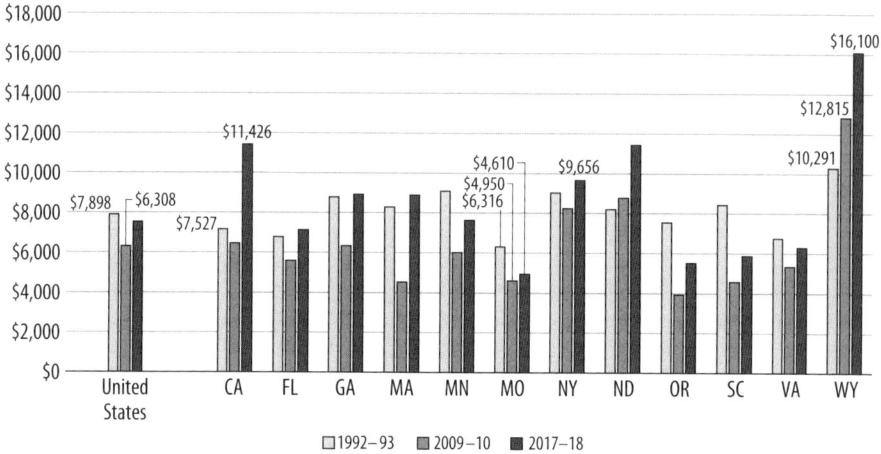

Figure 1.2. Public College and University Real Adjusted State Appropriations per FTE Student: United States and Selected States, 1992-93, 2009-10, and 2017-18. *Sources:* State Higher Education Executive Officers Association (SHEEO), *State Higher Education Finance (SHEF): FY 2018* (Boulder, CO: SHEEO, 2019), https://sheeo.org/wp-content/uploads/2019/04/SHEEO_SHEF_FY18_Report.pdf; Bureau of Labor Statistics, Consumer Price Index for All Urban Consumers (CPI-U), www.bls.gov.

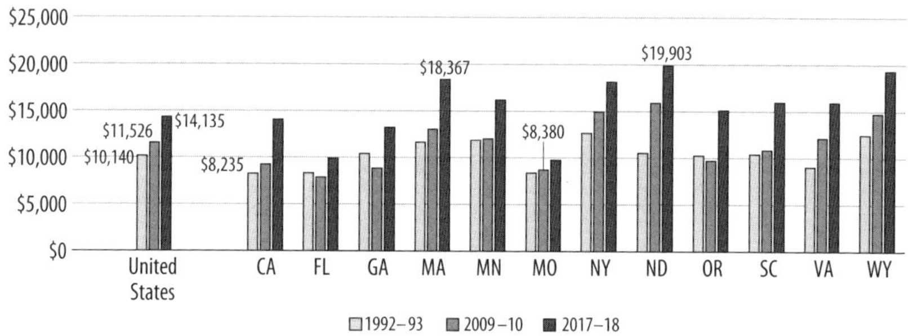

Figure 1.3. Public College and University Real Net Tuition and Real State Support Revenues per FTE Student: United States and Selected States, 1992-93, 2009-10 and 2017-18. *Sources:* State Higher Education Executive Officers Association (SHEEO), *State Higher Education Finance (SHEF): FY 2018* (Boulder, CO: SHEEO, 2019), https://sheeo.org/wp-content/uploads/2019/04/SHEEO_SHEF_FY18_Report.pdf; Bureau of Labor Statistics, Consumer Price Index for All Urban Consumers (CPI-U), www.bls.gov.

if the statewide board is coordinating in nature rather than having governance powers, or if an institution is a constituent part of a system of institutions? Does the presence of voting student members on a governing board affect the size of tuition and fee increases?

The empirical analysis in chapter 4 will be multivariate in character. That is, we will allow for the possibility that many different factors influence tuition and fee increases and the costs that public college and university students pay. Governance is one of those factors but hardly the only one. The level of funding provided to institutions by states is another, but despite the claims often made by higher education leaders, it is not as important as many of them would have us believe.

Armed with factual knowledge derived from our stratified sample of 275 four-year public institutions of higher education, we devote chapters 5 and 6 to evaluating proposals for change. We'll initially focus on reforms outside higher education and then segue to desirable changes inside academe. Many of these matters relate to how public college and university board members are identified and selected. Others relate to how they operate, the incentives they place in front of college and university presidents, and the metrics used to judge institutional performance. While doing so, we will address an obvious question—what knowledge, understandings, and appreciations are most important for members of governing boards to have in order for them do their jobs well? That is, how should states prepare their governing board members for the complex tasks awaiting them?

Having set the governing board scene, we will assess the major hypotheses concerning the causes of today's escalating cost increases in public higher education. There is no current higher education arena in which board members play a more central role than this. What are the most common explanations for the rapidly rising costs of higher education we observe, and how culpable are governing boards? How much culpability should be apportioned to stingy legislators? How can we change the cost-inflating dynamics we observe?

As we dissect the accumulated empirical evidence on the causes of higher education price inflation, we will find that what holds true on one campus may not be so on another campus, even one in the same state, or in one governed by the same board.

The focus throughout this book is on public rather than independent higher education. We adopt this focus not only because public institutions enroll approximately three-quarters of all college students, but also because it is within the public sector of higher education that citizens realistically enjoy the best opportunities to engender change. To be sure, many of the lessons we will draw will also apply to the independent sector of higher education. For good or ill, however, there are more public policy levers available to influence the behavior of public colleges and universities than exist in the private sector, where the legal status of independent institutions and their substantial variety make broadly applicable solutions difficult to specify.

We also confine our attention to four-year institutions. Two-year and community college governance systems are too numerous and too idiosyncratic to include in the same analysis as four-year institutions.

2 Governing Boards and Economic Mobility

> Well, we're moving on up, to the East Side.
>
> Theme song from 1970s TV sitcom *The Jeffersons*

> America's top universities are largely closed to the poor, merely helping well-off students remain well-off.
>
> Derek Thompson, "The Myth of American Universities as Inequality Fighters," *Atlantic Magazine*, August 31, 2017.

Public institutions of higher education have traditionally prided themselves on the positive roles they play in increasing the economic and social mobility of their students. Metaphorically, public colleges and universities are said to open doors of opportunity, enable graduates to climb the ladder of success, spring upward to greater things, and realize their potential.

There is more than fluff and spin to these metaphors. The City College of the City University of New York (CUNY) by itself can claim as graduates Colin Powell, Jonas Salk, Woody Allen, Henry Kissinger, Felix Frankfurter, Andy Grove, Ed Koch, Eli Wallach, Alfred Stieglitz, Edward G. Robinson, Bernard Baruch, Ira Gershwin, Upton Sinclair, Kenneth Arrow, Abraham Maslow, A. Philip Randolph, and Alan Dershowitz, to name only a few.

A single flagship state university, the University of California, Berkeley, includes on its list of alumni individuals such as Steve Wozniak, Earl Warren, Gregory Peck, Jerry Brown, Daniel Kahneman, Robert McNamara, Jack London, Betty Friedan, and Michio Kaku. Impressively, twenty-nine Berkeley graduates have earned a Nobel Prize.

Graduates of our nation's Historically Black Colleges and Universities (HBCUs) include Martin Luther King Jr., Thurgood Marshall, Oprah

Winfrey, Spike Lee, Toni Morrison, Alice Walker, Samuel L. Jackson, Marian Wright Edelman, Langston Hughes, Ralph Ellison, and Booker T. Washington.

An awareness of this impressive history was an important reason why a January 2017 article in the *New York Times* captured the attention of so many. The *Times* article, which was based on a seminal National Bureau of Economic Research (NBER) study of the impact of college attendance on income mobility between generations, detailed the percentage of college students who come from families in the bottom 60 percent and in the top 1 percent of the income distribution.[1] The *Times* supplied its readers with the ability to generate these income distribution data for specific campuses. One could plug in the name of a particular institution, say Kansas State University (KSU), and learn that in 2013, 1.6 percent of the KSU student body came from families in the upper 1 percent of the American income distribution, while 25.6 percent came from the bottom 60 percent of the income distribution. One also could glean from the NBER data that 29.6 percent of KSU students who came to the university from a family in the bottom quintile of the income distribution subsequently rose to the top income quintile.

Perhaps it did not surprise many that the NBER study (whose work has been extended significantly through Harvard University's Opportunity Insights project[2]) found that 38 independent institutions enrolled more students from the top 1 percent of the United States family income distribution than they did from the entire bottom 60 percent. At Washington and Lee University, for example, 19.1 percent of students came from families in the upper 1 percent of the income distribution, whereas only 8.4 percent came from the bottom 60 percent.

However, what discomfited and perhaps shocked those who inspected the data in greater detail was the extent to which the student bodies of public colleges and universities, especially flagship institutions, have increasingly tended de facto to segregate on the basis of family incomes. At Virginia's College of William and Mary, only 13.6 percent of the student body came to the historic Williamsburg campus from families in the lower 60 percent of the income distribution and only 1.6 percent from the bottom quintile. At the University of Michigan, which received almost 60,000 applications for undergraduate admission in fall 2017, the comparable statistics were 16.2 percent and 3.0 percent, respectively.

By contrast, at Mississippi Valley State University, where 2,310 individuals applied for admission in fall 2017, 86.9 percent of the student body came from the lower 60 percent of the income distribution and a mere 0.5 percent from the top quintile. The gap between Mississippi Valley State and the other institutions is indicative of the significant differences that exist in students' financial circumstances across American public higher education.

As admission selectivity declines, the presence of students from families in the top 1 percent of the income distribution drops off noticeably (table 2.1) and the presence of students from the lowest 60 percent of the income distribution climbs. Presumably, differences in the academic preparation and abilities of prospective students, the nature of the academic programs and environment on the campuses they attend, and their ability to pay are important determinants of this income stratification. Institutions and students mutually engage in a sorting process that ultimately results in greater proportions of students from upper-income families attending more selective institutions and greater proportions of students from lower-income families attending less selective institutions.

Table 2.1 Family Incomes of Students at Four-Year Public Colleges and Universities

		Percentage of students coming from families in:	
Institutional admissions selectivity category	Number of institutions	Top 1 percent of the income distribution	Bottom 60 percent of the income distribution
Elite or highly selective	30	2.9	27.3
Selective	370	0.9	46.1
Non-selective	74	0.6	57.4

Source: Raj Chetty, John Friedman, Emmanuel Saez, Nicholas Turner, and Danny Yagan, "Mobility Report Cards: The Role of Colleges in Intergenerational Mobility," NBER Working Paper 23618 (July 2017), www.nber.org/papers/w23618, MCR Table 2. See also Harvard University Opportunity Insights, https://opportunityinsights.org, for these data.

Deliberate or not, the economic sorting of students that occurs in American public higher education today is a gentile manifestation of segregation—not racial in this case,[3] but economic. Were we to include two-year and community colleges in our analysis, the extent to which sorting occurs on the basis of family income would be even more pronounced.

Why are we interested in these data? Because this is the world that governing boards have presided over and thus have wrought, whether or not they understand this to be so. With few exceptions, governing boards have voted unanimously in favor of the increases in tuition, fees, and other costs that have been so influential in stimulating the current economic stratification in public higher education. A recent study conducted by the advocacy foundation Partners for College Affordability and Public Trust found that over a two-year period, 99 percent of the members of Virginia public college governing boards voted in favor of the tuition and fee proposals presented to them.[4]

Governing boards are not solely responsible for the emergence of this world of structured inequality in higher education, but they do bear legal responsibility for its evolution. Pragmatically, the most plausible ways to remedy the situation usually reside within the traditional province and responsibilities of governing boards. But they cannot reasonably be expected to do so if they don't understand what has occurred and why. Thus, the emphasis in this chapter is on the economic stratification of student bodies.

How do the general findings of table 2.1 translate to individual institutions? The Harvard University Opportunity Insights data make it possible to assess the percentage of students coming from the lowest 60 percent of the income distribution for a broad range of four-year, public institutions (fig. 2.1). Several preliminary inferences can be drawn from these data. First, highly ranked flagship institutions have a substantial presence in the ten institutions with the lowest shares, while regional state colleges and HBCUs such as Mississippi Valley State dominate the listing of institutions that have the highest percentages.

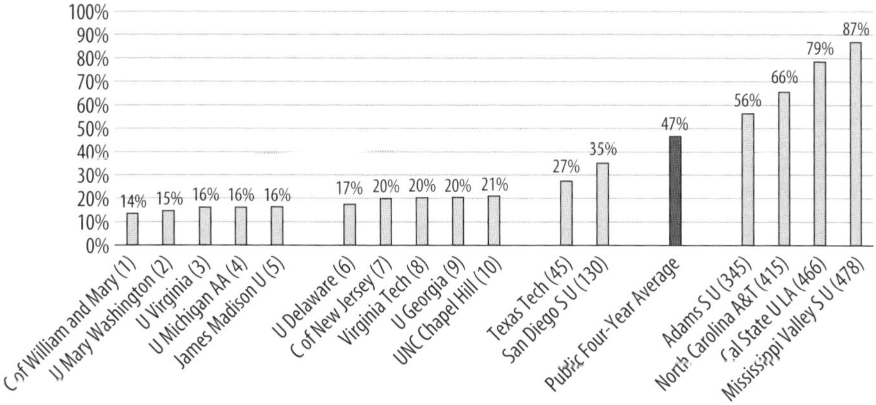

Figure 2.1. Percentage and Rank of Undergraduate Student Bodies Coming from the Bottom 60 Percent of the Family Income Distribution: Selected Public Institutions, 1999–2013. Note: The lower the percentage, the lower the institution's admission of lower-income students. *Source:* Harvard University Opportunity Insights, https://opportunityinsights.org.

The average institution among the study's 480 four-year public institutions enrolled 46.6 percent of its student body from families in the lowest 60 percent of the income distribution. Only two flagship campuses (New York's Stony Brook University and Idaho State University) enrolled more than this percentage.

Second, four of the five campuses with the lowest percentages are located in Virginia, where not so coincidentally each institution has its own governing board and the statewide coordinating board exercises rather limited powers. Institutional independence from statewide control, as we shall see, is an important consideration affecting college costs. Independence confers degrees of operational freedom that permit and even encourage a kind of campus entrepreneurship, the development of distinctive programs and campuses, and perhaps even a drive for exclusivity. Arguably, this independence of action has enabled Virginia's four-year public institutions to differentiate themselves and gain national attention. Clearly one size does not fit all in Virginia higher education.

It could also be the case, however, that having one's own governing board and the concomitant independence of decision-making emboldens colleges and universities to pursue admissions and financial aid policies that, over time, put them out of the financial reach of many of the very citizens who pay taxes to support them. Thus, an applicant from a lower-income family may not be able to afford to attend one of the more selective campuses without incurring significant debt.

Additionally, institutions granted considerable operational room to maneuver on their own often find the opportunity to earn premium revenues from enrolling healthy numbers of out-of-state students, who represent a demographic opportunity simply too tempting to resist. Whereas a variety of plausible arguments can be made in favor of enrolling nonresident students, when it occurs at selective institutions it often reduces the number of slots available to in-state applicants. Simply put, embracing revenue-enhancing out-of-state students may ultimately crowd out in-state students. In many states, the trade-off between in-state and out-of-state students has evolved into an issue that inflames the in-state citizenry and the media.

Third, if family income is the criterion, then the student bodies at four-year public institutions seldom look like the populations of the states in which they are located. The six out of ten Virginians who comprise the lower 60 percent of the income distribution in that state contribute only one out of every six students at the College of William and Mary, the University of Virginia, and James Madison University. Give or take a few percentage points, this situation exists at flagship universities across the country. At both the University of Alabama and University of Mississippi, for example, less than 30 percent of the undergraduate student bodies of these institutions come from the bottom 60 percent of the income distribution.

Fourth, it nevertheless remains the case that even highly prestigious institutions can choose a different admissions path over time. None of the highly ranked campuses of the University of California is in the bottom ten in figure 2.1, and one must proceed to number 48 on the list before the University of California, Santa Barbara, appears. The University of California, Berkeley, is 97th on the list, with 32.3 percent of its student body coming from the bottom 60 percent of the income distribution; University of California, Los Angeles, is 142nd, with 36.1 percent; and the University of California, Irvine, is 196th, with 40.5 percent.

The upshot is that even prestigious institutions can enroll substantially larger populations of talented lower-income students if they establish this as a priority. Even so, doing this successfully nearly always means they must offer generous financial aid to lower-income students and also support a variety of academic and social programs for these students, who frequently do not match the predominant campus mold.

Most flagship institutions in the United States (especially those deemed most prestigious) falter when confronted with these realities. They are imprisoned by their recent histories, their carefully cultivated institutional narratives, their own images of who they are or would like to be, and of course external rankings. Admitting more students from lower income quintiles would require them to reorder their internal spending priorities as well as those of their supporting foundations. At the same time, they might also find that admitting higher proportions of lower-income students causes rankings-sensitive metrics such as SAT scores to deteriorate.

In partial defense of those in power who choose not to attempt to reduce the economic stratification of their undergraduate student bodies, it must be acknowledged that declining rankings generally are poisonous to anyone deemed responsible. No college president relishes the job of explaining to his or her campus, governing board, alumni, and the media why the university declined in rankings, such as those published by the *U.S. News and World Report* or *Princeton Review*. As a consequence, security-conscious, rankings-sensitive college presidents typically issue rhetoric concerning the desire of their campus to enroll an economically diverse student body but rarely match their verbiage with action.

The Mobility Rating Index

The Harvard University Opportunity Insights data set, which includes information on more than 30 million college students and their families

In 2006, the University of Virginia (UVA) terminated its early-decision admissions program for freshmen out of concern that relatively few lower-income students used it. Early decision required conventional high school applicants to commit to UVA in December of their senior high school year, but this was well before they would know what financial aid they would receive. Many could not afford to make such a commitment until they knew whether they could afford to attend. In June 2019, UVA announced that it was restoring its early-decision admissions program but argued that this would not "unbalance the admissions playing field." A 2015 Jack Kent Cooke Foundation study, however, found that low-income students were much less likely to use early-decision admissions programs because of the financial uncertainty these programs imposed upon them.

Terry Nguyen, "UVA Eliminated Early Decision in 2006 to Level the Admissions Playing Field. Why Is It Coming Back?" *Chronicle of Higher Education,* May 30, 2019, www.chronicle.com/article/UVa-Eliminated-Early-Decision/246415.

between 1999 and 2013, revealed some conspicuous success stories. At CUNY's Baruch College, 46.8 percent of students who came from the lowest income quintile subsequently had risen to the top income quintile by 2014. CUNY's City College and Lehman College recorded 36.0 percent and 27.9 percent in this measure of intergenerational success, respectively, while on the other coast, California State University at Los Angeles posted a 29.9 percent success rate.[5] The four-year public college or university average for Opportunity Insights' 480 campuses was 23.2 percent.

These are potentially useful data, but the Harvard University Opportunity Insights scholars behind the study traveled an intriguing step further. It is a good thing, they reasoned, that some institutions exhibit high rates of success in moving students from the lowest income quintile (which they label P1, to indicate that it reflects the income quintile of the students' parents) to K5 (the 2014 income quintile of the students, who are termed "kids" in the study). They noted, however, that these same institutions usually do not admit many P1 students, so their success in moving students upward affects much smaller numbers of P1 students. This phenomenon is evident from data on the fifteen public institutions with the lowest P1 income quintile percentages and the percentages of students who move upward from the P1 income quintile of their parents to K5 quintile status (table 2.2). The average institution in table 2.2 can boast that 38.5 percent of its P1 income quintile students move up to the K5 quintile; however, the typical institution in this group enrolls only 2.6 percent of its student body from the P1 group. In other words, these institutions achieve considerable success in moving their lowest-income students upward, but they simply do not enroll very many of these individuals.

At Virginia Tech, for example, an impressive 47 percent of P1 students subsequently moved upward to the highest quintile (K5). Numbers such as these are the stuff that college presidents enjoy bragging about to whoever will listen and constitute the sort of information that alumni magazines trumpet. But this is only half of the story. In the case of Virginia Tech, only 2.84 percent of the student body came from P1. Like it or not, Virginia Tech and the other institutions profiled in table 2.2 have become stratified, income-exclusive institutions.

The Harvard University Opportunity Insights researchers developed a hybrid metric to take these competing pieces of information into account. They multiplied the decimal percentage of an institution's P1 student body times its P1 to K5 success rate; this new metric is available for the same selection of institutions profiled in table 2.2, but with a new set of other institutions that occupy the other end of the spectrum (table 2.3). One might debate what label to assign to this new statistic, but these researchers call it a "mobility rate." They argue that it measures the comparative ability of a specific campus to serve as an instrument of economic opportunity.

It is important that readers understand the mathematics of the Harvard University Opportunity Insights mobility rates because these rates have gained considerable attention. Specifically, the mobility index is an institution's decimal percentage of P1 to K5 success multiplied by the decimal percentage of students who come to that campus from a P1 household. Consider Georgia Tech as an example. At Tech, a laudable 57 percent of its P1 income quintile students moved upward to K5 by 2014.

However, only 3.23 percent of Tech's student body came from the P1 income quintile. Thus, Tech's computed mobility index is .57458830 × .032 33100 = .01857701, which typically is reported as a 1.86 mobility index value.

The average mobility index value in the study's sample of 480 four-year public institutions was 2.28. However, some institutions (such as CUNY's Baruch College) truly excelled according to this metric and achieved indices six times as high as the average. Others, such as the College of William and Mary, did not fare so well, primarily because they enroll very small proportions of lower-income students.

The University of Texas at El Paso, which serves a high proportion of Hispanic first-generation college students, recorded a mobility index score of 6.82, about four times higher than that of Georgia Tech. The critical difference? UTEP enrolled 27.7 percent of its student body from the ranks of P1, while the comparable percentage at Georgia Tech was only 3.2 percent. Thus, the mobility index reflects both what institutions are doing and what they are not doing in the realm of generating student income mobility.

The income mobility index data reported in table 2.3, when placed in the context of numeric goal posts provided by national averages, constitute valuable information that members of a governing board should know and understand. Why? Because these data help paint a picture that describes the extent to which their campuses are vehicles for economic mobility. Do specific institutions provide individuals with the opportunity to surmount their circumstances, or do they set existing social and economic arrangements in concrete?

Whether a typical public college or university board member knows many or any of these critical pieces of information about their campus is questionable. Our experience suggests that most public campus board members possess only impressionistic notions of the percentage of undergraduate students at their institution who spring from the lowest quintile of the income distribution. Usually, they know even less about how successful their campus is in moving these P1 (lowest income quantile) students to K5 (the highest income quintile).

If governing board trustees rely on the narratives promoted by their institutions, their lack of knowledge is understandable. Unfortunately, the always upbeat prevailing campus story lines relating to access, affordability, and economic mobility can be demonstrably misleading. Brochures and videos may say "we move people up the ladder" even while campus admissions, pricing, and financial aid policies maintain the status quo or even move the institution in the opposite direction. Alumni magazines in particular contribute to this distortion by highlighting individuals who have risen from difficult backgrounds to achieve success. Such individuals are worthy of the attention they receive, but their stories often are unrepresentative of the student body at large. More than a few institutions practice deception when they trumpet such cases because in so doing they deflect attention from the circumstances that cause their institutional mobility indexes to be mediocre. The reality is that unless a board member probes, he or she is likely to be uninformed on matters relating to admissions access, affordability, and mobility.

The Harvard University Opportunity Insights mobility index is quite new, so one can forgive most governing board members for being unaware of the rating of their campus. Now that it is available, however, who would deny that it is a critical metric that ought to occupy some of the attention of board members? After all, upward mobility data and income distribution information critically define the extent to which a campus is accessible, affordable, and an engine of social and economic mobility. How accessible is an institution to promising individuals who emanate from the bottom of the income distribution? If this is not among the major concerns of board members, then we argue it should be. Campus-specific data similar to those reported in tables 2.2 and 2.3 should be front and center concerns for board members.

Having highlighted the mobility index and sung its praises, we now issue several caveats. We start with its definition. The abstract of the original NBER study says that the mobility index measures the "fraction of students who come from families in bottom income quintile and reach the top quintile,"[6] but this does not turn out to be a precise definition. On hearing this description of the index, many might assume that the

Table 2.2 Rates of Success at Moving Students from Low-Income Families into the Highest Income Quintile at Fifteen Four-Year Public Campuses by 2014

Campus	% of P1 undergraduate students	% of P1 students who move to K5
U Mary Washington (VA)	1.27	60.7
College of William and Mary (VA)	1.35	38.9
James Madison U (VA)	1.85	40.4
U Delaware	2.23	39.0
Truman State U (MO)	2.61	28.8
Miami U (OH)	2.76	28.1
U Virginia	2.82	51.8
Virginia Tech	2.84	47.5
U Michigan-Ann Arbor	3.00	50.4
U Georgia	3.01	35.2
Longwood U (VA)	3.10	21.3
U Iowa	3.14	32.0
Colorado State U	3.16	35.4
Clemson U (SC)	3.17	37.8
Purdue U (IN)	3.18	31.5

Source: Harvard University Opportunity Insights, https://opportunity insights.org.

Notes: P1 = lowest parent income quintile. K5 = highest income quintile (for students themselves). These fifteen campuses are those with the lowest percentages of P1 undergraduates.

definition refers to the percentage of students who move from P1 to K5 at a specific institution. They might assume, for example, that Georgia Tech's mobility index is a lofty 57.5 percent, the share of its P1 students who move upward to K5. Not so. As we have seen, Georgia Tech's computed mobility index is only 1.86: its success rate (about 57.5 percent) multiplied by the portion of its students who come from P1 (for Tech, this is about 3.23 percent).

The Harvard University Opportunity Insights mobility index penalizes Georgia Tech and similarly situated institutions for not enrolling more P1 (lowest-income quintile) students. There may exist persuasive reasons for assigning such a statistical penalty, but one should understand that Georgia Tech is successful in creating upward economic mobility for its lowest-income students. Still, it also is true that the institution does not present this opportunity to very many lower-income students. The Har-

Table 2.3 Income Mobility Rates at the Fifteen Four-Year Public Campuses with the Lowest and a Selection of Institutions with Higher P1 Percentages

Campus	Mobility rate index		Mobility rate index
College of William and Mary (VA)	0.52	U Illinois System	2.12
Appalachian State U (NC)	0.54	U of Maryland System (except University College)	2.24
Utah State U	0.65	**Average of US institutions**	**2.28**
Longwood U (VA)	0.66		
James Madison U (VA)	0.75	Old Dominion U (VA)	2.37
Truman State U (MO)	0.75	U Louisiana at Lafayette	2.71
U Mary Washington (VA)	0.77	Jackson State U (MS)	2.97
Miami U (OH)	0.78	New Mexico State U	3.18
Grand Valley State U (MI)	0.79	Temple University	3.30
U Delaware	0.87	San Diego State U	3.66
Eastern Connecticut State U	0.89	Mississippi Valley State U	3.95
Westfield State U (MA)	0.90	Dickinson State U (ND)	4.10
Indiana U System	0.92	U California, Davis	4.44
Keene State C (NH)	0.95	U California, Berkeley	4.89
U Kansas	0.96	Florida International U	5.22
Eastern Illinois U	0.97	San José State U	5.43
Purdue U	1.00	UCLA	5.60
U Iowa	1.01	California State U, Northridge	6.32
U Cincinnati	1.04	U California, Riverside	6.01
U Georgia	1.06	U California, Irvine	6.77
Colorado State U	1.12	U Texas at El Paso	6.82
Clemson U	1.20	Stony Brook U	8.41
U Virginia	1.46	CUNY John Jay C	9.69
U Michigan-Ann Arbor	1.51	California State U, Los Angeles	9.92
U Connecticut	1.71	CUNY Lehman C	9.69
U Pittsburgh System	1.80	CUNY City C	11.72
U Nevada, Las Vegas	1.89	CUNY Baruch College	12.94
U Oklahoma	1.92		
U West Florida	2.00		

Source: Harvard University Opportunity Insights, https://opportunityinsights.org.

vard University Opportunity Insights mobility index attempts to take both factors into account.

Those using the mobility index should also be aware that it focuses on students who are income dependents of their parents or families for tax and financial purposes. Roughly 50 percent of undergraduates, however, are income *independent*—they are on their own. Hence, they are not part of the Harvard University Opportunity Insights study. If they were included, would this make a difference? Almost surely, because income-independent students are distinctive—they are more likely to be women, to work while attending college, to be members of a minority group, to live in poverty, and to enroll part-time.[7]

Additionally, the mobility index mixes part-time and full-time students together even though part-time students are much less likely to graduate and earn larger incomes as quickly as full-time students. Only about 52 percent of students who start a baccalaureate program graduate within six years, and this percentage has been falling.[8] Relatively few students ever earn a bachelor's degree if they attend only part-time. Ordinarily, some full-time attendance is a must if a student eventually wishes to earn a degree. In any case, the fact that the index does not differentiate between full-time and part-time students is a limitation. Consider that 92 percent of undergraduate students at the University of Oregon were full-time in 2017, while at nearby Portland State University, the full-time percentage was only 66 percent.[9] Yet the index does not differentiate between the circumstances of these two situations in this regard.

Further, the index seemingly struggles with students who transfer between institutions. At Portland State, for example, 14.4 percent of the 2017 undergraduate student body had transferred to that campus from another institution, while the comparable percentage at the University of Oregon was only 6.85 percent. Which institution should receive credit for the achievements of these transfer students—their earlier institution, their current institution, or perhaps their subsequent institution? The index largely assigns students to their most recent destination.

Finally, only indirectly does the index tell us anything about the affordability of an institution to its students. It is essentially an output measure that reflects the contributions of myriad inputs and influences, among them the incomes of students and their parents, the size of tuition and fees, the availability of financial aid, and academic majors of graduates. The index does not directly treat these matters except for parental income. Thus, it misses students who can't afford to attend an institution. They never become part of that institution's income mobility metric because they cannot afford to attend. The index measures what has been, not what might have been.

The *Wall Street Journal* and the *Times of London* have developed a model to rank universities. Fifteen separate performance indicators are used to generate the rankings, which in 2019 included 23 four-year public universities in the top 100 universities in the United States. However, none of the performance indicators measured the accessibility or affordability of the institutions to the citizenry. Student diversity received a bow but was included in an "environment" category that was weighted only 10 percent in the ranking. It is revealing that the *Journal* and the *Times* find it appropriate to rank and recommend a product (in this case, higher education) without reference to the price one must pay to acquire the product. This is akin to ratings that compare Lamborghini roadsters to Aston Martin Valkyrles. Perhaps this is interesting to a small set of automobile aficionados, but it is essentially irrelevant to nearly everyone else. In essence, the *Journal* and the *Times* assume that price is no object. This is an imaginary world.

These caveats are quibbles about which users of the Harvard University Opportunity Insights data set should be aware, but they should not distract us from the seminal nature and the high quality of the project's work. The study has provided invaluable, previously unavailable information on the roles academic institutions play in stimulating income mobility, and this information is based on a historically large sample of students and families. The insights the study continues to provide about individual institutions and our entire society deserve to become mandatory reading for college faculty and administrators as well as policy-makers such as governors and legislators.

But it may be the members of college governing boards who most need to become familiar with these income mobility data. Board members are legally responsible for the direction of their institution, and they urgently need to have a factual basis for their decision-making rather than consuming only the smooth institutional narratives presented to them by college and university administrators and their minions. These narratives usually avoid the ticklish questions concerning college access and affordability we have begun to pose here.

Reclassifying Institutions by Function and Mission

There is much more to be said about the Harvard University Opportunity Insights student and family income data, but in order to do so, we must find a more effective way to address the tremendous diversity of the approximately 700 four-year public institutions of higher education in the United States. The Harvard University Opportunity Insights study attempted to recognize institutional diversity by subdividing all of the more than 2,000 institutions in its sample into four groups based upon their admissions selectivity, as categorized in the 2009 edition of *Barron's Profiles of American Colleges*.[10]

The problem is that admissions selectivity does not capture many of the most critical features of institutions. Consider institutional size, which often is a critical differentiating factor in terms of institutional and governing board behavior. The campus-based institutions in the study include giant University of Central Florida (66,000 students) as well as struggling Cheyney University, an HBCU with only 725 students.[11] Even if these two institutions had the same admissions selectivity (although they do not), they would differ dramatically in their activities and challenges because of their differences in size.

Sometimes institutions have similar admissions standards but differ dramatically in their missions and activities. The 46,000-student University of Washington is a comprehensive doctoral research plus medical school institution that also pursues big-time intercollegiate athletics. It contrasts vividly with the 6,000-student Colorado School of Mines, which has a sharply focused mission and curriculum. These institutions differ in fundamental ways from each other even though their levels of admissions selectivity are similar.

Or, consider that South Dakota State University, a flagship, accepts 91 percent of its freshman applicants, while the College of New Jersey, a regional institution with a much more narrowly focused mission, accepts only 46 percent. Certainly, their admissions selectivity is an important aspect of these two institutions' identities, but their disparate missions define them more clearly.

While the eclectic nature of four-year public colleges and universities in the United States makes it a challenge to categorize them, we believe that institutional mission and programmatic breadth are superior to admissions selectivity as characteristics for categorizing institutions of higher education. We also contend that, within limits, more institutional categories are preferable to fewer. Consequently, we have placed each of the Opportunity Insights 480 four-year public institutions in one of six categories based upon its mission and programmatic breadth. Our goal is straightforward: we seek to avoid comparing metaphorical apples to oranges. We will use these categories throughout the remainder of this book.

The six institutional categories presented in figure 2.2 are self-explanatory with two exceptions. "*U.S. News* elite" refers to the 28 highest-ranked four-year public institutions identified in 2018 by *U.S. News and World Report* magazine. Prominent examples in the *U.S. News* elite category are the University of California, Berkeley, and the Universities of Michigan and Virginia.

The "non-flagship metro leader" category contains large public institutions located in the nation's most populous 150 metropolitan regions. These campuses, whose headcount enrollments average about 30,000, are not flagship institutions, but they have assumed influential roles in their regions and states and are often sources of educational innovation. Examples include George Mason University and Florida International University on the East Coast, the University of North Texas in the nation's midsection, and Portland State University in the West. Simply put, they have become players, and their peculiar evolutionary paths should not be ignored.

The institutions we have classified as "regional" were more often than not founded as teachers' colleges, and many have names containing a geographic direction—for example, Eastern Illinois University and the University of Southern Maine. Historically, they have served as portals for millions of students who have seen higher education as their ticket to upward economic and social mobility. Usually, this has meant these institutions charged lower prices and had more lenient admissions standards than flagship institutions. As we shall see, however, these circumstances

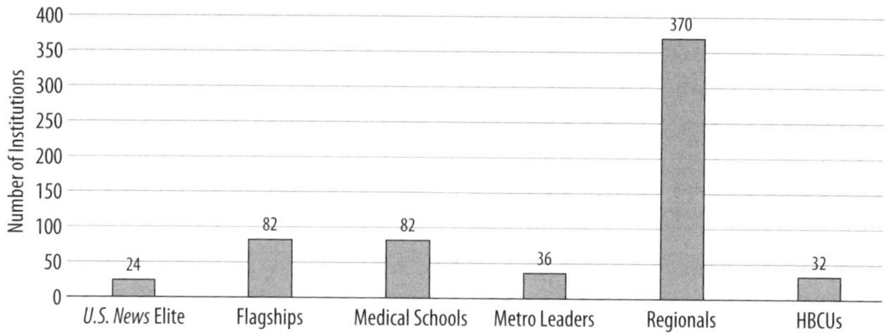

Figure 2.2. Categorizing Opportunity Insights' 480 Public Four-Year Institutions of Higher Education (Overlap Exists between the Categories). *Source:* Harvard University Opportunity Insights, https://opportunityinsights.org.

no longer describe a growing number of the regional institutions, some of which have become considerably more expensive selective institutions with statewide and regional student clienteles.

Note that a single institution might fit into several institutional categories, creating overlap. The University of Florida is both a flagship institution and a member of the *U.S. News* elite. All public HBCUs have been classified as regional institutions in our listing, but most regional institutions are not HBCUs. Most of the 82 institutions in the sample of campuses that boast a medical school are flagship institutions, but 26 (including Ohio's Wright State University and East Tennessee State University) are not. These and similar relationships explain why the sum of the institutions in the six categories exceeds the total number of institutions (480) being described.

Let's take an initial look at how the institutions in these six categories differ one from one another. According to data on the family incomes of students who attended an institution in one of the categories, 13.1 percent of the undergraduate students at flagship institutions come from families in the top 5 percent of the income distribution, while 6.3 percent come from the bottom quintile of the income distribution (table 2.4).

The fundamental message of table 2.4 rings loud and clear. The student bodies of four-year public institutions of higher education in the United States have become stratified on the basis of income. Only one in

Table 2.4 Family Incomes of Students Attending Four-Year Public Institutions of Higher Education in the United States, 2013

Institutional type	Number of institutions	Percentage of students coming from: Bottom 20% of the income distribution	Bottom 60% of the income distribution	Top 20% of the income distribution	Top 5% of the income distribution	Top 1% of the income distribution	Percentile rank of parents' income
U.S. News elite	24	5.0	26.2	46.8	16.7	2.6	69.1
Flagship	82	6.3	32.9	42.9	13.1	2.4	68.2
Medical school	82	7.7	36.1	39.9	11.4	2.0	66.1
Metro leader	36	9.5	42.3	32.9	7.6	1.1	61.9
Regional	370	12.5	50.1	24.5	4.5	0.6	56.6
HBCU	32	24.2	72.2	10.4	1.0	0.1	42.3
All	480	11.3	46.6	28.3	6.2	1.0	59.0

Source: Harvard University Opportunity Insights, https://opportunityinsights.org.

eleven four-year public college students comes from a family in the lowest quintile of the income distribution. At *U.S. News* elite institutions, only 5.0 percent of undergraduate students (about one in every 20) come from the lowest income quintile. Increasingly, lower-income students attend community colleges, go part-time at a regional or metro leader institution, or do not attend college at all.

To no one's surprise, regional institutions and HBCUs enroll proportionately more students from lower-income families than do the elite institutions, flagships, and universities with medical schools. Whereas the typical *U.S. News* elite institution enrolls only 26.2 percent of its student body from families in the lower 60 percent of the income distribution, for regional institutions the comparable number is 50.1 percent and at HBCUs it is 72.2 percent. At the other end of the income spectrum, the elite institutions enroll seventeen times as many students from the top 5 percent of the income distribution as do HBCUs and four times as many as regional institutions.

Metro leader institutions (the large non-flagship institutions located in large urban areas) occupy an in-between position. They enroll larger proportions of lower-income students than the elite and the flagship institutions but not as many as the regionals and far fewer than the HBCUs. Only one in every ten students at a metro leader institution comes from a family in the lowest income quintile. Some might regard this as ironic since an important reason for the founding of many of these institutions was to provide access to urban, place-bound, and often lower-income students.

The key to the income distribution data reported in table 2.4 is of course the incomes of the parents of the students. The average student at a four-year public institution comes from a family whose income places it in the 59th percentile nationally. This percentile rises to 68 at flagship institutions and to 69 at elite institutions. Four-year public colleges, especially those that are highly ranked, have gradually become the preserve of the well-to-do, and even many regional colleges now enroll student bodies that only faintly resemble the overall society they inhabit.

Let's give reality to the numbers in table 2.4 by focusing for a moment on a particular regional institution—Missouri's highly ranked,

6,200-student Truman State University.[12] Truman State enrolls only 2.61 percent of its student body from the lowest quintile of the family income distribution and rejects the admissions applications of one-third or more of those who apply. Between the 2000–01 and 2017–18 academic years, mandatory in-state undergraduate tuition and fees at Truman State increased 45.4 percent faster than the Consumer Price Index (CPI).[13] This translated to an average annual rate of increase 2.24 percentage points higher than the growth in the CPI. Institutions such as Truman State (once an open enrollment institution known as Northeast Missouri State Teachers College) have forfeited to community colleges their long-standing roles as inexpensive ladders of opportunity.

Truman State is hardly the only regional institution where an analogous scenario is to be found (fig. 2.3). Most of the regional colleges and universities listed in figure 2.3 have evolved into selective admissions institutions that receive far more applications than slots available and typically also enroll large numbers of non-resident students who pay premium prices. Enthusiasm and morale on these campuses are usually high, and most are viewed internally and externally as success stories. Nearly all, however, have departed from their origins and now leave to others the education of substantial numbers of lower-income students.

The evolution of four-year public higher education in general, and of these regional institutions in particular, toward less inclusive, higher-income student bodies is uniformly portrayed by the institutions as a highly positive development. Truman State's website, for example, touts its national rankings, the quality of its programs, and its attractive campus. None of these points of pride constitutes a falsehood. However, Truman gives little or no attention to the comparative absence of lower-income students on its campus.

The salient public policy question is whether it is wise for states to encourage the evolution of institutions such as Truman State, James Madison, the College of New Jersey, and Western Washington (to name a few) into campuses that are effectively closed to wide swaths of these states' citizenry. In some cases, the states in which these institutions are located have consciously decided to make these upwardly mobile institutions

Some of the regional institutions described in figure 2.3 might argue with their being assigned a regional classification because their student bodies have become statewide or even national in nature. However, none is a flagship institution, has a medical school, or is located in one of the 150 largest metropolitan areas.

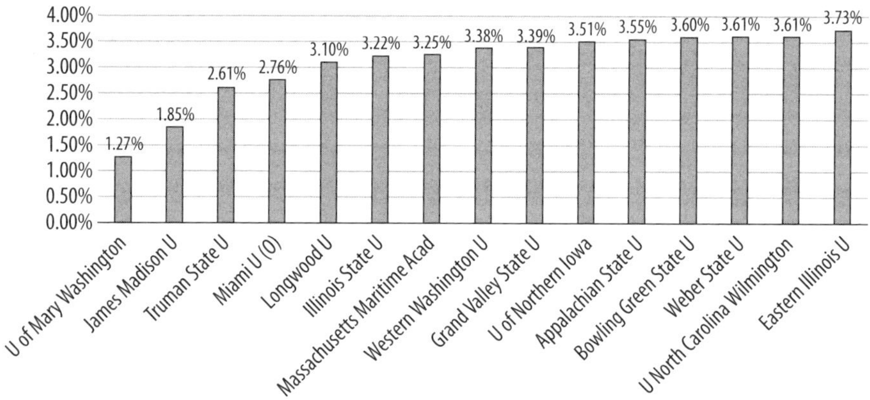

Figure 2.3. Percentage of Student Bodies at Selected Regional Institutions That Emanate from the Lowest Quintile of the Income Distribution: 2013. *Source:* Harvard University Opportunity Insights, https://opportunityinsights.org.

more exclusive, but more often this shift has been the practical result of a combination of high tuition prices, low student financial aid, deficient state appropriations, and ambitious administrators.

Changes in the roles of institutions seldom occur immediately. Consider that the state of Missouri's higher education appropriations per full-time equivalent (FTE) student declined 25.7 percent between FY 2008 and FY 2018.[14] There is a causal connection between the long-term decline in Truman State's state appropriation and its subsequent pricing behavior, and in turn between its pricing behavior and the nature of its student body. At Truman State, increases in grant-based financial aid have not kept up with tuition and fee increases. Thus, gradually over time,

Northeast Missouri State Teachers College morphed into Truman State University, which has become an institution that many lower-income students cannot afford to attend even if they are admitted.

The dynamics through which declining appropriations alter the nature of student bodies are hardly confined to Missouri. Over the same FY 2008 to FY 2018 period, state appropriations per FTE student nationally declined 11.2 percent.[15] These reductions were accompanied by significant increases in tuition and fees, which by FY 2018 accounted for 46.6 percent of total educational revenues in public higher education, up from 35.8 percent in FY 2008.[16] Grant-based financial aid to students did not keep up. The College Board reports that the average real, inflation-adjusted net price of attending a four-year public college or university increased 29.8 percent between FY 2008 and FY 2018.[17]

Higher net prices have promoted age and income stratification in higher education as a whole and at specific institutions. Two-year public colleges have increasingly become populated with older students. Forty-two percent of two-year public college students are 20 years or older, and 40 percent of them are financially dependent upon their parents or someone else. At four-year public institutions, 37 percent of full-time undergraduate students are 20 years or older, and 64 percent of them are financial dependents.[18] Further, as already reported in table 2.1, only 27.3 percent of the undergraduate students enrolled at institutions in Opportunity Insights' elite and highly selective admissions categories come from the lowest 60 percent of the family income distribution, whereas 57.4 percent of students enrolled at Opportunity Insights' nonselective institutions come from the lowest 60 percent of the family income distribution.

It should not escape readers that governing boards have presided over and approved the income stratification phenomenon that has occurred in public higher education. Individual board members may wring their hands over their votes and point their fingers at legislators, but virtually all of them vote affirmatively when confronted with budgets that raise student costs but skimp on student financial aid. Not all of the blame, of course, accrues to governing boards. In general, the same washing of hands applies to governors and state legislators. They may bemoan rising tuition and fees in their speeches to Rotary Clubs, but their fiscal actions and votes profoundly devalue their protestations.

We do, however, have some sympathy for governors and legislators, who face rising demands for a variety of services and, like it or not, have had to deal with stagnant or declining state revenues during and since the Great Recession. Nonetheless, legislators frequently treat public higher education as a bank account they can tap to balance state budgets in years when state revenues have been disappointing. They reason that colleges and universities (in contrast to the highway department or state social welfare agencies) can mitigate or avoid the impact of budget cuts by raising tuition and fees. Hence, legislators minimize perceived injury to their state as a whole by reducing higher education appropriations by larger proportions than those of most other agencies.

We hasten to point out that in the next chapter we introduce data showing that in every one of our institutional categories, the average institution increased its tuition and fees more than was necessary to compensate it for reductions of its state funding. Indeed, between 2003-04 and 2016-17, the typical institution raised its inflation-adjusted net tuition and fees per FTE student about $1,600 more than the cuts in its inflation-adjusted state appropriations per FTE student.[19] The increases were larger than appropriations cuts in forty-nine of the fifty states during this period, with only Missouri recording appropriations cuts greater than tuition and fee increases at the typical institution.

The income stratification that now characterizes public higher education and influences student access may be uncomfortable but is reality—and to some extent unavoidable given the economic factors just mentioned. It is time for us to address a central question posed by the Harvard University Opportunity Insights study—namely, is a public college or university student's future economic fate essentially determined by the income of his or her parents? To what extent is it possible for students to use their collegiate educations as the means to move upward from one income bracket to another?

Independent of the Harvard University Opportunity Insights project (https://opportunityinsights.org), CollegeNet has developed a Social Mobility Index (www.socialmobilityindex.org) for institutions that considers five factors: tuition, the economic background of students, graduation rates, the early career salaries earned by students, and college endowments. CollegeNet's ranking of institutions in its Social Mobility Index generates results similar to those of the Harvard University Opportunity Insights project.

Probing Income Mobility and Board Responsibility

Let's stipulate that incomes are unequally distributed in the United States and that the undergraduate student bodies of American four-year public colleges and universities are stratified on the basis of the family incomes of the students. Two significant questions emerge. First, does this student sorting on the basis of incomes make any difference? Second, to what extent does the family income of a student's parents effectively determine where the student attends college and ultimately the future income destiny of that student?

The answers to these questions are more nuanced than some might believe. Excepting the elite institutions, the institutional types that perform best in terms of the Harvard University Opportunity Insights mobility index are the metropolitan leaders, the regionals, and the HBCUs (fig. 2.4). Each outperforms flagship institutions and those with medical schools. Several of the mobility index best performers in our institutional categories are shown in figure 2.5, while those that performed the worst are shown in figure 2.6.

We need to look more closely at these data, however. Six University of California (UC) campuses are in the *U.S. News* elite (top twenty-five) institution classification. They have pursued admissions policies that have emphasized access across income classes. In 2016–17, 31 percent of beginning undergraduate enrollees at the six UC campuses received a federal Pell Grant. Pell Grants are a useful thermometer of student financial need. To be eligible to receive a Pell Grant, one's family income must be less than $50,000, but in

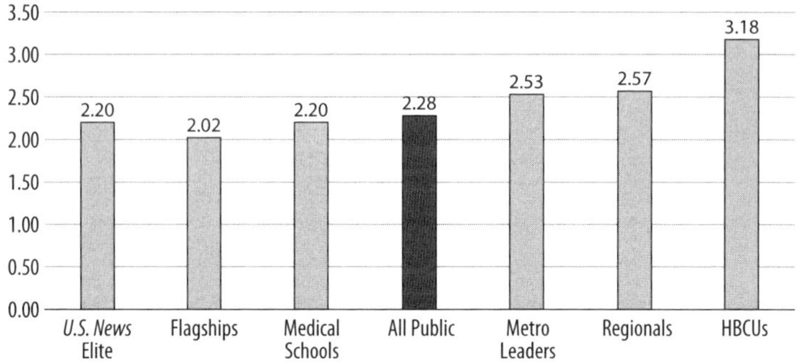

Figure 2.4. Average Mobility Indexes by Institutional Category, 2014. *Source:* Harvard University Opportunity Insights, https://opportunityinsights.org.

fact the great majority of Pell Grant dollars go to students whose family incomes are less than $20,000.[20] At UC Irvine that year, where only 14 percent of undergraduates were recorded as being white, 38 percent of beginning undergraduates received a Pell Grant, and 88 percent of that group were full-time students who graduated within six years.[21]

The University of California Pell Grant recipient percentages contrast visibly with the remainder of the elite institutions, where the average share of students receiving Pell Grants was only 17 percent, and with the other non-UC flagship institutions, where the average was 24 percent. As a consequence, when one removes the UC campuses from consideration, the mobility index of the elite institutions falls by 22 percent, from 2.20 to 1.72.

In general, the non-elite, non-flagship institutions receive higher mobility index grades from Harvard University Opportunity Insights. The non-elite institutions have a larger impact on society in this arena because proportionately they enroll far more P1 income quintile students than the elite and the flagships. Historically Black Colleges and Universities are stars in this regard; their average mobility index is 3.18.

Even so, elite and flagship public institutions typically report much higher success ratios for the lower-income students who come to them than do other institutions. This carries interesting implications. For example, if you are a lower-income student, then as a practical matter, if you can gain admission to an elite institution or flagship state university and can

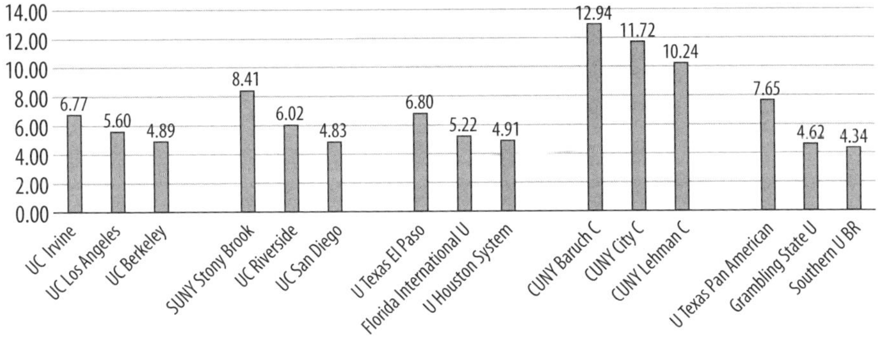

Figure 2.5. Best-Performing Mobility Index Institutions by Institutional Category. *Source:* Harvard University Opportunity Insights, https://opportunityinsights.org; and authors' calculations.

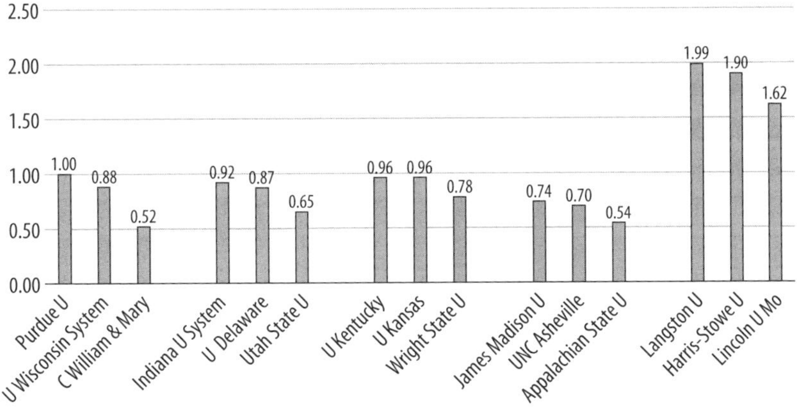

Figure 2.6. Worst-Performing Mobility Index Institutions by Institutional Category. *Source:* Harvard University Opportunity Insights, https://opportunityinsights.org; and authors' calculations.

afford to attend it, such an institution typically offers the best prospects for lifting you from the P1 income quintile to the K5 income quintile.

From society's standpoint, however, the elite and flagship public institutions (excepting the University of California campuses) are usually parsimonious in allocating admissions slots to talented but financially struggling students. Whatever their rhetoric, providing many opportunities for income mobility to large numbers of lower-income students is

Pell Grants have declined in value. In 1975, the maximum Pell Grant covered 79 percent of the cost of attending a four-year public university; by 2018, it covered only 29 percent of that cost.

Danielle Douglas-Gabriel, "Hits and Misses in the House Higher Education Bill," *Washington Post,* October 16, 2019, www.washingtonpost.com/education/2019/10/16/hits-misses-house-higher-education-bill.

not high on their lists. Today, most elite and flagship public institutions practice some form of admissions and financial aid optimization, behavior similar to the pricing practices airlines follow to extract the most revenue from their passengers. Campuses size up the market and assess what educational costs applicants with varying characteristics are willing and able to pay. An applicant's access to financial aid and ability to borrow clearly enter this decision mix as do his or her standardized test scores, racial and ethnic background, gender, desired major, and perhaps location. What emerges is an "optimal" freshman class that enables the institution to earn a given amount of net revenue (after institutionally based financial aid has been deducted) and simultaneously satisfy specific academic and demographic goals. As numerous observers have noted, seldom does this process benefit lower-income applicants and students. The models used by a typical campus nearly always make it desirable for that campus to admit more wealthy applicants.[22]

Thus, whereas individual lower-income students might have reason to prefer the elite and the flagships, economically conscious state governments and citizens might do well to direct resources elsewhere. If their goal is to improve the lot of the largest number of lower-income students, then the non-elite institutions are their best bets. It follows that resource allocations focused on this goal should reflect this reality and favor the non-elite unless the elite (excepting the University of California campuses) change their tune.

The groups that could cause—even force—the elite and the flagships to change their tune are their own governing boards. If governing boards appoint the right campus leaders and provide them with appropriate incentives, then even elite and flagship institutions will gradually change their behavior. By and large, the current incentive structures placed in front of university presidents by their boards do not reward behaviors that increase access and affordability, and therefore they fail to generate more social and economic mobility in society. We will have more to say about this phenomenon in chapter 5.

Governors and state legislators have the authority to mandate changes in the behavior of elite and flagship institutions (and ambitious regionals as well) but are typically reluctant to do so. Interference from above in the daily operations of public colleges and universities is a risky enterprise, and not only because such actions smack of discredited Soviet-style methodologies. Adventures in micromanagement on campuses seldom end well in the long term. Far better that those who hold legal responsibility for direction—that is, members of governing boards—focus on making appropriate policies and establishing the right set of administrative incentives. In their power to effect change on a local level, governing board members sit in the catbird seat. As they do so, however, they must be careful to devote themselves to making policy and to assessing results rather than attempting to control daily operations, which are properly the province of the president and the campus. This is a narrow and perhaps precarious path for boards and board members to traverse, and not all prove capable of doing so.

3 Who's in Charge and Does It Make Any Difference?

Who's in charge here, anyway?

Adam Zimmerman, *Who's in Charge Here, Anyway? Reflections from a Life in Business* (1997)

Statewide coordinating boards, the number of governing boards in a state, and methods for selecting governing board trustees each have significant, independent effects on net tuition and fee revenue.

Robert C. Lowry, *American Journal of Political Science* (2001)

Public higher education (our primary focus in this book) in the United States is remarkably varied, more so than in most other developed counties. Although the federal government provides large amounts of funding for specific aspects of higher education (including especially student financial aid, research and development, and outreach efforts in areas such as agriculture), primary responsibility for the funding and supervision of public higher education resides with the states. In this regard, the United States visibly contrasts with most nations of the world, including China, Japan, the Middle East, and Western Europe, where national leadership, standards, and funding are de rigueur.

While there are fifty states in the Union, there are many more than fifty different systems of public higher education in the United States because higher education is sliced and diced in multiple ways in some states. California provides an instructive example. Since 1960, there have been three major subdivisions in California public higher education: the University of California, the California State University, and the California Community Colleges. The California Postsecondary Education Commission was created to oversee this conglomerate.

In 2011, however, California governor Jerry Brown judged the Postsecondary Commission "ineffective" and wiped out its entire General Fund appropriation, ending its existence.[1] Each of the three systems, which in 2018–19 together enrolled more than 2.7 million headcount students, now negotiates more or less independently with the governor and legislature concerning its own governance and budget.

Governor Brown's assessment of the commission as ineffective may or may not have been on target, although it has been echoed by others.[2] But his harsh evaluation does linger. Here we address the governor's challenging assessment by responding to four questions:

- How do states assign responsibility for governing higher education?
- How do states populate the governing boards or other bodies that carry out those responsibilities?
- How do states prepare the individuals who become members of the governing boards or other bodies responsible for higher education?
- What evidence is there that how states answer any of the first questions makes any difference in outcomes?

In the remainder of this chapter, we explore the state of knowledge concerning each of these questions. The answers are critical to recognizing the manner in which American public higher education has evolved over time and how we can influence its future. How we choose to structure and govern higher education does make a difference.

How Do the States Structure Responsibility for Higher Education?

In American public higher education, authority usually is distributed rather than concentrated. In most states, constitutions or legislatures delegate substantial authority to public college and university governing boards that therefore hold legal responsibilities for public college campuses. Parenthetically, it is worth noting that the Education Commission of the States (ECS) and the State Higher Education Executive Officers Association (SHEEO) are the authoritative go-to sources for the most current and comprehensive data on how states structure and distribute the power to make decisions concerning public colleges and universities.

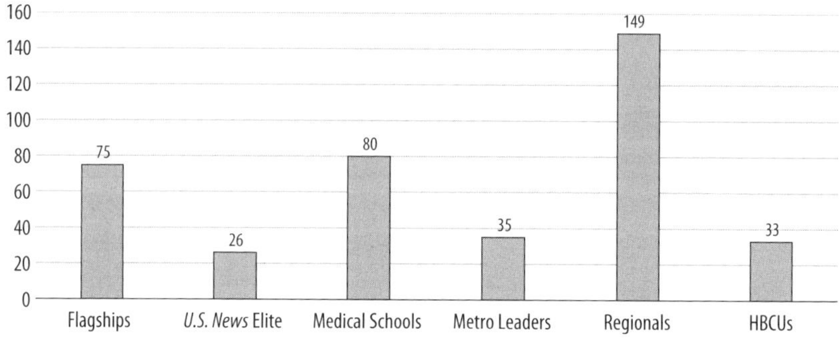

Figure 3.1. The 275 Public Four-Year Institutions of Higher Education in Our Sample (Overlap Exists between the Categories)

We use a stratified sample of 275 four-year public institutions of higher education to provide the primary basis for our analysis, and we again subdivide these institutions into our six categories. This sample and the six institutional categories are presented in figure 3.1, and the classifications are designed to reflect the diversity of twenty-first-century American public higher education. Approximately 700 four-year public institutions of higher education exist in the United States; our sample of 275 includes more than 39 percent of that group and more than 65 percent of the four-year public institutions included in the Harvard University Opportunity Insights study. Data unavailability is the primary reason for an institution's exclusion from this study.

All states save Wyoming are represented in the sample by at least two institutions. California supplies 14 members of the sample—appropriate because the Golden State enrolls approximately one in every six of the nation's college students.

At times, public higher education governance structures seem to defy categorization. Each state's governance structure exhibits its own quirks, and on occasion what appears to be a straightforward governance model is sharply modified in practice. The presence of an especially influential governor, legislator, governing board chair, or university president, for example, alters power relationships. Informal relationships built over the years may trump statutory processes. Alumni connections can open doors. Apart from the influence of individuals and personalities, however, a state's fiscal condition ultimately may have more to do with whether a governor or governing board supports, penalizes, listens, or dictates. If there is a moral to this story, it is that governance relationships change over time and sometimes appear to do so without reference to statutory and constitutional considerations.

As already noted, significant differences sometimes exist within states in terms of how public universities are governed. It is one thing to be one of thirty colleges plus seven universities governed by the Minnesota State Colleges and Universities system (St. Cloud State University is one of that group) and quite another to be the dominant University of Minnesota Twin Cities campus that is governed by the University of Minnesota Board of Regents. Such contrasts help explain why governance differences among institutions inside a state can be as substantial as those between states.

The data in table 3.1 bring some order to the disparate public university governance arena. These data are derived from a 2019 study published by the Education Commission of the States (ECS), and it is to the ECS that individuals desiring more detailed information should repair.[3]

Of the 275 institutions in our sample, 108 (39 percent) operate in states in which no statewide coordinating or governing board exists for public higher education (table 3.1). The institutions in these states have their own governing boards and typically deal directly with the governor and the legislature. The remaining 167 institutions in the sample are located in states that have either a statewide coordinating board or a statewide governing board for higher education.

Coordinating boards typically are tasked with providing a statewide view, and sometimes a national view, of the higher education needs of their state, and they are supposed to have the best interests of their state at heart. Such boards may be called upon to opine on the merit of institutional proposals in matters ranging from proposals for new degree programs and tuition and fee increases to requests for new construction. Many coordinating boards are tasked with administering statewide financial aid programs and assembling data, such as persistence and graduation

In New York State, the state's budget, including its allocations to public higher education, were historically determined by "three men in a room"—the governor, the speaker of the New York Assembly, and the Senate majority leader. As one knowledgeable observer commented, "many would-be decision makers with plausible claims to leadership are simply frozen out," and "bills favored by one of the big three are introduced with little discussion or explanation and then zip through to enactment in a matter of days." Political and economic reality sometimes differs dramatically from apparent statutory and constitutional strictures where university governance and budgets are concerned.

Alan Ehrenhalt, "The Albany Triopoly," *Governing* (November 2006), www.governing.com/topics/mgmt/Albany-Triopoly.html.

rates, that are thought to define institutional performance. On occasion, they exercise some authority over private colleges as well. Examples of coordinating bodies include the Indiana Commission for Higher Education and Massachusetts's Board of Higher Education.

"Coordinating" usually means, however, that final authority with respect to a decision resides elsewhere. Formal decision-making authority may rest with a statewide governing board that exercises authority over all four-year higher education in a state. In our sample, ECS identifies 109 institutions as having a statewide governing board that wields the authority to say yes or no to institutional proposals, including budgets, tuition, and fees (table 3.1). Examples are New York's State University of New York (SUNY) Board of Trustees and the University of North Carolina Board of Governors.

Many states have opted for boards governing systems of institutions, which either group similar institutions together or incorporate institutions that have the same generic name even though they may have very different missions. In our sample, 159 institutions are governed by boards that oversee systems of institutions. The Board of Trustees of the California State University system and the Arizona Board of Regents, respectively, exemplify these different strands of the systems governance model,

Table 3.1 Major Governance Models in Our Sample

Governance model	Number of institutions
No statewide board	29
Statewide coordinating or governing board	137
Statewide governing board	109
Systemwide board	159

Source: Education Commission of the States, "50-State Comparison: State Postsecondary Governance Structures," March 5, 2019, www.ecs.org/50-state-comparison-postsecondary-governance-structures.

Note: Overlap exists among governance types, so the number of institutions represented here exceeds the sample of 275. For example, Colorado State University's flagship Fort Collins campus has its own board of governors, but that board is also responsible for two other Colorado State institutions (Colorado State University-Pueblo and Colorado State University Global). There also is a Colorado Commission on Higher Education, which is a statewide higher education coordinating board.

which are appropriately viewed as semi-centralized in nature because other public university systems exist in both states.

Overlap obviously exists among the governance models identified in table 3.1. Radford University aptly illustrates this point. Radford has its own Board of Visitors, which holds the legal authority to operate the institution; at the same time the State Council of Higher Education for Virginia (SCHEV) functions both as a coordinating board and as an agency that exercises some decision-making authority in areas such as programmatic approval.

Nonetheless, insofar as governance is concerned, in virtually every state, the proverbial rubber meets the road in the respective state legislatures. The old adage nearly always applies: Whoever has the gold, makes the rules. If legislators do not like what is happening in public higher education or are dismayed by occurrences on a specific campus, they can soon change the behavior they find obnoxious by tightening institutional purse strings or by excising a specific program or even an individual's salary from a university's budget. Few governing boards and college presidents have the ability to resist such messages, whether positive or negative. Further, in most states, legislators have some ability to influence or determine the membership of university governing boards and thereby the identity of a university's leadership. We have more to say about this circumstance below.

A Look at Previous Studies Linking Governance Structures to Institutional Behavior

It is plausible that the various ways the 50 states and the 275 institutions in our sample have chosen to organize and operate university governance influence their behavior and thereby impact the welfare of students and citizens. Only a handful of studies have attempted to investigate such links. Arguably, the most rigorous of these studies (Robert Lowry's groundbreaking 2001 article in the *American Journal of Political Science*) necessarily relied on evidence from the previous century,[4] and nothing in the same genre as his study has appeared since then. Examining the impact of governance arrangements on college costs, Lowry found that tuition and fees were lower at institutions where members of the governing board either were directly appointed by public officials or were elected as opposed to being nominated and then confirmed by a legislative body. He concluded that these arrangements made board members more connected and thus more responsive to public officials, whom he assumed were interested in controlling the growth of tuition and fees.

Legislators may wish to control public institution tuition and fees, but countervailing winds might also exist. When tax collections stagnate or fall, legislators tend to regard public higher education as a soft target where they can impose major budget cuts because they presume the institutions can make up for the cuts by increasing tuition and fees. In these situations, legislators essentially invite their public colleges and universities to increase tuition and fees in response to budget cuts, and the institutions typically respond by doing so, often by substantial amounts.

Tangential subsequent work by Mclendon et al. (2009) and Tandberg et al. (2017) addressed the influence of modes of governance and political factors on overall state funding for higher education.[5] These two studies found—no surprise—that political factors loomed large in state funding for public higher education and that relationships such as those between the state higher education executive officers and the governors and legislators were important to the setting of tuition and fee levels. Institutional funding is higher in administrations where there is a friendly, closer relationship between the state higher education executive officers and the governors and legislators.

The absence of recent empirical evidence on the impact of governance on tuition and fee inflation is notable and a bit unexpected given the national surge in tuition and fees to which we referred in chapter 1 and the mobility data we presented in chapter 2. It seems natural to ask what role governing boards have played in this scenario. After all, the escalation of college costs has caused many people to raise questions about the ultimate worth of public higher education and sometimes to express doubts about whether pursuing a college degree is really a good investment.

One reason for this dearth of scholarly studies on the connection of governance models to college and university behavior is the challenge of identifying and assessing precisely what public colleges and universities do. One cannot assess and critique the cost of a commodity unless one knows what that commodity is. One can see what a highway department does, measure traffic congestion, and track potholes. Higher education is less amenable to tracking metrics.

Not only do public colleges and universities supply what we usually term higher education, but they also provide many other products and services, including housing, food, entertainment, health services, and job placement. Visualize a university as a multi-product firm, but one where historically it has been difficult to measure the size and importance of this firm's inputs and outputs. What precisely does a university "produce," and which inputs are responsible for its outputs? Are universities in the business of generating knowledge, or producing knowledgeable citizens, or supplying individuals capable of filling available job openings, or providing entertainment such as football teams, or all of these? These are only some of the considerations that focus on the raison d'être for public higher education. It will suffice for us to observe that even on campuses with well-identified missions, there is seldom agreement on the social and economic purposes of higher education, and even less concurrence with off-campus views on these matters.[6]

The anonymous wag who once opined that "a faculty member is someone who thinks otherwise" hit the proverbial nail on the head. Seldom is there agreement on campuses about what higher education is or what it should be doing. Moreover, what a public college or university does changes over time, and so do ideas about what it should be doing.

In this book we avoid some of these complexities by focusing deliberately on an aspect of institutional behavior that is both measurable and important: tuition and fees. This is hardly the only measure of institutional performance, but how institutions price what is arguably their most important product—undergraduate education—is a critical metric that we can use to help assess differences in inter-institutional performance. In all but two states (Florida and Louisiana), tuition and fees and increases at public institutions of higher education must be approved by their governing boards.

In Florida and Louisiana, state legislatures set the published "sticker price" tuition and fees that one sees in catalogs, but these bodies exercise only partial control over other variables, such as institutional grants, that ultimately determine the net price students pay. Net price determination continues to be largely the province of administrators and governing boards, and practice here varies substantially from campus to campus. Thus, in 2016-17 the average net price paid by an in-state undergraduate student at Florida A&M in Tallahassee was $13,529, and the comparable net price tag at cross-town Florida State University was $16,450—21.6 percent higher.[7]

The duties of most public institution governing boards extend well beyond undergraduate education and undergraduate tuition and fees, but the prices administrators and governing boards decide to charge undergraduate students offer an obvious and important window from which we can observe and assess the impact of these governing boards. In addition to tuition and fees, we will examine several other interesting "measurables" including each institution's ratio of administrative expenditures to instructional expenditures, faculty teaching loads, class sizes, and persistence and graduation rates.

How Public University Boards Are Populated

Given the many different governance models within American public higher education, it should come as no surprise that the same lack of uniformity exists with respect to the manner in which the members of public university governing boards come to their posts. Most often (in 250 of our 275 cases), some or all of the members of governing boards are nominated by the state's governor, but in only 162 of these instances (64.8 percent) does the governor nominate all the members of the board. In nearly all states, legislatures have some input: either legislators must approve some or all individuals nominated for membership on public university governing boards, or, in 13 percent of our institutions, they themselves select some or all board members.

The unavoidable lesson is that legislators usually have their hands in the politics and economics of public higher education.[8] The Association of Governing Boards (AGB) put it succinctly: "Politics cannot be removed from public trusteeship."[9] This is especially true given that nearly all public university governing board posts are sought after by substantially more citizens than there are slots available. As a consequence, in most states, political contributions to the election coffers of the governor or key legislators are taken for granted as constituting a semi-mandatory prerequisite for nomination. There is a symbiotic relationship between legislators and governors in this regard. Both raise money and in friendly times cooperate with each other. On the one hand, legislators want their constituents nominated or appointed to posts by governors, and they do not relish gubernatorial vetoes of their pet legislation. On the other hand, governors hope to see their legislative programs and nominations treated favorably and therefore do not casually ignore the governing board membership recommendations of influential legislators.

One might be invited to board membership simply on the basis of one's achievements and reputation, or perhaps because of an institution's need for specific expertise, or perhaps because a scandal has erupted and governors and legislators are "sending in the troops" (the language of a president who found himself in this situation) to do damage control. Sterling qualifications, however, are by no means a necessary condition for nomination to many governing boards. Institutions may push forward the names of individuals who could make major financial gifts to an institution. Indeed, this criterion may loom larger in a campus's nomination calculus than anything else, including intrinsic interest by the individual in serving on the board. Still, institutional preferences may not matter if the individuals being considered have records of opposition to the governor and key legislators. This is the political equivalent of being labeled untouchable, and, not surprisingly, such individuals seldom end up seated on boards.

Other complications can derail an individual's membership on a public university governing board. Of special import and concern from the standpoint of public policy are situations in which the nominations of potentially influential board members raise possible conflicts of interest. For example, nominees may be doing (or wishing to do) business with the universities they would govern, they may own strategically located properties near university developments, they may have an interest in developing intellectual property, or they may seek *gratis* use of university facilities and resources. True, universities and states nearly always have statutes and rules that discourage or prohibit such situations, but adept individuals are often able to find ways to achieve the legal separation necessary to enable them to join a governing board. It is not that American higher education is experiencing an epidemic of such conflicts, but it is naïve to suggest that such episodes do not occur. When they do, they may be swept under the proverbial rug because of the perceived importance of the individuals involved.[10]

The institutions categorized as metropolitan leaders sometimes face an interesting variant relating to possible conflicts of interest. The intensely regional roots of these campuses can understandably cause regional political leaders, including mayors and city managers, to seek influence over the institution's activities, perhaps by determining where branch campuses and outreach programs are or can be located. What better way to accomplish this objective than to get appointed to the institution's board? When this occurs, it can work to the institution's advantage in the short run because the support of the mayor or city manager greases the skids for the desired project. This scenario may not sit well, however, with the other mayors and city managers in the region, who want to know why they have been ignored. Further, when decision time comes, the question becomes, Whose interests will the mayor or city manager put first—those of the campus or those of the city?

The preceding scenario also applies to the appointment of legislators, legislators' spouses or offspring, and legislative aides to governing boards. Why do they wish to be on the governing board, and whom do they ultimately represent? Possible conflicts may diminish when it is former legislators and public officials who join a governing board, but they may be accentuated if these individuals become employees of the institution. Such individuals could turn out to be "can't be fired" employees whose primary interest is pumping up the value of their state employee pension.

While not without controversy, it has become commonplace for governing boards to appoint former elected or prominent appointed officials as campus presidents. This is a venerable tradition and includes names such as Dwight Eisenhower (Columbia), David Boren (Oklahoma), Kenneth Starr (Baylor), Robert Gates (Texas A&M), Janet Napolitano (University of California system), Rebecca Blank (Wisconsin-Madison), Mitch Daniels (Purdue), Margaret Spellings (North Carolina), John Engler (Michigan State), and Richard Myers (Kansas State). Without a doubt, such individuals come to their posts with enabling connections and may serve as useful interpreters of legislative activities and preferences. But their records of achievement are mixed, and some find it difficult to discard their former roles. Few, however, would quarrel with the excellent performances of Rebecca Blank (a former US secretary of commerce) at Wisconsin-Madison, Mitch Daniels (a former head of the US Office of Management and Budget and former governor of the State of Indiana) at Purdue, or Richard Myers (a former chairman of the Joint Chiefs of Staff) at Kansas State.

Although not evincing open conflicts of interest, some individuals, when they join their governing board, bring with them a full-throated agenda for action. This might involve making personnel changes up to and including getting rid of their university's president or its football coach; initiating or abolishing specific academic programs; ending, limiting, or even expanding affirmative action in admissions and hiring; establishing or expanding a branch campus in a specific location; or changing the complexion of speakers who make presentations on the campus. There is nothing intrinsically wrong with board members harboring such enthusiasms or championing such endeavors; public higher education governing board members are a manifestation of American democracy, and its four-year colleges and universities should lend an ear to them because to some degree board members are the de facto voice of the people. Even so, single-issue board members can become problematic because they may be uninterested in the overall welfare of the institution they govern. Their highly focused passion is often the engine that motivates them to curry legislative favor and importune governors on specific issues, sometimes independent of the institution's president and the overall board.

The passion of single-issue board members motivates them to be more interested in board membership than most citizens, and hence they may pursue board nominations with single-minded energy. After being appointed to the board, if they succeed (or do not succeed) in attaining their goal, their interest in participating in governance may flag. A challenge confronting the president and other board members is to harness and redirect the energy of such board members and broaden their perspectives and knowledge bases.

Nomination leading to confirmation by a governor or legislative body is not the only way to become a member of a governing board. Some governing board members are directly appointed or elected by other bodies, such as the state legislature or an institution's alumni association. The University of Michigan's Board of Regents, for example, consists of eight members, all of whom are elected at large in biennial statewide elections. In 2018 two slots were open, and several candidates (including the two eventually elected) ran on platforms that emphasized controlling the institution's tuition and fee increases.

In New York, North Carolina, and South Carolina, legislators elect some or all of the members of flagship university governing boards. In

At a large public university, a new board member walked into the president's office with a copy of the university's catalog, from which he had assembled a list of approximately two dozen courses that he insisted should be deleted from the catalog and dropped from the curriculum. At the top of his list was a course in Marxian Economics, whose deletion was justified, he asserted, because such a course would be a study of demonstrably failed economic thought. The president responded by explaining that while the university's governing board did possess the legal authority to take such action, doing so would likely set in motion a wave of negative publicity that would focus not only on the university but also on the new board member himself. The *Chronicle of Higher Education,* the *New York Times,* the *Washington Post,* and the *Wall Street Journal* would all cover the story, the president observed, and the tone of their coverage was likely to be exceedingly negative. Critical editorials would follow. Hence, the situation might not play out as the new board member hoped. After some time passed, the board member dropped his request.

these states, as in Michigan, those desiring appointment court legislators, make strategic financial contributions, and woo alumni organizations. The endorsement of a university president may help or hinder in such situations.

The Penn State University Board of Trustees presents an intriguing hybrid model that involves a combination of elections and other mechanisms. At Penn State, nine board members are elected by alumni, six are elected by state agricultural societies, six are elected by a board representing business and industry, six are appointed by the governor, and three are elected by the board itself. Penn State has turned out to be the most expensive public university in the country in terms of the average annual net price paid by its students. In 2016–17, in-state undergraduates at Penn State's flagship campus paid an average of $25,346.[11] It is not clear, however, that this elevated price necessarily reflects Penn State's governance structure because the Commonwealth of Pennsylvania's financial support for public higher education on a per-student basis has been the second lowest in the country.[12] To some extent, tuition has substituted for state financial support in Pennsylvania.

Some individuals are ex officio members of college boards by virtue of the offices they hold. In Alabama, the governor is an ex officio member of the boards of all four-year public universities in the state; moreover, this is true nationally for approximately one of every six public college boards. Usually, such membership is not meaningful because governors do not have the time or interest to attend board meetings. However, ex officio status becomes more interesting if a governor chooses to send a representative in his or her place. Whether or not these representatives have a vote in meetings (and states differ in this regard), their presence can alter behavior. It is difficult for board members and a university president to plot legislative strategy or comment candidly about state conditions, politics, or budgets when a representative of the governor's office is present. Of course, one or more conventionally appointed members of the board might already be reporting tidbits to gubernatorial and legislative offices. Wise presidents and senior administrators learn to watch their tongues.

Much more could be written about the origins, goals, and internal workings of governing boards, and Robert Scott's recent *How University Boards Work* provides an excellent tour of the subject.[13] Scott's perspective is valuable because he served with success as a statewide higher education official and as a long-serving college president in both the public and independent sectors. Our focus here, however, is different from his because we zero in on the empirical connections between governance and governing board decision-making. We want to know whether the peculiar ways in which higher education governance is structured in the states and the manner in which governing boards are populated in these states make any difference in behavior, particularly in terms of tuition and fees determination. Does it make a difference in board decision-making if a state has a coordinating or governing board for public higher education? Or if an institution is part of a system? Do board members behave differently if they are elected rather than appointed? Or if they represent the alumni? Providing answers to such questions is central to this book.

A First Look at Governance and Tuition and Fees

Succeeding chapters will provide detailed multivariate empirical evidence that connects governing board structures and membership characteristics to specific board behavior. We hope to whet your appetite, however, with some intriguing bivariate empirical evidence that outlines and clarifies what is to come.

To do so, we examine real net public tuition and fee increases per full-time equivalent student between the 2003–04 and 2016–17 academic years and segment these data by institutional type (fig. 3.2). The term "real" means inflation-adjusted; all of the dollar values presented in figure 3.2 are expressed in 2016 dollars (that is, 2016 purchasing power) and are therefore comparable across the years. "Net" means that institutional grants have been subtracted from the tuition and fee revenues collected by each institution. Thus, if annual tuition and fees are $12,000, but the institution grants a student a $2,000 scholarship that does not need to be paid back, we use a net figure of $10,000. It would be deceptive to pretend that the institution is actually collecting $12,000 from the student.

The data in figure 3.2 depict in-state (resident) students only. In subsequent chapters, we will also deal with non-resident students.

"T&F" refers to mandatory tuition and fees paid by in-state undergraduate students; it does not include special discipline-specific fees that might be paid by engineering students, nursing students, and the like.

"Per FTE student" means that the dollar values in the figure have been computed on the basis of full-time equivalent students. The conventional methodology for doing so assumes that 30 semester hours of coursework represents one full-time equivalent undergraduate student for one year.[14] The institutional types are the same as those used previously.

The data in figure 3.2 are organized to reflect the differing ability and willingness of various types of institutions to collect increasing amounts of tuition and fees from their undergraduate student bodies. Over this thirteen-year period, the *U.S. News* elite raised their net real tuition and fees by an average of $6,033 per FTE student. Flagship institutions (a grouping that contains nearly all of the elite) raised their tuition and fees

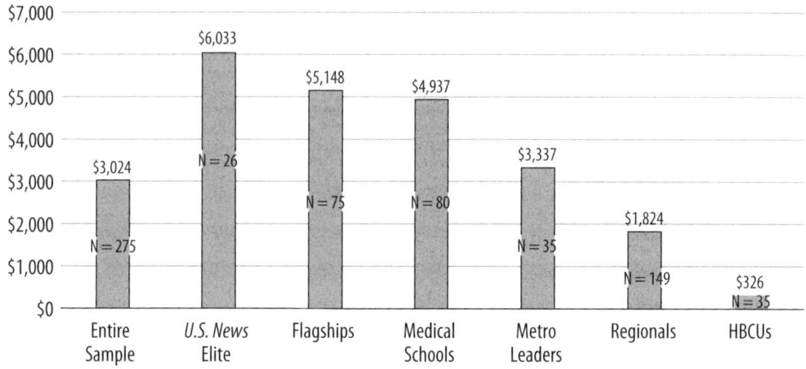

Figure 3.2. Change in Real Net Public In-State T&F per FTE Student by Institutional Type, 2003-04 to 2016-17. *Sources:* Integrated Postsecondary Education Data System (IPEDS), https://nces.ed.gov/IPEDS; *U.S. News and World Report*, "U.S. News Best Colleges," https://www.usnews.com/best-colleges; State Higher Education Executive Officers Association (SHEEO), *State Higher Education Finance: FY 2018*, https://sheeomain.wpengine.com/wp-content/uploads/2019/04/SHEEO_SHEF_FY18_Report.pdf.

by a lesser amount, $5,148 per FTE student. In descending order after that came institutions with medical schools (this classification probably is a proxy for research activity), the large-enrollment metropolitan area leader institutions, regional state colleges and universities (often former teachers' colleges), and Historically Black Colleges and Universities (HBCUs). It is noteworthy that, alone among the various institutional types, the HBCUs ended the period collecting far less inflation-adjusted revenue per FTE student than did the institutions in any other category.

What explains the tuition and fee behavior we observe in figure 3.2? Certainly, the existing literature suggests that individual institutional reputations for excellence and students' ability to pay are important determinants. Thus, institutions that have price-making power usually take advantage of that power to increase their net tuition and fees more rapidly than institutions that do not enjoy such influence. In general, flagship institutions possess price-making ability, and for the elite among them, this is especially true.

In chapter 2, we reported Harvard University Opportunity Insights data that focused on the family incomes of students attending four-year public colleges and universities. Let's review some of these numbers. Only 15.0 percent of undergraduates at the University of Virginia came from families in the lowest 60 percent of the income distribution, while 8.5 percent came from the top 1 percent. At the University of Michigan-Ann Arbor, the comparable percentages were 16.5 percent and 9.3 percent. These are significant numbers in many ways, but economically speaking, they mean that these campuses have considerable ability to increase their tuition and fees without experiencing major backlash from students and families. The online tool College Navigator reports that there were 64,917 applicants for admission to UM's fall 2017 freshman class, of whom 23 percent were admitted. In-state undergraduates at UM in 2017-18 paid an average net price of $16,856, but those whose families earned $110,001 or more annually paid an average net price of $25,040.[15] Economists label this "price discrimination" because the same product is sold to different customers at different prices, and there is no cost justification for doing so. To economists, price discrimination of this sort is unmistakable economic evidence of market power.[16]

Next, we begin to address questions relating to governance and its effect, if any, on the level of undergraduate in-state tuition and fees (fig. 3.3). For our sample, the average institutional increase in real, net tuition and fees per FTE student was $3,024 during this period. Differences in governing structures and practices do appear to make a difference. When no statewide coordinating or governing board existed in the state, the average institutional increase in real, net tuition and fees was $3,998—nearly $1,000 higher than the average. When statewide coordinating boards were present, tuition and fee increases were slightly below the average, at $2,994. When statewide governing boards were present, the increases were $238 (7.9 percent) below the average at $2,786. These intriguing relationships suggest that the presence of statewide boards does constrain institutions and their boards, at least insofar as tuition and fee increases are concerned. We will investigate these possibilities further when we report our multivariate analyses.

Institutions with some elected board members also recorded a very high average increase ($3,633); however, only 23 of our 275 institutions

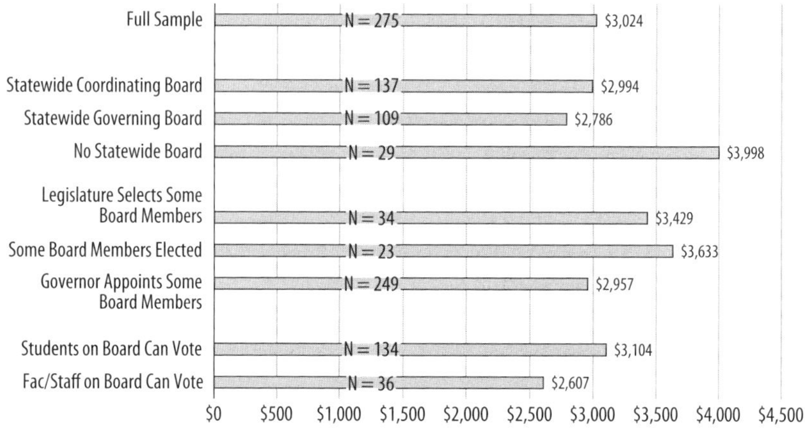

Figure 3.3. Change in Real Net In-State Four-Year Public T&F per FTE Student by Governance Type: 2003-04 to 2016-17. *Source:* Education Commission of the States (ECS), "50-State Comparison: State Postsecondary Governance Structures," https://www.ecs.org/50-state-comparison-postsecondary-governance-structures.

fit into this category. When legislators appoint or elect some board members, the average increase in real, net tuition and fees was $3,429. These two results suggest that neither voters nor legislators effectively constrain the behavior of the individuals they appoint or elect as board members.

Where students, faculty, and staff were members of a governing board and could vote, tuition and fee increases were within $80 to $417 of the average. However, as is true for all of the other board member classifications reported in figure 3.3, we cannot infer cause and effect.

Several additional caveats are appropriate with respect to the provocative bivariate data analysis reported in figure 3.3. Only 29 institutions make up the subsample of institutions operating in states that have no statewide coordinating or governing board. Only 23 institutions are included in the "some board members are elected" subsample, and this group includes the Universities of Delaware, Michigan, Minnesota, Nebraska, Nevada, and New Hampshire as well as Michigan State, Penn State, Purdue, and Wayne State (Michigan). The institutions are atypical when considered in the context of the entire national population of approximately 700 four-year, public colleges and universities. Hence, their presence in the "elected" subsample has the potential to push the real net tuition number upward for reasons that have nothing to do with the election of board members. For these flagship institutions, other factors could be at work, such as their allure and price-making power as well as the wealth of their students and families. We will consider the roles and impacts of these factors in the next chapter. For now, one should regard the data reported in figure 3.3 as intriguing or suggestive but certainly not conclusive.

A First Look at State Appropriations

Tuition and fee revenues are important, but they constitute only one part of the revenue structure of a modern public institution of higher education. State appropriations are another important source of financial sustenance. A common lament among many university presidents and governing board members is that persistent reductions in state appropriations have injured their institutions and left them with no choice but to increase tuition and fees. The SHEEO provides partial support for this contention. Between the 2008 and 2018 fiscal years, real state funding on public higher education per FTE student fell on average by 11.2 percent, although this funding fell only 4.3 percent over the twenty-five-year period 1993–2018. Nevertheless, total institutional revenue per FTE student (the sum of net tuition and fees per FTE student plus state appropriations per FTE student) rose 6.4 percent during the 2008–18 period, signaling that real net tuition and fees rose more than was necessary to counteract state funding reductions. This was the story in forty-eight states during this period; only in Missouri and Wisconsin did public higher education institutions register average reductions in total institutional revenue per FTE student.[17]

Let us now take the tuition and fee data presented in figures 3.2 and 3.3 and add to them the modifying economic influence of state appropriations for the period 2003–04 to 2016–17. As we already have observed, between 2003–04 and 2016–17 the average institution in our sample increased its real net tuition and fee collections per FTE student by $3,024. During the same period, the typical institution in our sample suffered a decline in its real state appropriations per FTE student of $1,420 (table 3.2).

Stephen Burd of New America is one of the harsher critics of public higher education: "Over the last 20 years, state disinvestment and institutional status-seeking have worked together, hand in hand, to encourage public colleges and universities to adopt the enrollment management techniques of their private college counterparts. For many of these schools, that has meant using their institutional aid dollars strategically in order to lure affluent out-of-state students to their campuses, rather than spend these funds on in-state students who can't afford to go to college without the help."

Stephen Burd, The Out-of-State Student Arms Race" (Washington, DC: New America, 2015), www.newamerica.org/education-policy/policy-papers/out-of-state-student-arms-race.

In net terms, the representative institution ended the period $1,605 per FTE student better off in real, inflation-adjusted terms. This means that the typical institution (or, to be more precise, 208 of our 275 institutions) raised its tuition and fees more than the amount necessary to counteract reductions in its state funding. The only general exception to this dictum were the institutions in the HBCU group, which had to cope with both declining tuition and fee collections and declining state appropriations.

The plight of the HBCUs is worthy of additional comment. Historically Black Colleges and Universities long have been viewed as offering both learning opportunities and a congenial learning and social atmosphere to students who otherwise might not have access to higher education. We observed in chapter 2 that the Harvard University Opportunity Insights study collectively assigned them above-average mobility indexes. These institutions do have the ability to change the social and economic circumstances of their students.

In recent years, however, their relative market position in higher education has deteriorated. Community colleges underprice them, while state colleges and universities with predominantly majority student bodies have become more welcoming and attractive to African American students. Further, many metro leader and flagship state universities now offer lower net prices than the HBCUs. The state of South Carolina provides an illustration. The average net price paid in 2017-18 by an in-state undergraduate student whose annual family income ranged between $0 and $30,000 was $10,819 at the flagship Columbia campus of the University of South Carolina, but $20,488 for a similarly situated student at the HBCU South Carolina State University.

These competitive circumstances plus the financials presented in table 3.2 have produced a challenging competitive environment for HBCUs. These are among the reasons why FTE enrollment declined at approximately 60 percent of the HBCUs in our subsample between 2003-04 and 2016-17 and the average HBCU in our subsample lost more than 3 percent of its FTE students. We will give additional attention to the HBCUs in our subsequent multivariate analysis.

Final Comments

The data presented above do not permit us to reach any strong conclusions, but they do pique our interest in the relationships between gover-

Table 3.2 Tuition and Fees and State Support per FTE Student at 275 Public Four-Year Colleges and Universities, 2003-04 to 2016-17

		Real change from 2003-04 to 2016-17		
Category	Number of institutions	Net tuition and fees per FTE student	State support per FTE student	Net overall change in dollars available per FTE student
Full sample	275	$3,034	–$1,420	$1,605
There is a state coordinating board	137	$2,924	–$1,835	$1,089
There is a state governing board	109	$2,786	–$519	$2,267
Own board sets tuition and fees	128	$3,194	–$1,780	$1,414
No statewide board	29	$3,998	–$2,535	$1,463
Students on board can vote	133	$3,104	–$1,607	$1,497
Some board members are elected	21	$3,633	–$1,786	$1,846
U.S. News elite	24	$6,033	–$2,424	$4,268
Flagship	70	$5,148	–$2,390	$2,768
Medical school	80	$4,810	–$2,548	$2,262
Metro leader	35	$3,337	–$2,037	$1,243
Regional	148	$1,824	–$853	$962
HBCU	35	$326	–$927	–$1,027

Source: State Higher Education Executive Officers Association (SHEEO), *State Higher Education Finance (SHEF): FY 2018* (Boulder, CO, 2019), Tables 3 and 4, https://sheeo.org/wp-content/uploads/2019/04/SHEEO_SHEF_FY18_Report.pdf.

Note: HBCU = Historically Black College and University

nance structures and tuition and fee increases. This is an important area of investigation. There has been a tendency for some involved in debates over higher education funding to deploy relatively unsophisticated tools that assume that a one-dollar decline in state support leads to a one-dollar increase in tuition and fees. Only a few observers (Jeffrey Selingo deserves a blue ribbon) have correctly noted that the relationship is more complicated. Opined Selingo in a 2017 op-ed, "The precise impact of state budget cuts on student tuition has never been clear—a drop in one doesn't usually lead to an equal increase in the other."[18]

We will take these complications into account in chapter 4, where we will also estimate the impact of various governance models on tuition and fees. Does governance really make a difference in tuition and fee pricing behavior?

4 Tuition and Fees, Governing Boards, and State Financial Support

College cost increases we have observed are "not even particularly unusual."

Robert B. Archibald and David H. Feldman, *Why Does College Cost So Much?* (2011)

Almost every board vote to increase tuition is unanimous. How can rate-setting—one of a board's most important and consequential responsibilities—happen with almost no dissent?

Patrick Callan, *Real Clear Education* (May 22, 2018)

When asked why tuition and fees have been increasing so rapidly on America's public college and university campuses, national higher education officials, governing board members, and university presidents most often point their fingers at penurious governors and tight-fisted legislators. These parties, they claim, have failed to maintain, much less increase, state financial support. Consequently, higher education leaders aver that they have been forced, albeit reluctantly, to increase tuition and fees in order to maintain academic quality.

There is some truth to this scenario. A February 2019 edition of the *Hechinger Report* headlined that inflation-adjusted ("real") collective financial support by the states for public higher education had declined by $9 billion over the previous decade.[1] While the essence of this information was correct—state support has been declining in real terms—the estimate was slightly more than double the actual decline (which was about $4.466 billion).[2] Nevertheless, neither of these numbers constitutes good news for public higher education.

As we will demonstrate in this chapter, however, the financial picture for public higher education is not so grim as represented. The primary reason is that rising net tuition and fee collections have typically more than offset state funding declines. We will have much more to say about this below.

Although there are several ways to measure the financial condition of public higher education, we believe the best data concerning state funding are those produced by the State Higher Education Executive Officers Association (SHEEO). The SHEEO data on state financial support for public higher education are especially useful because they cover more than three decades. Further, they are careful to exclude momentary developments such as Great Recession–era funding received from the federal government as a part of the American Recovery and Reinvestment Act of 2009 as well as specific non-instructional allocations made by the states for research and medical schools.

We use SHEEO funding data in this chapter and express all financial values in terms of 2016 prices.[3] To make valid comparisons and arrive at valid conclusions over time, adjusting state support levels (or tuition and fees) for price changes is an absolute necessity. It is also essential to adjust for full-time equivalent (FTE) student enrollment in order to take account of the significant increases in enrollment on most public university campuses over the past quarter century. Thus, we rely on SHEEO's data on FTE student enrollment by state to help generate state funding per FTE student.

The most identifiable, and arguably the most consequential, objective of four-year public colleges and universities is to educate students, and this is our focus here. Even if this were not true, however, in nearly every state the majority of state higher education funding is tied to this purpose. Thus, our focus on state funding per FTE student and tuition and fees per FTE student gets at the heart of the matter for both states and students.

In chapter 1, we showed that a representative four-year public college or university in a typical state ended the 1992–93 to 2016–17 time period with more real dollars to spend per FTE student than at the beginning of this time span. Indeed, the only state that was an exception to this observation was Missouri. Interestingly, however, this improvement in spendable

---

We readily acknowledge that public colleges and universities do many things in addition to educating students. Research and public service are prime among these other activities, but some of the largest financial commitments of campuses are to other activities such as intercollegiate athletics. One might consider the football team of an institution such as the University of Alabama a public service, but doing so would require some flexibility in the definition of the term "public service."

---

dollars did not come about because the typical state increased its real funding per FTE student—only nineteen of the fifty did so over this twenty-five-year period. Instead, it occurred because four-year public institutions generally increased their tuition and fees to more than cover any reductions in state support.

Over the twenty-five-year period 1992–93 to 2016–17, four-year public institutions in the United States gained an average of $2,753 more to spend per FTE student (table 4.1)—even after taking overall price inflation into account. In only one state—Missouri—did the typical public institution of higher education end this period with fewer real dollars per FTE student available to spend. Even after we deduct financial grants made to students (but not loans to students, which must be paid back), inflation-adjusted *net* tuition and fee revenues increased substantially more on a typical campus than was necessary to compensate for cuts in state funding.[4]

Without question, students on virtually every campus in every state were battered by the tuition and fee increases imposed upon them. Although the financial damage associated with declining state funding was unequally distributed across institutions, the brutal truth is that most campuses transferred their financial pain to their student bodies and to those students' families.

Thus, it is difficult to make the case that four-year public institutions of higher education have been systematically injured financially over the past thirty years. Instead, it is their students and those students' families that have been wounded. But most institutions have downplayed or hidden the extent to which they succeeded in transferring any state-imposed financial agony to their students.

Would the United States as a whole and the individual states now be better off if the states had been more generous with their funding in recent decades? That is, if most institutions in most states had not experienced reductions in their state funding, would society broadly speaking have been better served?

We believe the answer is "yes," at least in the abstract, although the precise details underlying this assessment depend upon how institutions would choose to spend the additional dollars provided, the disciplines students decide to study, the precise needs of each state, and the like.[5] Economic evidence informs us that higher education accomplishes a variety of good things for society as a whole and not just for the students who attend college.[6] Thus, incremental higher education is connected to a variety of desirable spillover effects that range from additional tax revenues and lower crime rates to reduced reliance upon social welfare programs.[7] In the language of economists, there are positive externalities associated with higher education—ripple effects that benefit even those far removed from campus.

However, not all spending for all campus purposes is created equal. The use of additional state funds to restrain tuition and fee increases or to reduce the costs facing lower-income students frequently yields considerable social benefits. For example, a recent study of the economic impact of Pell Grants found a rate of return approximating 7 percent.[8] This is attractive in a world in which the yield on thirty-year US government bonds hovers below 3 percent. Pell Grants, then, are not simply a redistributive giveaway but instead an intelligent investment of public funds.

However, incremental expenditures on campus amenities, such as climbing walls and lazy rivers, or on "improvements" that increase the number of administrators per student, or minimize faculty contact with students, or increase subsidies for intercollegiate athletics may be difficult to defend. *USA Today* reported that in 2016-17 the University of Connecticut apparently subsidized its intercollegiate athletics teams to the tune of $42 million over and above the revenue generated by these programs.[9] This massive subsidy translates to more than $2,180 per undergraduate student at U Conn—slightly in excess of $72 per credit hour.[10] One must perform mental contortions to believe either that such expenditures do not result in higher tuition and fees or that the average undergraduate student at U Conn somehow derives $72 per credit hour of net benefits from U Conn's intercollegiate athletic teams.

Our focus in this book is on the role that governing boards have played in generating the numbers shown in table 4.1. In one sense, the role of governing boards is undeniable: their members collectively voted in favor of the tuition and fee hikes that produced these results. However, multiple other factors also come into play, and as we noted in chapter 3, many trustees have been inserted into governance roles for which they are ill prepared. We will have more to say about this phenomenon.

Table 4.1 Changes in Tuition and Fees and State Support per FTE Student for All Fifty States, 1992-93 to 2016-17

State	Change in real net tuition and fees per FTE student	Change in real state support per FTE student	Difference
Alabama	$7,726	$80	$7,806
Alaska	$3,598	$2,871	$6,469
Arizona	$5,094	−$3,100	$1,994
Arkansas	$2,473	−$923	$1,550
California	$952	$1,340	$2,292
Colorado	$5,486	−$1,388	$4,098
Connecticut	$6,549	$1,287	$7,835
Delaware	$9,078	−$1,073	$8,005
Florida	$1,185	$351	$1,536
Georgia	$2,249	$136	$2,385
Hawai'i	$4,697	−$169	$4,528
Idaho	$2,210	−$1,051	$1,159
Illinois	$5,308	$6,157	$11,465
Indiana	$5,507	−$666	$4,841
Iowa	$4,603	−$4,534	$69
Kansas	$4,106	−$1,188	$2,918
Kentucky	$3,864	−$933	$2,931
Louisiana	$1,771	−$474	$1,297
Maine	$4,478	−$789	$3,689
Maryland	$3,630	$198	$3,828
Massachusetts	$2,327	$609	$2,936

(continued)

Table 4.1 (continued)

State	Change in real net tuition and fees per FTE student	Change in real state support per FTE student	Difference
Michigan	$7,922	−$2,448	$5,474
Minnesota	$5,106	−$1,457	$3,650
Mississippi	$2,586	$1,058	$3,644
Missouri	$1,180	−$1,366	−$186
Montana	$3,849	−$498	$3,350
Nebraska	$3,949	$1,098	$5,047
Nevada	$2,519	−$1,737	$782
New Hampshire	$3,635	−$1,116	$2,519
New Jersey	$6,265	−$3,845	$2,420
New Mexico	$2,366	$514	$2,880
New York	$2,661	$647	$3,307
North Carolina	$2,496	−$701	$1,795
North Dakota	$5,072	$3,254	$8,327
Ohio	$2,943	−$731	$2,212
Oklahoma	$3,941	−$3,505	$435
Oregon	$5,478	−$2,024	$3,454
Pennsylvania	$5,362	−$2,895	$2,467
Rhode Island	$3,270	−$130	$3,140
South Carolina	$5,340	−$2,560	$2,779
South Dakota	$5,140	$1,620	$2,955
Tennessee	$3,263	$682	$3,801
Texas	$2,638	−$1,511	$385
Utah	$3,367	$65	$3,432
Vermont	$5,051	−1,494	$3,557
Virginia	$4,951	−$463	$4,489
Washington	$3,119	−$1,577	$1,542
West Virginia	$3,912	$131	$4,043
Wisconsin	$2,310	−$1,382	$928
Wyoming	$412	$5,809	$6,221
Average for the United States	**$3,316**	**−$371**	**$2,753**

Sources: State Higher Education Executive Officers Association, *State Higher Education Finance Data, FY 1980–FY 2018,* https://sheeo.org/wp-content/uploads/2019/04/SHEEO_SHEF_FY18_Nominal_Data.xlsx; Integrated Postsecondary Education Data System (IPEDS), https://nces.ed.gov/IPEDS.

Notes: We have adjusted both state funding and tuition and fees for annual changes in prices using annual July values of the Consumer Price Index (CPI-U). No medical school or specific research funding is included in the calculations, and medical school students are not counted in the student FTE. Tuition and fees are for in-state students. Any state financial aid to independent institutions is not included.

The Nature of Our Sample

The primary basis for our empirical analysis consists of annual observations of critical variables describing the characteristics and activities of 275 four-year public institutions of higher education for fourteen academic years, beginning with 2003–04 and ending with 2016–17. Our original intent was to use the twenty-five-year time horizon that we relied upon in table 4.1, but key institution-specific data for that period were not available for many institutions. This study-period decision is representative of the practical choices one must make when doing large-sample empirical work.

Our sample reflects the diversity of four-year public American institutions of higher education (table 4.2). One institution might appear in multiple categories. For example, UCLA is a member of the *U.S. News* elite colleges and universities, is a flagship university, has a medical school, and is located in a large metropolitan area.

Let's look at the tuition and fee and funding data for a representative subsample of our 275 institutions (table 4.3). Comparable tuition and fee and state funding data were available for 271 of the 275 institutions for

Table 4.2 Number of Institutions and FTE Students by Institutional Category

Institutional category	Number of institutions	Average number of FTE students, fall 2016
U.S. News elite, 2017	25	39,207
Flagship	75	27,466
Regional	149	9,162
HBCU	33	4,244
Medical school	80	28,145
Non-flagship metro leader	35	25,014
Located in a largest 150 metro census area	108	23,929
Rural location	45	4,764
Statewide coordinating board	137	15,810
Statewide governing board	108	15,538
Systemwide board	160	16,654

Source: Governance categories reflect the categorizations of the Education Committee of the States, "50-State Comparison: State Postsecondary Governance Structures," https://www.ecs.org/50-state-comparison-postsecondary-governance-structures, accessed June 2019. Data are from the Integrated Postsecondary Education Data System (IPEDS), https://nces.ed.gov/IPEDS, and National Center for Education Statistics, College Navigator, https://nces.ed.gov/collegenavigator.

Note: Some categories overlap; see table 3.1.

both 2003-04 and 2016-17. Fully 205 of these institutions (76 percent) ended the period better off in real terms per FTE student than when they started it. The *average* institution was able to increase its real net tuition and fees by $3,024 per FTE student, while sustaining cuts in real state financial support of $1,420 per FTE student. After accounting for inflation, the average institution in this sample ended up $1,605 per FTE student better off. Note, however, that this is an average; some institutions in some states ended the period worse off. It is not easy to generalize about the financial circumstances of America's four-year public institutions of higher education.[11]

Thus, at the end of our fourteen-year study period, the typical institution in the sample had more money to spend per FTE student even after taking price inflation into account. Some might attribute this to falling college enrollments, which diminished or held constant the number of FTE students that must be funded. This has been a factor; legislatures have not had to struggle quite so much to fund their colleges and universities. Nevertheless, although the fall of 2018 became the eighth consecutive year that overall headcount college enrollments fell in the United States, it is only since the fall of 2016 that this has occurred among four-year public institutions. It therefore does not explain what we have found here. The major victims of falling college enrollments have been four-year for-profit institutions and community colleges.[12]

The data do tell us something of importance about the power of institutional brand names and position. Consider figure 4.1, which is based on the data in table 4.3 and reports the average change in adjusted net revenues experienced by institutions in five categories—*U.S. News* elite, flagships, metro leaders, regionals, and HBCUs. The elite institutions have a substantial ability to charge higher prices, and they do. The increase in their net real tuition and fee revenues (institutional grants have been removed) was almost double that of the metro leader institutions and more than triple that of the regional colleges and universities. Their increases dwarfed those of the HBCUs.[13]

Insofar as the elite and flagship institutions are concerned, the data presented in figure 4.1 reflect their status, branding allure, and price-making

Table 4.3 Changes in Tuition and Fees per FTE Student for a Representative Subsample of Institutions, 2003-04 to 2016-17

Category/institution	Change in real net tuition and fees per FTE student	Change in real state support per FTE student	Difference
U.S. News elite			
Georgia Tech	$7,031	–$3,999	$3,032
UCLA	$9,674	–$9,925	–$250
U Michigan-Ann Arbor	$6,085	–$4,499	$1,586
U Texas-Austin	$2,645	–$460	$2,185
Elite group average	$6,033	–$3,151	$2,882
Flagship			
Montana State U	$3,005	$715	$2,290
Oregon State U	$3,633	$2,927	$706
U Alabama	$7,504	–$4,186	$3,318
U Kentucky	$6,612	–$7,623	–$1,011
U Missouri-Columbia	$2,755	–$4,615	–$1,860
U New Hampshire	$3,667	–$2,255	$1,412
U North Dakota	$3,286	$2,004	$5,290
U South Carolina-Columbia	$5,259	–$5,050	$210
Flagship group average	$5,148	–$2,437	$2,711
Metro leader			
George Mason U	$4,916	–$947	$3,968
Portland State U	$1,668	–$35	$1,634
U Central Florida	$1,666	–$1,117	$549
U Cincinnati	$4,698	–$2,562	$2,136
U Wisconsin-Milwaukee	$2,185	$2,686	–$501
Metro leader group average	$3,377	–$2,038	$1,339
Regional			
Adams State U	$4,662	–$3,510	$952
Cal State U Fresno	$214	–$2,753	–$2,539
CUNY City College	–$615	$1,051	$436
James Madison U	$3,871	–$346	$3,525
Nicholls State U	$3,180	–$2,356	$824
Pittsburg State U	$1,943	–$1,334	$609
Weber State U	$1,212	$194	$1,406
Regional group average	$1,824	–$873	$952
HBCU			
Alabama A&M	$3,993	$1,554	$5,547
Delaware State U	$2,119	$5,515	–$3,396
Florida A&M	$797	$1,986	$2,783
Norfolk State U	$196	$1,795	$1,990
HBCU group average	$326	$211	$537
Average for 271 institutions	**$3,024**	**–$1,420**	**$1,604**

Sources: Integrated Postsecondary Education Data System (IPEDS), https://nces.ed.gov/IPEDS, and authors' calculations.

Note: Tuition and fees are for in-state students.

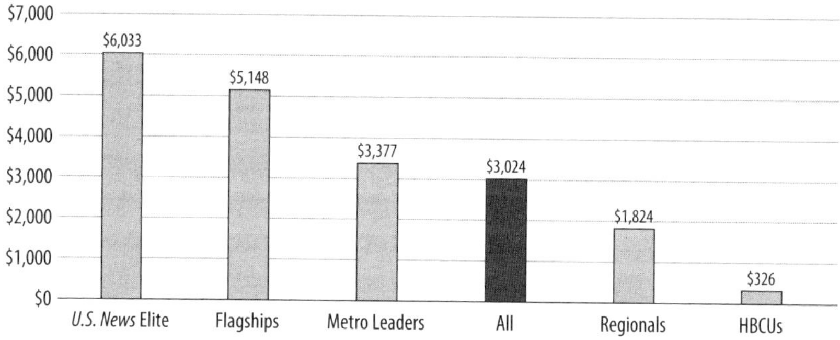

Figure 4.1. Net Gains in Real Net Tuition and Fee Revenue per FTE Student by Institutional Type, 2003–04 to 2016–17. *Sources:* Integrated Postsecondary Education Data System (IPEDS), https://nces.ed.gov/IPEDS, and authors' computations.

power. In effect, figure 4.1 is a thermometer that registers raw institutional clout.

Even so, the ability of the elite institutions to charge higher prices can also make them more inviting targets for budget-cutting governors and legislators. They easily sustained the largest absolute dollar reductions in real state financial support per FTE student. As a governor once told one of the authors, "They [meaning the elite and flagships] can charge any price they want. Our cuts will cause them some discomfort but really won't make much different to them in a couple of years."

This claim may well be true with respect to the total operating revenues of the elite and flagship institutions, but it ignores the impact of these actions upon students and their families. Students, especially lower-income students, are being progressively priced out of the elite and flagship markets by cost increases that have not been matched by need-based financial aid. What may not appear to be a problem in a single year evolves into an accessibility issue if states pursue (or allow) such policies over longer periods of time.

Furthermore, reductions in state funding may stimulate institutions to increase the proportion of non-resident students they enroll. This is a blowback effect that many state budget makers tend to ignore but that is always lurking in the background. Do we believe there is a connection between the University of Alabama's losing $4,186 per FTE student in state funding between 2003–04 and 2016–17 and its ramping up of its out-of-state student enrollment to approximately 65 percent? Absolutely!

The data in figure 4.1 also make it clear that it would be a major mistake to conflate the price-making ability of the elites and flagships with the remainder of public sector campuses. This is a lesson that should be heeded by public policy makers in general, and governors, legislators, and board members in particular. One should not confuse the elite flagships' situations with those of regional state colleges.

Institutions that are neither elite nor flagships and not located in a metropolitan area are subject to very different market positions and financial circumstances. Most lack price-making power, and many serve lower-income student clienteles that struggle with affordability. Currently, a significant proportion of the regionals are experiencing enrollment declines, not least because they have found it difficult to compete for students with the elite and flagship institutions even though they often offer lower net prices. This is yet another consequence of the crisis in access and affordability that increasingly grips American public higher education. All too often, budget makers believe they can take action in isolation and ignore the ripple and spillover effects of their decisions.

In partial defense of state budget makers and analysts, it should be acknowledged that they face many competing demands, for both their attention and the revenues they allocate. For better or worse, critical state budget decisions tend to be shoehorned into brief periods of time, sometimes as fleeting as an unrecorded minute-long conversation between key participants. Theirs is not an easy job. Nevertheless, they should concede that Newton's third law of motion also applies to budgets: for every action, there is an equal and opposite reaction. As much as possible, budget decision-makers need to arm themselves ahead of time with an understanding of the reactions and consequences that their actions are likely to stimulate. It does not appear most have done so in the tuition and fee arena.

Specifying Our Primary Empirical Model

Our primary multivariate empirical analysis focuses on the determinants of the change in the real net tuition and fee collections of our 275-observation sample of institutions on an FTE basis between 2003-04 and 2016-17. Our typical estimating equations[14] will follow this model:

$$\text{change in real T \& F per FTE}_{ij} = a + \sum_{i=1}^{n} b_{ij} X_{ij} + e \tag{4.1}$$

where $i = 1, 2, \ldots, n$ independent variables,
$j = 1, 2, \ldots, 275$ institutions,
a = constant term,
b_{ij} = estimated partial regression coefficient for an explanatory variable,
X_{ij} = vector of n variables for the $j = 275$ institutions, and
e = stochastic error term.

Categories of Independent Variables

Our dependent variable—that is, what we seek to explain—is the change in real net real tuition and fee revenue per FTE student. This is a variable that reflects both demand and supply influences as well as governance issues; therefore, our estimating equations include variables that reflect such factors. We categorize our explanatory variables as follows:

- State funding
    - Change in real state funding per FTE student, 2003-04 to 2016-17
- Ability to pay
    - Opportunity Insights parental income percentile
    - Beginning student Pell Grant percentage
    - Percentage of graduates in science, technology, engineering, and math (STEM) disciplines
- Nature and size of the market
    - Percentage change in public K-12 school enrollment, 2000-15
    - Prices charged non-resident students

- Quality of the product or service produced
    - Six-year graduation rate for students who began in 2011
    - Retention rate from freshman to sophomore year
    - Incomes earned by graduates after graduation
- Characteristics of the institution
    - Percentage undergraduate enrollment
    - Percentage in-state enrollment
    - Brookings standardized SAT/ACT test score
    - Real administrative costs per FTE student in 2016
    - Institutional type dummy variables: *U.S. News* elite, flagship, metro leader, regional college or university, or HBCU
- Nature of governance
    - Statewide coordinating board dummy variable
    - Statewide governing board dummy variable
    - Systemwide board dummy variable
    - Percentage of board appointed by the governor
    - Percentage of board that is elected
    - Students have a vote on the board dummy variable
    - Numerical size of the institution's critical board

Determinants of the Changes in In-State Tuition and Fee Increases, 2003–04 to 2016–17

Let's begin by observing that the zero-order[15] Pearson correlation coefficient between the change in real tuition and fees per FTE student and the change in real state appropriations per FTE student was only −0.175 during the 2003–04 to 2016–17 period (fig. 4.2). Prima facie, this suggests that tuition and fee increases over this fourteen-year period may not have had quite as much to do with reductions in state support as some contend.[16] This finding underscores that state funding is only one of a much larger set of factors that influence the level of tuition and fees we observe on campuses. Therefore, one must employ multivariate analysis to determine whether the relationship between state funding and tuition and fees is sustained when other influences on tuition and fees (for example, the size of the incomes of the students' parents) are considered.

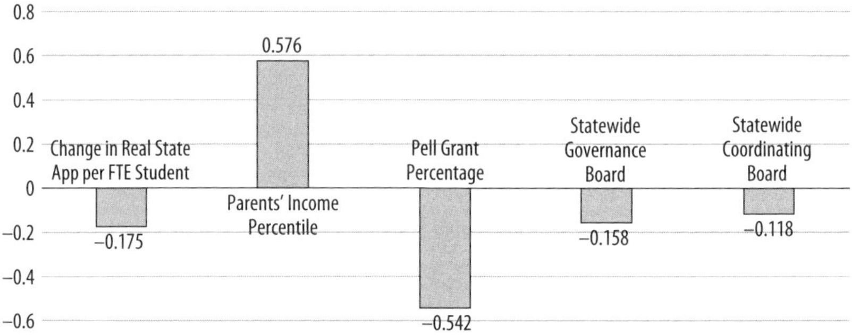

Figure 4.2. Pearson Zero-Order Correlation Coefficients for the Change in Real Tuition and Fees per FTE Student, and Selected Variables, 2003-04 to 2016-17. *Source:* Authors' calculations based on State Higher Education Executive Officers Association (SHEEO), *State Higher Education Finance: FY 2018*, https://sheeo.org/wp-content/uploads/2019/04/SHEEO_SHEF_FY18_Report.pdf, Tables 3 and 4.

Also of interest in figure 4.2 is the 0.576 correlation between the change in real tuition and fees per FTE student and parents' income percentile. The other side of this coin is the −0.542 correlation between the change in real tuition and fees per FTE student and the share of beginning students on campuses that are receiving Pell Grants. These correlations signal that ability to pay is likely an important determinant of tuition and fee increases.

The correlations between tuition and fee increases and statewide coordinating and governing boards are negative, though not impressively large. Our interest here is in determining the extent to which statewide agencies constrain tuition and fee increases compared with circumstances in which institutions have their own board and hence do not report to a statewide board.

It would be statistical folly to attempt to include all the possible independent (explanatory) variables listed in our predictive equation. Hence, let us start with a focused estimating equation in which we attempt to explain the change in real net tuition and fees over our time period for our sample of institutions by means of the following variables:

- State funding
    - Change in real state funding per FTE student, 2003-04 to 2016-17

- Ability to pay
  - Opportunity Insights parental income percentile
  - Beginning student Pell Grant percentage
  - Percent of graduates in STEM disciplines
- Nature and size of the market
  - Percentage change in public K-12 school enrollment, 2000-15
  - Prices charged non-resident students
- Quality of the product or service produced
  - Incomes earned by graduates after graduation
  - Percentage of students who move from the lowest income quintile to the highest income quintile after graduation
- Characteristics of the institution
  - Percentage undergraduate enrollment
  - Real administrative expenditures per FTE student in 2016
  - Institutional type dummy variables: elite, flagship, and HBCU
- Nature of governance
  - Statewide coordinating board dummy variable
  - Statewide governing board dummy variable
  - Systemwide board dummy variable

The estimation results in table 4.4 reveal that changes in real state appropriations over the period 2003-04 to 2016-17 were not even close to being a statistically significant determinant of changes in real net tuition and fees. The exceptionally weak performance of state funding as a possible stimulus for tuition and fee increases is eye-opening. Few would deny that state funding levels influence tuition and fee increases in a single year because the reaction of campuses to state funding cuts often is immediate. The evidence in table 4.4, however, suggests that over a sufficiently long time period the relationship between the two ebbs substantially, at least partially because campuses raise tuition and fees even in years when their real funding per FTE student increases. The years following the Great Recession in 2008 illustrate this situation: net real tuition and fee revenues per FTE student continued to increase even when reductions in state funding had largely disappeared (fig. 4.3).

Table 4.4 Determinants of the Changes in Real In-State Tuition and Fees at Four-Year Public Colleges and Universities, 2003-04 to 2016-17

Variable	Coefficient	Standard error	Absolute value *t*-statistic	Two-tailed probability
Constant	2,675.44	2,192.17	1.22	.2236
Change in real state appropriations per FTE student	.0368	.0721	0.51	.6098
Change in real non-resident T&F per FTE student	.1031	.0290	3.56	.0005
Parental income percentile	60.03	22.05	2.72	.0070
Pell Grant percentage	−25.13	14.15	1.78	.0771
Percentage of graduates in STEM disciplines	31.72	9.88	3.21	.0015
Percentage of undergraduate enrollment	−76.13	15.57	−4.89	.0000
Percentage change in K-12 enrollment	14.95	13.32	1.12	.2631
Percentage of students who move from lowest income quintile to highest after graduation	101.39	51.62	1.96	.0508
Real administrative costs per FTE student, 2016	.2511	.1133	2.21	.0277
Elite dummy	2,720.31	707.93	3.84	.0002
Flagship dummy	841.59	461.63	1.82	.0697
HBCU dummy	23.66	633.40	0.04	.9702
Statewide coordinating board dummy	−685.76	482.54	1.42	.1567
Statewide governing board dummy	−1,139.55	521.09	2.19	.0298
Systemwide board dummy	−150.74	246.63	0.61	.5417
Interaction term between elite and flagship	−2,902.79	1,017.59	2.85	.0048

Source: Authors' calculations based on data from State Higher Education Executive Officers Association (SHEEO), *State Higher Education Finance (SHEF): FY 2018* (Boulder, CO, 2019), https://sheeo.org/wp-content/uploads/2019/04/SHEEO_SHEF_FY18_Report.pdf; and National Center for Education Statistics, Integrated Postsecondary Education Data System, https://nces.ed.gov/ipeds.

Notes: The dependent variable is change in real net tuition and fee revenue per FTE student, 2003-04 to 2016-17. White heteroscedasticity correction made. $N=230$; R^2 adj. = .560; $F=19.18$ (.0000). T&F = tuition and fees; STEM = science, technology, engineering, and math.

The regression results reported in table 4.4 underscore the role that ability to pay plays in determining both absolute levels of tuition and fee and increases in those charges. The income of a student's parents is a strong, positive predictor of increases in net tuition and fees, as is the percentage of students who graduate in STEM disciplines and therefore often end up occupying high-paying jobs. In the case of parental income, a climb in parental incomes that increases the campus average by five per-

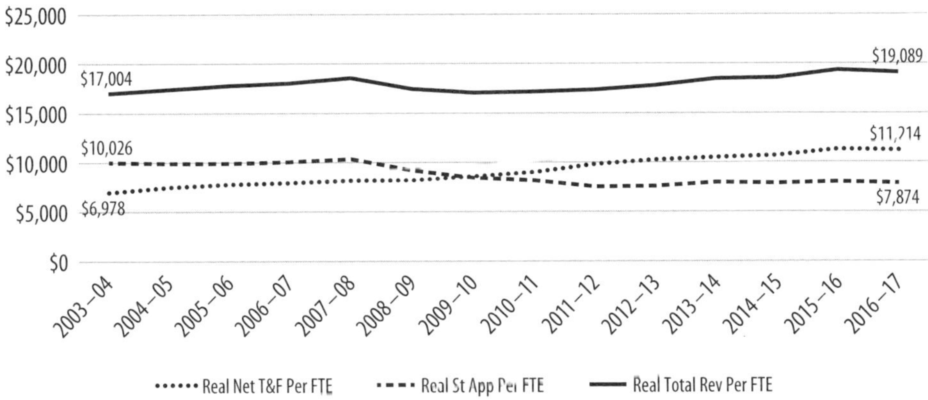

Figure 4.3. Net Tuition and Fee Revenue per FTE Student and State Appropriations per FTE Student: 275 Four-Year Public Institutions, 2003-04 to 2016-17. *Source:* State Higher Education Executive Officers Association (SHEEO), *State Higher Education Finance: FY 2018*, https://sheeo.org/wp-content/uploads/2019/04/SHEEO_SHEF_FY18_Report.pdf.

centile points is on average associated with a $300 increase in net tuition and fee income collected per FTE student. A 5 percentage point increase in the share of graduates in STEM disciplines is associated with a $122 increase in net tuition and fee revenue per FTE student.

Let's provide some institutional perspective for these estimates. The $300 + $122 = $422 increase in net tuition and fee revenue per FTE student translates to $118.16 million over our fourteen-year period for a single institution with 20,000 FTE students.

In contrast, an increase in the percentage of Pell Grant students reduces our typical institution's ability to raise tuition and fees. The negative impact on real net tuition and fee collections over our period is only $7.0 million, but this does not take account of the cost of additional programs and advising that must be tailored to first-generation, lower-income students if they are to survive and prosper on a typical medium- to large-sized four-year public campus. (Institutions that need instruction or example in this regard should visit the University of California's Irvine campus, which both admits and graduates large numbers of first-generation, lower-income students.)

Explicitly or implicitly, we presume that institutions critically assess the ability-to-pay variables we have cited when they make tuition and fee recommendations. They fear making tuition and fee increases that will damage enrollment and perhaps provoke adverse public reactions, but they simultaneously covet the additional revenues provided by tuition and fee increases.

As time passes, individual campuses gradually drift in the direction of charging what their particular traffic will bear even though they usually cloak their decisions with nebulous paeans to academic quality and improved educational results. In the end, the motivating principle usually is the institution's ability to earn additional revenue to enable it to absorb state financial cuts and beyond this to launch new programs or improve existing ones. For a large swath of public colleges and universities, the fact that these tuition and fee increases may price some (or perhaps many) students out of their institution and effectively deny access to a large segment of their state's population has not proven to be a deterrent.

This analysis helps explain why American public higher education has become increasingly stratified based on student and family incomes. Becoming more exclusive is associated with a financial payoff, while improving access to lower-income studies usually carries a financial penalty. With apologies to Bob Dylan, it is not difficult to see which way the financial winds have been blowing in public higher education, and this helps explain why so many institutions have walked away (often surreptitiously) from admitting and serving lower-income students.

Whether members of college governing boards understand the mathematics we have just presented is not clear, although we suspect that intuitively many do. They likely understand viscerally that upper-income students are less expensive to serve than lower-income students and that admitting more lower-income students might threaten standardized test scores, rankings, and the like. This might help explain their willingness to increase tuition and fees whenever asked to do so by administrators.

Board members who vote "yes" to tuition and fee increases can pat themselves on the back for defending the fiscal solvency of their campus, or even improving it. That such policies gradually change the character of the campus student body is not necessarily something they either recognize on their own or hear from campus administrators. Once again, we observe that the data presented in chapters 1 and 2 that document the income stratification of four-year public higher education are not widely understood or publicly discussed.

Which brings us back to the subject of governance. Three of the variables in the estimating equation presented in table 4.4 represent or reflect the presence (or absence) of various governance structures—the existence of a statewide coordinating board, the existence of a statewide governing board, and the existence of a systemwide board that is responsible for multiple institutions. These variables are expressed as binary dummy variables, where 0 indicates the absence and 1 indicates the presence of one of these modes of governance. Implicitly, the excluded category consists of institutions that have their own dedicated governing board. The coefficients can thus be viewed as reflecting the financial impact of not having one's own board but instead having one of these other governance arrangements.

The negative coefficients on all three of these variables could be interpreted as suggesting that governance supervision from above or afar can restrain tuition and fee increases. Especially consider the negative coefficient (-$1,139) on the statewide governance board variable. This coefficient is statistically significant at the .05 level. The estimated coefficient tells us that net tuition and fee collections per FTE student at the typical institution would be $1,139 lower over the fourteen years if that institution's action were subject to the approval of a statewide governance board. For an institution with 20,000 FTE students, this change would result in $22.96 million in reduced tuition and fee collections over fourteen years, or an average of $1.64 million annually.

The –$685 coefficient reflecting the presence of a statewide coordinating board is not statistically significant at the .10 level. The systemwide board coefficient (reflecting an institution governed by a board that deals with multiple institutions) has a negative sign but is not statistically significant.[17]

The regression results reported in table 4.4 tell us that the structure of higher education governance inside a state makes a difference. Institutions with their own dedicated governing board (but no statewide governance supervision above them) raise tuition and fees more aggressively than institutions whose actions are subject to inspection and approval at a statewide level. Plausible reasons for this phenomenon include a desire at the statewide level to "treat everyone the same"; possible constraining directives to statewide boards from governors and legislators, who have more needs to consider than those of a single institution; and the reduced ability of a charismatic president to persuade and co-opt more distant statewide board members with whom he or she does not have constant contact.

Another variable in the estimating equation presented in table 4.4 is the percentage of the student body composed of undergraduates at an institution. The higher this percentage, the lower the institution's commitment to graduate students and research. This variable captures institutional mission and campus complexity as well. The coefficient of this variable is negative and statistically significant at .01 level. Holding other things constant, this estimated coefficient tells us that institutions that focus intentionally on undergraduate students tend to increase their undergraduate tuition and fees less than those institutions whose attention is often directed elsewhere.

A rather different variable is the percentage change in K-12 public school enrollment in each institution's state between 2000 and 2015. This variable is designed to represent changes in the size of the potential admissions pie from which an individual institution cuts its slice. The coefficient has the expected positive sign but fails to achieve statistical significance at even the .10 level, perhaps because non-resident enrollment has assumed much greater importance. Consider that in fall 2017 slightly more than 30 percent of undergraduate students at the elite institutions were non-residents. This means these institutions do not have to pay as much attention to their home state market as they did in the past.

Institutional mission and type make a difference. We have included three dummy variables in our table 4.4 estimating equation. They represent the elite institutions, flagship institutions, and HBCUs. The largest coefficient ($2,720) belongs to the variable representing the institutions in the *U.S. News* elite group (which numbered 28 in 2017). The $2,720

Does the extent to which income is distributed unequally in a state influence its financial support for higher education? This is an interesting possibility raised by a reviewer of this book. There is, however, no evidence of this in our sample. The simple correlation coefficient between states' Gini coefficients (which measure the inequality of a state's income distribution) and changes in states' real appropriations per FTE student between 2003-04 and 2016-17 is only −.008. When a Gini coefficient independent variable was inserted into our predictive equations, it explained nothing.

coefficient, which is significant at the 0.01 level, is a raw representation of the pricing power of the elite institutions, and this coefficient is more than triple the estimate for flagship institutions, whose coefficient is significant at the .10 level. The average FTE student body size of a member of the elite was almost 40,000 in 2017. Let's assume that the average size of the undergraduate student body of a member of the elite over our fourteen-year period was 30,000 FTE. Then, by this metric, the average value of elite status was worth more than $81 million over the study period in terms of additional net tuition and fees.

Our analysis supports the hypothesis that elite and flagship institutions have both developed brands that endow them with price-making power. Clearly, some of these institutions have much more such power than others. There is a difference between the draw exercised by the University of Michigan-Ann Arbor (UM) and that of many other flagship institutions, particularly those located in less populated states. In the fall of 2018, UM received 64,917 applications for undergraduate admission. This circumstance endowed this highly regarded institution with price-making power. One may well consider our $81 million measure of the average annual value of elite status to be very much a lower-bound estimate for UM.

The estimates also show that HBCUs as a group effectively have no pricing power compared with our excluded category, regional state colleges and universities, of which they also are members (table 4.4). This reflects the reality that changes in their tuition and fee structures have failed to have much impact on their net revenues.

One of the more interesting independent variables in the estimating equation presented in table 4.4 is the change in the real net tuition and fees charged out-of-state undergraduate students, whose estimated coefficient is positive and significant at the .01 level. But here's the rub: if an institution can charge out-of-state students hefty price premiums for their attendance, then it does not have to be quite so attentive to current or prospective in-state students or worry so much about their reactions to higher tuition and fees.

Non-resident students serve an attractive source of additional revenue and can be an enrollment buffer for institutions in states with declining demographics. The University of Illinois (UI) provides a case study in this regard. The College Navigator reports that the university's flagship campus in Urbana-Champaign charged out-of-state students $31,664 in tuition and fees in the fall of 2018, more than double the price it charged in-state students. UI offered these out-of-state students only minimal institutional-based financial aid so that it earned approximately $16,500 more from a typical out-of-state student than from an Illinoisan. This was worth an incremental $141 million to UI in 2018 alone, a critical addition to its revenue given the wretched financial condition of the state of Illinois and the numerous cuts in state financial support UI has suffered in recent years.

In New England, many institutions have undergraduate student bodies that are predominantly non-resident (the University of Vermont's 79 percent and the University of New Hampshire's 59 percent are examples). Viewed nationally, these also are high-tuition institutions for in-state students. In 2018–19, Vermont's published tuition and fees for in-state students were a hefty $18,276 and had increased by 121.0 percent (an average of 5.56 percent annually) since the 2000–01 academic year. By contrast, UV's published out-of-state tuition and fees were $42,516, and these had risen 114.6 percent since 2000–01.[18]

There is no definitive evidence that either UI or UV used their ability to extract premium tuitions from non-residents to subsidize lower tuitions for their resident students. In fact, the opposite appears to be true. Therefore, the highly significant positive coefficient on the out-of-state tuition and fee variable in table 4.4 provides support for the hypothesis that an institution's ability to charge non-resident students high prices in turn enables and drives higher prices for resident students.

One of the more intriguing results reported in table 4.4 relates to the influence of real administrative costs per FTE student on tuition and fees. The coefficient on real administrative costs is positive and statistically significant at the .05 level. This suggests that increased administrative expenditures have exerted upward pressure on tuition and fees. We will return to this issue in a section below.

Taking a Closer Look at Governing Boards

Whether it is a statewide coordinating or governing board or a system-wide board, a board's membership can vary in potentially important ways. Data from the Education Commission of the States report what proportion of board members are appointed by governors, what proportion are elected, whether student members can vote, and how many members can vote.[19] From these data, we have developed four testable hypotheses.

Some observers believe that boards hold the purse strings tighter when governors appoint many or all of the members of those boards, and that those who are elected to board membership are more likely to be loyal alumni who may be more responsive to the cost-increasing requests of an institution's administrators.[20] With respect to the latter notion, status as an alumnus or alumna is often cited by candidates for governing boards as an important qualification in states such as Michigan and Pennsylvania, where some or all trustees are elected.

Students have the right to vote on almost one-half of the four-year public institution governing boards in the United States today. Might their views of student self-interest cause them to advocate restraint in tuition and fee increases and motivate them to vote accordingly? Or is it the case that students seldom hold board membership long enough to gain a firm understanding of the complexities of their duties and therefore often end up deferring to administrators?

Our own observations suggest the possibility that the larger a board is in size, the more likely it is to be dominated by the president and senior administrators and hence the more likely it is to approve cost-increasing proposals. This assertion is an empirical proposition, and in tables 4.5, 4.6, 4.7, and 4.8 we test it, along with the three other informal hypotheses we developed above. The regression results we report below are based upon the regression specification we used in table 4.4.

The first hypothesis concerns the effect that gubernatorial appointments to boards have on tuition and fees (table 4.5). At 162 of our sample of 275 institutions, governors appoint 100 percent of the members of governing boards, and in 26 cases they appoint none. The average share of board

Table 4.5 Influence of Governor-Appointed Board Members on In-State Tuition and Fees at Four-Year Public Colleges and Universities, 2003-04 to 2016-17

Variable	Coefficient	Standard error	Absolute value *t*-statistic	Two-tailed probability
Constant	3,502.76	2,451.87	1.43	.1546
Change in real state appropriation per FTE student	.0334	.0716	0.46	.6412
Change in real non-resident T&F	.1047	.0290	3.61	.0004
Parents' income percentile	52.42	24.28	2.16	.0320
Pell Grant percentage	−26.63	14.63	−1.82	.0702
Percentage of graduates in STEM fields	23.67	10.40	2.28	.0239
Percentage of students who move from lowest income quintile to highest after graduation	96.11	52.43	1.83	.0682
Percentage of undergraduate enrollment	−61.22	16.64	3.68	.0003
Real administrative costs per FTE student	.2321	.1134	2.05	.0419
Percentage change in K-12 enrollment	14.26	13.63	1.05	.2968
Elite dummy	2,851.39	722.48	3.95	.0001
Flagship dummy	862.47	452.59	1.91	.0581
HBCU dummy	−79.41	625.83	.13	.8991
Statewide coordinating board dummy	−810.71	543.10	−1.49	.1370
Statewide governing board dummy	−1275.68	603.11	−2.12	.0356
Systemwide board dummy	−225.64	267.40	−0.84	.3997
Interaction term between elite and flagship	−2,999.54	1,024.00	2.93	.0038
Percentage of board appointed by governor	−4.43	4.13	1.07	.2848

Source: Authors' calculations based on data from State Higher Education Executive Officers Association (SHEEO), *State Higher Education Finance (SHEF): FY 2018* (Boulder, CO, 2019), https://sheeo.org/wp-content/uploads/2019/04/SHEEO_SHEF_FY18_Report.pdf; and National Center for Education Statistics, Integrated Postsecondary Education Data System, https://nces.ed.gov/ipeds.

Notes: The dependent variable is the change in real net tuition and fee revenue per FTE student, 2003-04 to 2016-17. White heteroscedasticity correction made. $N=230$; R^2 adj. $=.560$; $F=18.13$ (.0000). T&F = tuition and fees; STEM = science, technology, engineering, and math.

members appointed by governors is 79.54 percent. The coefficient of the variable representing the percentage of board members appointed by governors is small, has a negative sign, and is not statistically significant. Hence, we cannot demonstrate that giving governors more power to appoint public university board members has a restraining influence on the net tuition and fee revenues at four-year public institutions collectively.

A modest proportion of board members (6.23 percent) at institutions is elected rather than appointed. Only thirteen campuses have all the members of their governing boards elected—prominent among them are the Universities of Colorado, Michigan, and Nebraska, as well as Michigan State and Penn State. Regression results reveal, however, that the election of board members has no perceptible influence upon tuition and fee determination (table 4.6). Hence, it does not appear that elected trustees turn out to be overly enthusiastic, pliable, and effective advocates for their institutions or that they exhibit excessive deference to administrative proposals to increase tuition and fees.

A resounding majority of the institutions in our sample have student members on their governing boards, but in only 134 of our 275 cases (less than half) do the student members have voting privileges. Moreover, there is no evidence that student trustees who do have a voting franchise on boards actually exercise any additional discipline over tuition and fee increases (table 4.7); indeed, their presence has no significant impact upon tuition and fee decisions.

The evidence supports the view that the larger the size of a governing board, other things held constant, the more likely it is that this board will vote for tuition and fee increases (table 4.8). The coefficient on the board size variable is positive (though of moderate size) and statistically significant at the .05 level. A larger board plausibly diminishes communication among board members and perhaps their commitment to active board membership as well. Eckel and Trower hypothesize that "as boards grow larger, trustee engagement wanes."[21] We provide the first empirical evidence on this issue here.

Tables 4.5 through 4.8 represent the first large sample attempt by any researcher to date to connect the characteristics of governing boards to

Table 4.6 Influence of Elected Board Members on In-State Tuition and Fees at Four-Year Public Colleges and Universities, 2003-04 to 2016-17

Variable	Coefficient	Standard error	Absolute value *t*-statistic	Two-tailed probability
Constant	2,598.32	2,211.71	1.17	.2414
Change in real state appropriation per FTE	.0388	.0716	0.54	.5833
Change in real non-resident T&F	.1061	.0284	3.73	.0002
Parents' income percentile	64.91	22.57	2.88	.0044
Pell Grant percentage	−26.13	14.42	1.81	.0713
Percentage of graduates in STEM fields	24.38	11.22	2.17	.0308
Percentage of students who move from lowest income quintile to highest after graduation	116.13	53.98	2.15	.0326
Percentage of undergraduate enrollment	−63.02	16.39	3.85	.0002
Real administrative costs per FTE student	.1692	.1174	1.44	.1512
Percentage change in K-12 enrollment	29.11	26.94	1.08	.2810
Elite dummy	2675.1	759.66	3.52	.0005
Flagship dummy	897.92	484.20	1.85	.0651
HBCU dummy	337.36	670.62	0.50	.6156
Statewide coordinating board dummy	−841.76	504.30	1.67	.0966
Statewide governing board dummy	−1,216.16	533.34	2.28	.0236
Interaction term between elite and flagship	−2,700.39	1,070.68	2.52	.0124
Percentage of board elected	−6.92	6.21	1.11	.2665

Source: Authors' calculations based on data from State Higher Education Executive Officers Association (SHEEO), *State Higher Education Finance (SHEF): FY 2018* (Boulder, CO, 2019), https://sheeo.org/wp-content/uploads/2019/04/SHEEO_SHEF_FY18_Report.pdf; and National Center for Education Statistics, Integrated Postsecondary Education Data System, https://nces.ed.gov/ipeds.

Notes: The dependent variable is the change in real net tuition and fee revenue per FTE student from 2003-04 to 2016-17. White heteroscedasticity correction made. $N = 230$; R^2 adj. = .551; $F = 17.50$ (.0000). T&F = tuition and fees; STEM = science, technology, engineering, and math.

their actions and decisions. Our results suggest that the presence of a statewide coordinating board, and especially a statewide governing board, are substantially more important in restraining tuition and fee cost increases than how the members of governing boards reach their positions. We also find evidence in favor of the hypothesis that large board sizes are associated with greater tuition and fee increases.

Table 4.7 Influence of Voting Student Board Members and In-State Tuition and Fees at Four-Year Public Colleges and Universities, 2003–04 to 2016–17

Variable	Coefficient	Standard error	Absolute value *t*-statistic	Two-tailed probability
Constant	2,772.78	2,265.20	1.22	.2223
Change in real state appropriation per FTE student	.0440	.0729	0.60	.5466
Change in real non-resident T&F	.1068	.0285	3.75	.0002
Parents' income percentile	61.64	22.29	2.77	.0062
Pell Grant percentage	−26.84	14.23	1.89	.0607
Percentage of graduates in STEM fields	25.30	11.36	2.23	.0269
Percentage of students who move from lowest income quintile to highest after graduation	107.56	54.79	1.96	.0509
Percentage of undergraduate enrollment	−63.03	16.64	3.79	.0002
Real administrative costs per FTE student	.1579	.1189	1.33	.1858
Percentage change in K-12 enrollment	32.13	29.11	1.10	.2711
Elite dummy	2,698.30	766.28	3.52	.0005
Flagship dummy	858.20	473.34	1.81	.0712
HBCU dummy	372.15	673.14	0.55	.5809
Statewide coordinating board dummy	−769.35	495.71	1.55	.1222
Statewide governing board dummy	−1166.52	532.62	2.19	.0296
Interaction term between elite and flagship	−2,729.44	1,060.26	2.58	.0107
Student board members can vote	168.51	284.44	0.59	.5542

Source: Authors' calculations based on data from State Higher Education Executive Officers Association (SHEEO), *State Higher Education Finance (SHEF): FY 2018* (Boulder, CO, 2019), https://sheeo.org/wp-content/uploads/2019/04/SHEEO_SHEF_FY18_Report.pdf; and National Center for Education Statistics, Integrated Postsecondary Education Data System, https://nces.ed.gov/ipeds.

Notes: The dependent variable is the change in real net tuition and fee revenue per FTE student from 2003-04 to 2016-17. White heteroscedasticity correction made. $N=230$; R^2 adj. = .549; $F=18.39$ (.0000). T&F = tuition and fees; STEM = science, technology, engineering, and math.

We note in passing, however, that we were unable to obtain large sample data relating to other characteristic of board members, such as their gender, race or ethnic background, and age. These concerns provide an agenda for future research.[22]

How Tuition and Fee Increases Influence Aspects of Institutional Performance

One plausible reason to increase tuition and fees is to use the additional funds to improve academic quality and performance. To test such

Table 4.8 Influence of Governing Board Size and In-State Tuition and Fees at Four-Year Public Colleges and Universities, 2003-04 to 2016-17

Variable	Coefficient	Standard error	Absolute value *t*-statistic	Two-tailed probability
Constant	1,696.09	2,195.46	0.77	.4407
Change in real state appropriation per FTE student	.0341	.0716	0.48	.6346
Change in real non-resident T&F	.1010	.0284	3.56	.0005
Parents' income percentile	55.87	23.34	2.50	.0131
Pell Grant percentage	−20.86	13.97	1.49	.1370
Percentage of graduates in STEM fields	24.70	10.64	2.32	.0212
Percentage of students who move from lowest income quintile to highest after graduation	103.58	50.79	2.04	.0426
Percentage of undergraduate enrollment	−59.30	16.19	3.66	.0003
Percentage change in K-12 enrollment	12.25	13.41	0.91	.3619
Elite dummy	2,587.59	701.11	3.69	.0003
Flagship dummy	973.86	451.66	2.16	.0322
HBCU dummy	−435.68	656.08	0.66	.5074
Statewide coordinating board dummy	−496.35	500.77	0.99	.3227
Statewide governing board dummy	−1,076.25	525.15	2.05	.0417
Systemwide board dummy	−231.56	246.60	0.94	.3488
Interaction term between elite and flagship	−2,787.71	990.42	2.81	.0053
Size of critical board	48.52	21.54	2.25	.0253

Source: Authors' calculations based on data from State Higher Education Executive Officers Association (SHEEO), *State Higher Education Finance (SHEF): FY 2018* (Boulder, CO, 2019), https://sheeo.org/wp-content/uploads/2019/04/SHEEO_SHEF_FY18_Report.pdf; and National Center for Education Statistics, Integrated Postsecondary Education Data System, https://nces.ed.gov/ipeds.

Notes: The dependent variable is the change in real net tuition and fee revenue per FTE student from 2003-04 to 2016-17. White heteroscedasticity correction made. $N=230$; R^2 adj. = .565; $F=18.48$ (.0000). T&F = tuition and fees; STEM = science, technology, engineering, and math.

a hypothesis, however, one must be willing to measure (or attempt to measure) academic quality and performance. We have no definitive means to accomplish this; we do, however, have access to a variety of common metrics that are often cited as measures of quality and performance colleges and universities:

1. the full-time student retention rate in 2016;[23]
2. the six-year graduation rate of students who began their undergraduate careers in 2011;[24]
3. the national percentile rank of the incomes earned by graduates;[25]
4. the percentage of students who come from families in the lowest quintile of the income distribution and made it to highest income quintile after graduating;[26]
5. the student-faculty ratio in 2016;[27] and
6. real administrative costs per FTE student in 2016.[28]

We will shortcut our presentation of this evidence by pointing out that in only two of our six cases did the variable representing the change in real net tuition and fees per FTE student attain statistical significance. Further, the variable representing the change in real state appropriations per FTE student failed to attain statistical significance in any of the six instances. Thus, over this fourteen-year study period, there was only a modest connection between tuition and fee revenue and quality and performance measures and no apparent connection between state appropriations and any of the measures of quality and performance.

Our basis for these statistical conclusions is regression equation estimations that follow the models presented in tables 4.4 through 4.8, except that now the dependent variable in each case is one of the six specific measures of academic quality or performance noted above.

The four independent variables that consistently *did* attain statistical significance in our analysis were parents' income percentile, a Brookings Institution measure that harmonizes Scholastic Aptitude Test and American College Test scores into a single variable,[29] the percentage of graduates in STEM disciplines, and HBCU status.

Student Retention

The dependent variable in this analysis is the institutional student retention rate for undergraduates moving from their freshman to sophomore years. Retention is measured for the year 2016. Parents' incomes and the Brookings test score variable were statistically significant with the expected positive signs on the coefficients. The HBCU dummy variable was statistically significant at the .05 level. Thus, once one accounts for differences in parental income, Pell Grant status, and standardized test scores, HBCUs perform well.

Interestingly, the coefficients on the statewide coordinating and governing board variables were negative in this regression. Some presidents with whom we have discussed this result believe that "institutions on their own" have a superior ability to respond to campus-specific circumstances.

Graduation Rates

The dependent variable in this estimate is the six-year graduation rate of each institution for undergraduate students who began their undergraduate careers in 2011. This metric is potentially problematic because of the difficulty of dealing with transfer and part-time students. However, it is commonly cited in the higher education literature.

Parental income and standardized test scores once again were highly significant factors. Holding other things constant, higher real net tuition and fee revenues were positively associated with higher graduation rates. This was the only dimension of institutional performance where tuition and fee collections bore any statistical relationship to institutional performance.

Graduating More (or Fewer) Students Than Expected

The circumstances and culture at some institutions cause them to graduate a higher percentage of their enrolled students than one might expect. Most of the campuses of the California State University system have reputations as outperforming the graduation rates that would be expected based on the incomes of the households of their students, their standardized test scores, and the like. In contrast, some flagship state universities in the plains and Rocky Mountains (the University of North Dakota, North Dakota State University, the University of Montana, and Idaho State University) have earned reputations of underperforming expectations with respect to graduation.

We explored these relationships by estimating an expected six-year graduation rate for full-time students who began their studies at each institution in our sample in 2011 and were pursuing a baccalaureate degree. We then compared each institution's predicted rate with its actual graduation rate in 2017. Our predictive equation explained almost 80 percent of the variance in institutional graduation rates and unsurprisingly revealed that parental income and standardized test scores are strong predictors of actual graduation rates. HBCUs consistently overperformed with respect to their graduation rate expectations, whereas the elite and flagship institutions as a group showed no facility for exceeding graduation rate expectations.

Further, the reputations of some institutions for exceeding graduation rate expectations and others for falling short were confirmed by our estimates. For example, our estimating equation predicted a 62 percent graduation rate for California State University at Fullerton; its actual graduate rate was 76 percent. Our model predicted a 40 percent graduation rate for Idaho State University, but its actual rate was only 29 percent.[30]

There is considerable fodder here for members of governing boards. Do they know their institution's graduation rate and how it compares to those of similar institutions? Do they incentivize their campus presidents and administrators to improve performance in this arena? Do they understand that tuition and fee collections and state appropriations have relatively little to do with an institution's ability to exceed (or fall short of) graduation rate expectations? With respect to this latter question, once one has accounted for family income levels and standardized test scores, our analysis tells us that most of the things that produce higher graduation rates relate to campus culture and commitment.

Institutions develop traditions in this regard. Some campuses see helping students graduate as a high priority, while on other campuses graduation rates gradually become peripheral to other considerations such as funded research and intercollegiate athletics.

These are matters about which members of governing boards should be informed—both before they assume their positions as trustees and subsequently as they exercise their duties. We believe concern over graduation rates is a part of trustees' fiduciary responsibility.

Incomes Earned by Students

The dependent variable in this case is a Brookings Institution estimate of the percentile rank nationally of the incomes earned by students of each institution after graduation. A host of independent variables were statistically significant in this regression, including strongly positive relationships with the incomes of students' parents, the percentage of students graduating in STEM disciplines, and the extent to which an institution enrolls proportionately more graduate students than undergraduates.

Student Income Mobility

It is one thing to talk about the absolute incomes that students earn after they graduate and quite another to address the ability of specific campuses to endow students with the ability to move above their parents' income category. The dependent variable we use to measure this latter phenomenon is the percentage of students graduating from each institution who move upward from the lowest income quintile (as measured by their parents' income classification) to the highest income quintile.

The elite institutions exhibit the highest percentages of success in this regard; the problem is that most elite institutions do not admit many students whose parents are in the lowest income classes. We discussed this distinction in chapter 2. Harvard University Opportunity Insights researchers chose to deal with this phenomenon by developing a mobility index that in effect penalizes institutions that do not choose to admit many lower-income students. When this adjustment is made, the apparent superiority of the elite institutions disappears, and the most statistically significant determinants of student income mobility become each institution's graduation rate and the percentage of Pell Grant students that it admits.

HBCUs once again performed well with respect to this metric. Holding constant factors such as parental incomes, standardized test scores, and STEM discipline status, HBCUs exhibit the ability to move their graduates up the income scale.

Student-Faculty Ratios

This dependent variable is the ratio of FTE students to FTE faculty at each institution. Over the past decade this ratio has gradually declined nationally. That is, the average faculty member at the institutions in our sample is teaching somewhat fewer students now than in past years. We cannot explain why.

Notably, our estimating equation explained only 16.57 percent of the variance in campus student-faculty ratios, and so it is fair to conclude that local customs and idiosyncrasies likely have more to do with student-faculty ratios on a specific campus than tuition and fee revenues, state appropriations, institutional type, or governance arrangements. If tuition and fee increases were designed to lower student-faculty ratios, we found no evidence of this.

Administrative Costs

The dependent variable here consists of real administrative costs per FTE student in 2016—a specification that allows us to indirectly test a popular explanation for rising tuition and fees: administrative bloat. Much has been written over the years about the alleged tendency of campuses to hire unnecessary administrators, who arguably contribute little to educational quality and results but do add to institutional operating costs. We do not lack for anecdotal evidence in this arena. Consider economist Mark Perry's disclosure that the University of Michigan employed a minimum of 82 full-time diversity officers whose total compensation in 2018-19 was $10.63 million, or an average of $129,631 per position.[31]

Large-sample studies, however, have not always found administrative complexity to be increasing, though certain types of administrative posts (primarily managerial and professional workers such as information technology specialists) have clearly increased more rapidly than the number of FTE students. McClure and Titus's rigorous look at the spending of 164 public research universities found that both state appropriations and tuition and fee revenue were positively associated with levels of administrative spending.[32] Still, the overall number of headcount employees in higher education per FTE student has not changed much since the turn of the century.[33]

With this background in mind, we present table 4.9, in which real administrative expenditures per FTE student in 2016 are made a function of our usual independent variables. At least two regression coefficients are worthy of mention in this regression. First, the estimated coefficient on the tuition and fee variable is positive and statistically significant at the .01 level. This result is by all odds an embarrassing result for four-year public colleges and universities because it suggests that they have been using higher tuition and fee collections to fatten their administrative ranks. It does not appear that governance structures (statewide governing boards, for example) have had anything to do with this practice, although one could interpret the results to suggest that institutions that are part of systems (where one governing board deals with multiple institutions, such as in the California State University system) reduce on-campus administrative expenditures. Whether there is a net gain to society in this arrangement is not clear.

The other intriguing coefficient in table 4.9 relates to HBCUs. Holding other things constant, HBCUs spend substantially more on administration than other institutions ($2,154 per FTE student in 2016, according to our estimate), and the estimate was statistically significant at the .0001 level. IPEDS data tell us that the average ratio of administrative to instructional expenditures in 2016 was 0.429 at HBCUs but only 0.193 at flagship institutions.[34] This result supports the inference that HBCUs are heavily administered, perhaps over-administered—a tradition that HBCU veterans told us could be traced to the role that HBCUs historically played in providing employment to individuals who were shut out of other job opportunities. The findings suggest that HBCUs continue to respond in this context.

Little or No Evidence of Increased Measured Quality

Overall, we found no strong positive connection between the substantial increases in real tuition and fees per FTE student that occurred between 2003-04 and 2016-17 and the measures of institutional quality and

Table 4.9 Explaining Real Administrative Expenditures per FTE Student, 2016

Variable	Coefficient	Standard error	Absolute value t-statistic	Two-tailed probability
Constant	2,179.08	1,507.62	1.45	.1498
Change in real net T&F per FTE student	.1178	.0449	2.62	.0094
Change in real state appropriation per FTE student	.0214	.0481	0.44	.6572
Parents' income percentile	3.59	17.18	0.21	.8349
Pell Grant percentage	12.94	8.80	1.47	.1426
Percent of Graduates in STEM Fields	−7.76	8.03	0.97	.3349
Percentage of students who move from lowest income quintile to highest after graduation	7.51	27.34	0.27	.7839
Percentage of undergraduate enrollment	−4.25	11.510	0.37	.7122
Percentage change in K-12 enrollment	21.28	6.61	3.22	.0015
Standardized admissions test index	320.64	167.98	1.91	.0576
Elite dummy	762.12	636.53	1.20	.2325
Flagship dummy	342.16	247.21	1.38	.1678
HBCU dummy	2,154.18	467.98	4.60	.0000
Statewide coordinating board dummy	−300.27	303.82	0.99	.3241
Statewide governing board dummy	189.62	328.99	0.58	.5650
Systemwide board dummy	345.28	183.12	1.89	.0607
Interaction term between elite and flagship	101.59	767.07	0.13	.8934

Source: Authors' calculations based on data from State Higher Education Executive Officers Association (SHEEO), *State Higher Education Finance (SHEF): FY 2018* (Boulder, CO, 2019), https://sheeo.org/wp-content/uploads/2019/04/SHEEO_SHEF_FY18_Report.pdf; and National Center for Education Statistics, Integrated Postsecondary Education Data System, https://nces.ed.gov/ipeds.

Notes: The dependent variable consists of real administrative expenditures per capita in 2016. White heteroscedasticity correction made. $N=230$; R^2 adj. = .276; $F=6.49$ (.0000). T&F = tuition and fees; STEM = science, technology, engineering, and math.

performance. In only two of six cases did tuition and fee collections have a statistically significant relationship with the quality and performance measures we introduced, and in one of these instances the sign on the coefficient suggested that higher tuition and fee collections *damage* performance. This finding is antithetical to the argument that tuition and fee increases were essential to maintain or improve the quality of educational offerings and institutional performance.

Finally, to the extent that a statewide coordinating or governing board existed among the sample of 275 institutions, it was sometimes negatively associated with performance measures. It is not clear why this might be true. One could argue that statewide boards inhibit innovation and discourage distinctive campus-centric approaches that are tailored to a student body. This is a possibility, but we believe further detailed research is required before much more can be said.

A Look at Non-Resident Tuition and Fees

Non-resident (out-of-state) students[35] constitute valued sources of enrollment and revenue for many four-year public colleges and universities. Some campuses, especially regional institutions, enroll few non-resident students. A scant 1 percent of undergraduate students at Texas's Stephen F. Austin State University claimed non-resident status in 2017, while only 2 percent of undergraduates were non-residents at two California State University campuses (Chico and Los Angeles). At two other Texas institutions (Tarleton State and Texas State) and two New Jersey university campuses (Richard Stockton and William Paterson), non-residents made up only 2 percent of undergraduates.[36] At the other end of the spectrum, 79 percent of undergraduate students at the University of Vermont were from out of state in 2017, while comparable numbers were 68 percent at Delaware State University and the University of Alabama, and 66 percent at North Dakota State University.[37]

The extent to which institutions rely upon non-resident students for enrollment and revenue involves a strategic choice that is influenced by each institution's location, branding, programs, campus facilities, and pricing. Over an extended time, most of these factors can be influenced or determined by the campuses themselves. Thus, the University of Alabama decided to recruit non-residents students; a dozen or more regional institutions (notably Vermont's Keene State College, Ohio's Miami University, and Pennsylvania's Indiana University) and certain HBCUs (such as Delaware State University and Oklahoma's Langston University) gradually changed their admissions profiles and now enroll 60 percent or more non-resident students.[38] These regional institutions are exceptions to the general rule, however. At the typical regional institution, only 19.4 percent of students are non-residents, compared with 35.2 percent at the flagships, 32.2 percent at the HBCUs, 29.1 percent on the elite campuses, and

15.0 percent at the metro leaders. Only a few metro leader institutions, such as Portland State University and Temple University, have more than 30 percent non-resident students.

In this section, we focus on explaining the change in real non-resident tuition and fee revenues per FTE student at the institutions in our sample between 2003–04 and 2016–17. Our regression results appear in table 4.10. Not surprisingly, out-of-state tuition and fee charges turn out to be more difficult to explain than in-state rates, primarily because we do not know the states from which these students come and go for individual campuses. The state of Illinois, for example, has been hemorrhaging college students to other states that seem more dynamic and prosperous. In 2016, a phenomenally high 46.6 percent of its college students ventured to out-of-state institutions for their educations.[39] However, we do not know precisely where in the state these students came from, specifically where they landed, or how long they stayed. In general, we know less about out-of-state students' backgrounds and circumstances than we do for in-state students.

The signs on coefficients of the independent variables in table 4.10 are as expected, but, except for the institutional dummy variables, the variables typically lose some of their explanatory power.

Holding other things constant, elite status is associated with charging non-resident students $5,767 more than non-resident students attending a non-elite institution. The elite have an ability to attract and retain non-resident students even though they charge them notably high prices. Ohio State is a representative institution in this regard; the tuition and fees it charges non-resident students are triple those paid by Ohio residents; the absolute difference between the two is about $20,000. Still, this is small potatoes compared with the University of Virginia, where the gap between in-state to out-of-state tuition and fees is approximately $31,000, or the University of Michigan Ann Arbor, where it is more than $34,000.

Out-of-state tuition and fee premiums generate hefty sums of money for all elite campuses and nearly all flagship campuses. At the University of Michigan, the non-resident pot of gold approximated $498 million in 2018–19.[40] Small wonder that 49 percent of undergraduate students in Ann Arbor are non-residents.

But not all institutions face the same situations. The distinctive circumstances of HBCUs are worthy of comment. Almost one in every three undergraduate students at a four-year public HBCU is a non-resident and therefore is liable to pay a non-resident price premium. Either this increases their cost of attendance, or it forces the institutions they attend to supply more financial aid to convince these individuals to attend. Perhaps both occur.

The dynamics of the HBCU situation are not clear. Why do African-American high school graduates in, say, Maryland choose to attend public HBCUs in Virginia, while similarly situated individuals in Virginia cross the Potomac River to attend public HBCUs in Maryland? Why don't they stay in their homes states, where they will pay much lower tuition and fees?

Whatever the reasons, this behavior is expensive for students and families and increases the financial pressure on them. This is not a small consideration. The average national percentile rank of the incomes of parents of HBCU students is only 42, whereas it is 68 at the flagships.[41] Consequently, many HBCU students struggle to pay their higher education expenses, and this struggle is accentuated when many choose to increase those expenses by leaving their home state to go to college. The brand magnetism of some HBCUs may offer a partial explanation.

The phenomenon of students choosing to attend an HBCU in another state also exerts pressure on the target HBCU to discount its tuition. In addition, non-resident students are more likely to drop out or transfer,[42] and this factor depresses the retention and graduation rates of the typical HBCU.

Summarizing What We Have Learned about the Influence of Governance on Costs

This is a data-dense chapter because most of the issues we address are ultimately empirical in nature. However, the number crunching has yielded significant benefits. In summary, we find the following:

- While reductions in state appropriations have undoubtedly resulted in increases in tuition and fees at four-year public colleges and universities in specific years, over a longer period of time (fourteen years in

Table 4.10 Determinants of Changes in Net Out-of-State Tuition and Fee Revenues, 2003–04 to 2016–17

Variable	Coefficient	Standard error	*t*-statistic	Two-tailed probability
Constant	−821.04	4,688.13	0.18	.8611
Change in real in-state T&F per FTE student	.4941	.1783	2.77	.0061
Change in real state appropriation per FTE student	−.125	.0794	0.6	.1097
Parents' income percentile	134.10	46.72	2.87	.0045
Pell Grant percentage	11.75	28.11	0.42	.6763
Percentage growth in K-12	64.39	26.41	2.44	.0156
Percentage of graduates in STEM disciplines	27.21	23.68	1.15	.2519
Percentage of students who move from lowest income quintile to highest after graduation	144.85	96.37	1.50	.1343
Percentage undergraduate students	−33.90	35.11	0.97	.3354
Real administrative expenditures per FTE student	.3213	.2104	1.53	.1283
Elite dummy	5,767.55	1,433.42	4.02	.0001
Flagship dummy	1,431.15	844.71	1.69	.0917
HBCU dummy	750.98	1,216.14	0.62	.5376
Statewide coordinating board dummy	598.92	890.62	0.67	.5020
Statewide governing board dummy	−1,136.92	923.67	1.23	.2197
Systemwide board dummy	−145.78	575.51	0.25	.8003
Interaction term between elite and flagship	−5,471.72	1,578.79	3.47	.0006

Source: Authors' calculations based on data from State Higher Education Executive Officers Association (SHEEO), *State Higher Education Finance (SHEF): FY 2018* (Boulder, CO, 2019), https://sheeo.org/wp-content/uploads/2019/04/SHEEO_SHEF_FY18_Report.pdf; and National Center for Education Statistics, Integrated Postsecondary Education Data System, https://nces.ed.gov/ipeds.

Notes: The dependent variable is the change in real non-resident tuition and fee revenue per FTE student from 2003-04 to 2016-17. White heteroscedasticity correction made. $N = 230$; R^2 adj. = .414; $F = 11.13$ (.0000). T&F = tuition and fees; STEM = science, technology, engineering, and math.

this case), they do not explain the acceleration of tuition and fees at four-year public institutions we have observed in recent years.

- Even if one adopts the view that the tuition increases invoked in years when state support was constant or increasing were required as "makeup," the magnitude of tuition and fee increases on the typical campus on average have exceeded the amount of state funding cuts.
- In forty-nine of fifty states, the typical institution had more real dollars to spend in 2016-17 than it had in 1992-93. And between

2003-04 and 2016-17, 76 percent of the institutions in our sample ended the period with more real dollars to spend per FTE student than at the beginning of the period. Over this fourteen-year span, the average institution became $3,024 better off in real terms per FTE student. Elite public institutions ended the period better off by $6,033; flagships, by $5,148; metro leaders, by $3,377; regional institutions, by $1,824; and HBCUs, by $326.

- On average, the presence of a statewide coordinating board or a statewide governance board—or both—constrained tuition and fee increases during these years. While estimates in this regard are sensitive to the regression specification chosen, our baseline estimate tells us that the presence of a statewide governing board reduced net tuition and fee collections per FTE student by $1,139 (see table 4.4). For an institution with 20,000 in-state FTE students, this translates to $22.78 million in reduced tuition and fee collections over the fourteen-year study period, or an average of $1.63 million annually per institution. The corresponding estimate for a statewide coordinating board is a $685 reduction in net tuition and fee collections per FTE student, which produces an estimated reduction of about $13.7 million per institution total over the fourteen years.
- We cannot show that tuition and fee behavior has been sensitive to whether members of governing boards are appointed by a governor or elected by the public.
- Our results do not support the hypothesis that when students exercise a voting franchise on a governing board, tuition and fee increases are moderated.
- Modest but intriguing evidence suggests that increases in the size of governing boards result in larger tuition and fee increases.
- We found no statistical evidence that the substantial increases in real tuition and fees per FTE student that occurred between 2003-04 and 2016-17 had any consistent impact on six measures of institutional quality and performance. We examined quality and performance measures in the form of retention rates, graduation rates, post-graduation earned incomes, income mobility, student-faculty ratios,

and expenditures on administration. On the one hand higher tuition and fee increases were associated with higher graduation rates, and on the other hand they were also strongly associated with increased administrative expenditures.

- In the estimating equations where we attempted to explain variations in the six measures of institutional quality and performance, the Brookings standardized test index (which harmonizes the SAT and ACT tests into a single metric) performed well in nearly every equation, as did parental incomes. All else being equal, gifted, wealthy students tend to perform better in a variety of collegiate contexts, and so do the institutions they attend.
- Once other control variables were introduced, institutional type (for example, identifying an institution as a flagship) was not important as a predictor of either quality or performance.
- By a wide margin, the least successful estimating equation was that dealing with student-faculty ratios. In short, we could not explain the variations in institutional student-faculty ratios that were present in the data. The adjusted R^2 statistic for this equation was an anemic .17. We surmise that local customs, traditions, and binding factors such as union contracts have more to do with the selection of instructional models (and student-faculty ratios) than do funding levels.
- When the governing boards coefficients did prove statistically significant with regard to quality and performance measures, they typically had negative signs, potentially suggesting that statewide governance results in the deterioration of quality and performance. This is an argument the authors have heard many times from presidents and board members, who chafe at the restrictions placed on them by statewide entities. If this claim is valid, then this is the other side of the proverbial statewide governance coin. We found strong evidence that statewide boards, especially those with governance authority, inhibited cost increases. Our latest evidence, while tentative, suggests there may be some quality and performance costs attached to constraints on tuition and fee increases. More research on this issue is needed.

5 We Can Do Better I

Governing Boards, Legislatures, and Governors

> Too many [trustees] have seen their role narrowly defined as boosters, cheerleaders, and donors. They should ask the questions that need to be asked and exercise due diligence. They must not be intermittent or passive fiduciaries of a billion-dollar industry critical to the preparation of America's next leaders.
>
> From *Governance for a New Era* (2014), Benno Schmidt, Chair

> The more any quantitative indicator is used for social decision-making, the more subject it will be to corruption pressures and the more apt it will be to distort and corrupt the social processes it is intended to monitor.
>
> Campbell's Law, from Donald T. Campbell, "Assessing the Impact of Planned Social Change," *Evaluation and Program Planning* (1979)

Outside of campus, the recipe with the greatest potential to contain burgeoning college costs and enhance access and affordability is deceptively simple. It includes the following courses of action: (1) put into law the principle that the fiduciary relationship of board members specifically includes a duty toward citizens, taxpayers, and students as well as the university itself; (2) maintain and improve the quality of individuals who gain board membership; (3) continually orient and train board members; (4) change the prevailing incentive structures that influence the behavior of trustees and senior administrators; and (5) increase transparency so that all parties can make more informed decisions.

Alas, each of these courses of action is easier said than done. There are multiple reasons for this, but a core difficulty is that few states have enunciated clearly what their public colleges and universities are supposed to be doing. Teaching, research, and public service, yes, but how much of each and to what ends? To mold minds? To prepare students for jobs? To push back the frontiers of knowledge? To change society? To broaden opportunity? To elevate the value of students' degrees? To serve the citizens of their state? To entertain? To critique and challenge the society around them?

A typical state avoids answering these questions directly by supporting a university system that consists of a diverse set of institutions—"We have one for everybody," a senior legislator told us somewhat unenthusiastically. Consider, for example, the state of Washington, which supports the University of Washington in Seattle, a 46,000-student multiversity that has developed in the tradition of Clark Kerr,[1] as well as the contentious 3,000-student Evergreen State College, which bills itself as a progressive liberal arts institution offering a nontraditional, interdisciplinary curriculum that students create for themselves. Or contrast the circumstances of the 1,500-student St. Mary's College of Maryland, which describes itself as "the national public honors college," with the 40,000-student University of Maryland, College Park. Same states, but very different institutions.

Members of governing boards usually deal with the assertion that they ought to focus on a specific task (such as preparing students for jobs) by responding, "Well, we already do this." And this is often an accurate response. Like Topsy, American public institutions of higher education "just growed"[2] and now are involved in myriad activities that include running restaurants, motor pools, television networks, child care, law enforcement, entertainment, athletics, K-12 laboratory schools, training for military officers, alumni activities, and placement services, in addition to the traditional triad of teaching, research, and public service.

The old adage that humorously warns us "He who doesn't know where he is going will get there every time" applies to many governing boards, if not to public higher education itself. By default, governing boards have presided over a world in which individual campuses often go their own way, gradually defining their own distinctive missions and paths in response to their own desires and administrative proposals, as well as those of the audiences they most directly serve. What is best for society is a secondary consideration in many of these institutional evolutions; what is good for the campus and key campus constituencies dominates.

"In 2017, the University of Virginia reported an operating budget of almost $3.2 billion, assets of $11.2 billion and liabilities of more than $7.8 billion. The university includes UVA Global LLC, a wholly owned subsidiary based in Shanghai; an athletics enterprise with 25 programs and $24 million in revenues and expenses; a police force with 67 officers; an investment company that manages resources from 25 tax-exempt foundations, each with its own board . . . a top-ranked medical center with . . . more than 12,000 employees, and its own budget of almost $1.5 billion . . . a recycling business; a mental healthcare provider. Incidentally, UVA also educates around 16,000 undergraduates and 6,500 graduate and professional students each year."

Adams Daniel and Chad Wellmon, "The University Run Amok!" *Chronicle of Higher Education,* July 29, 2018, www.chronicle.com/article/Why-the-University-s/244010.

How does this happen? Part of the problem is that governing board members come and go. Sometimes, when a new governor is elected, board memberships experience a complete turnover. Amid these governance changes, senior administrators often persist and veteran campus constituencies retain their clout. Unless constrained by mission, statewide governance arrangements, money, or some other pertinent circumstance, the interests of these long-term participants come to dominate as the years pass. It is a sophisticated form of regulatory capture—that is, the takeover of a regulatory body by the very groups it is supposed to be regulating.

To be sure, many of the concerns of long-term campus constituencies such as faculty are admirable. Most faculty governance groups typically are interested in enrolling students with higher test scores; they advocate higher salaries and generous, fully funded fringe benefits; they support improved, up-to-date classrooms and laboratories; and they plump for more time for research. Problems can arise, however, when their desires turn out to be inconsistent with the welfare of students and citizens, whose interests may be more closely tied to their ability to access and afford higher education. Someone must pay for the things desired by the long-term constituencies, and the evidence introduced thus far reveals

One president to whom we spoke kiddingly likened his institution's status in his state to that of North Korea. "We stretch the regulations knowing they [the statewide board] may not react because what we are doing is on the border line," he said referring his institution's foray into engineering curricula. "We label programs differently, hire faculty, enroll students, and then eventually confront them with reality. We raise outside money to avoid being dependent upon them. As long as our violations are not huge, they tend to wag their fingers at us a bit but don't do anything about it."

that students and families are usually the constituency that carries the largest portion of the burden of doing so.

Some (although certainly not all) of these problems can be averted if institutions have clearly defined missions that identify what they are supposed to be doing (and not doing). Even so, dozens of examples reveal a remarkable ability of institutions to morph around and over the seeming strictures of mission statements. Much depends upon the focus and determination of any governing boards that are involved.

Fiduciary Status

Black's Law Dictionary defines a fiduciary as "one who owes to another the duties of good faith, trust, confidence, and candor."[3] One of the Latin roots of the word is *fiducia,* meaning a position of trust.[4] A fiduciary is expected to exhibit loyalty to his or her clients as well as to care for their best interests. But as Felix Frankfurter put it in a 1943 United States Supreme Court opinion, "To say that a man is a fiduciary only begins analysis; it gives direction to further inquiry. To whom is he a fiduciary? What obligations does he owe as a fiduciary?"[5]

Among the considerations relevant to determining fiduciary duties are the ages, sophistication, and vulnerability of those affected.[6] In the case of public higher education, the primary customers are students, who are young, typically not financially sophisticated, but often impressionable and therefore vulnerable. Their vulnerability reflects the reality that higher education is both a *trust market* and an *experience market.* In trust markets, non-expert customers have little choice but to trust the advice they are given by those serving them. Thus, when a physician writes a prescription for specific drug, nearly all her patients will accept her advice and obtain the drug. Or, when an auto mechanic tells the owner of car that just has been towed into his garage that the car needs a new transmission, the car owner is likely to follow his advice. Neither the patient nor the car owner has enough information to decide otherwise.

Analogously, students and families have little choice (or at least believe they have little choice) but to trust faculty, administrators, and staff, particularly when the students are lower-level undergraduates. They don't know or understand all the intricacies of university life and therefore defer to the individuals whom they regard as experts to steer them into the correct majors and courses, recommend the most appropriate textbooks, discuss the places where they can live, and so forth. Implicitly, students and families also put their trust in their institution's governing board to "do the right thing." Students and their families do not expect public campus trustees to take actions that are not in their best interest; indeed, they likely expect the contrary.

Higher education also is an experience market because it is difficult for students to know or evaluate the worth of the education they are receiving until they actually experience it. Only then can students decide they do not enjoy economics but love chemistry, or that Professor Jones really is a great teacher, or even that their investment in higher education is not doing for them what they hoped it would and therefore is not worth it. They often do not understand their opportunity costs—that is, what alternatives they have surrendered that would have provided them superior outcomes (net benefits) vis-à-vis what they have experienced. For example, perhaps a different major would have provided them with a better job outlook or greater income. Once again, students must rely upon faculty, administrators, staff, and governing boards to protect them and understand their situation while they gain experience and hopefully hone their abilities to assess the value of their campus experience.

In a word, students (and their families) are *vulnerable* and therefore must trust members of governing boards to act wisely, as true fiduciaries, on their behalf. The need for fiduciary status is amplified by the financial stakes involved. For most undergraduate students, their investment in higher education is easily the largest and most important financial commitment of their lives to this point and usually will rank in the top two or three most important investment decisions of their entire lives.

Scharffs and Welch note, "In its strongest formation, the duty of loyalty requires that a fiduciary put aside his own interests and act in furtherance only of the interests of a beneficiary."[7] Not only should board members recognize they have a fiduciary relationship to students, but others on campus—administrators, faculty, and staff—should understand that they too are obligated to consider the best interests of their students.

A series of federal court decisions have established significant fiduciary duties on the part of institutions of higher education toward their students,[8] but these decisions have substantially overlooked the role of governing boards. One might expect the question of board members' specific fiduciary duties toward students to have been resolved long ago, but in fact this issue has yet to be rigorously defined or legally tested.[9] The Association of Governing Boards of Universities and Colleges (AGB) may assert that "fiduciary duty is the law" because all states have some form of fiduciary law on their books.[10] Nevertheless, it is not clear that these laws apply to the trustees of public college and university governing boards, and it certainly is not clear that the fiduciary responsibilities of trustees encompass the costs of higher education in general, or tuition and fees in particular.

This is why action at the state level is required. Every state should adopt legislation that unambiguously establishes a fiduciary relationship between governing boards on the one hand and citizens and students on the other hand. Furthermore, as a condition of their service, members of governing boards should be required to sign a statement declaring that they recognize this fiduciary relationship. It would be difficult for any prospective board member (or board) to construct a plausible argument why he or she should not be a fiduciary on behalf of citizens and students.

If nothing else, the public discussions and legislative maneuvering connected to a governing board's fiduciary proposal would be illuminating.

Although such an idea may appear to some to be a motherhood-and-apple-pie proposal, some influential campuses will seek ways to delay or defeat such legislation (although they are unlikely to do so publicly). They understand that it would change the dimensions of their playing field.

The Need to Clarify Institutional Missions

Another fundamental way for states to improve the performance of their systems of higher education is to clarify their expectations for public higher education as a whole or for an individual institution. What do we want higher education to accomplish, and how will we measure its performance?

California does better than most states by clearly specifying the missions of campuses within its three-tier system of higher education—the University of California, California State University, and the California Community Colleges system. This legal clarity has diminished the mission creep that has plagued so many other states; moreover, it may have made it easier for board members to make informed decisions. California is no better than any other state, however, when it comes to assessing performance.

At the opposite end of the spectrum, the Commonwealth of Virginia says little about the missions of its four-year institutions. The Virginia Constitution says merely, "The General Assembly may provide for the establishment, maintenance and operation of educational institutions which are desirable for the intellectual, cultural and occupational development of the people of this Commonwealth."[11] This lack of detail constitutes license for Virginia's four-year public campuses to do nearly anything that intrigues their ambitious administrators, faculty, and trustees, so long as they can fund it. Virginia provides no guidance to its public university board members concerning what it means to have either a defined institutional mission or a fiduciary relationship to citizens and students.

On occasion, institutions end up pursuing goals that seemingly bear little or no relationship to their mission statements. As Charles Clotfelter of Duke University has pointed out in his influential book *Big-Time Sports in American Universities,*[12] most university mission statements completely ignore intercollegiate athletics even though on some campuses, "sports" may involve hundreds of millions of dollars of annual expenditures. This gap between an institution's mission and its actions was perhaps among the reasons why the *Chronicle of Higher Education* critically reviewed Louisiana State University's opening of a $28 million renovation of a facility providing plush amenities to football players even while the university's flood-damaged library went unrepaired.[13] What did this imply about the institution's priorities, the *Chronicle* asked, suggesting the answer was that football has attained virtually untouchable status on the LSU campus.

Yet the story of intercollegiate athletics at LSU is more complicated than it might first appear. In 2017, LSU's athletic programs generated a $16 million surplus of revenues over expenditures.[14] Thus LSU's governing board (its Board of Supervisors, whose members are appointed by the governor) can respond truthfully that intercollegiate athletic programs do not reduce academic expenditures; furthermore, they can point to an agreement whereby a portion of LSU athletic profits are transferred to the academic side of the institution.[15] We note this to underscore the complexities that trustees often must consider when making decisions.

The relevant governance question, however, is whether LSU's governing board would have sufficient political clout to rein in the university's intercollegiate athletic programs, even if it wished to do so. The answer is uncertain. Meanwhile, what is clear is that LSU ranked 140th in *U.S. News and World Report's* 2019 national ranking of best universities.[16]

Whatever an institution's mission or the fiduciary relationship of its governing board to the public, the best governing board members are those who can see the big picture. This need recalls the ancient fable of the blind men and the elephant. In this story from the Indian subcontinent, a half-dozen blind men encounter an elephant and begin to touch it to find out what it is. Each man touches a different part of the elephant's body (tusks, trunk, feet, tail, and so on). When the men begin to describe their interactions with the elephant, each has a very different perception, based upon his own experience. After all, an elephant's trunk is very different from its leg. As each man listens to his companions' dramatically

A highly regarded sitting college president told us that he had interviewed to become the president of a flagship state university that boasted a highly successful (and profitable) football team. He emerged as the preferred candidate, but at what was supposed to be his final meeting with the institution's governing board before his appointment, he asked if the president was in charge of intercollegiate athletics. "Yes, of course," was the chorus from the board. He noted that the institution's football coach was widely regarded externally as an NCAA rule-breaker and then asked, "What if I decided I needed to fire him?" This question provoked consternation. Early the next morning he was informed by the search firm coordinating the process that the board had decided he was "not a good fit for the institution."

different descriptions of this thing that none can see, the descriptions he hears fail to match his personal experience. Each man begins to doubt and distrust the others. Collectively, they start to quarrel over the true essence of this animal called an elephant, and eventually some of them even come to blows. (Setting aside the fisticuffs, this parable may describe the dynamics of a faculty senate meeting on many campuses.)

Almost needless to say, governors, legislators, and responsible board members need to see the entire elephant, not simply its trunk or ears. This means they must listen to others and be open to other perspectives. It should be apparent, however, that defining the elephant is less thorny when institutional missions are clear and fiduciary duties have been established.

A Need to Refashion the Membership of Governing Boards

Our discussion in the previous section assumed that board members had already been appointed or elected. Let's backtrack and consider productive opportunities for improving the processes by which individuals join governing boards. We have already seen that governors are responsible for appointing all the members of the governing boards at about two-thirds of the institutions in our sample, and they appoint some of the board members in 91 percent of these cases. In 13 percent of cases, some or all board members are elected.

Board appointment and election procedures are and always will be political in nature, but the final outcome can be improved by enhancing the roster of individuals considered by governors, political parties, and alumni groups for governing board posts. Ideally, a nonpartisan group of distinguished individuals within the state will identify a group of candidates for the consideration of governors, legislators, and voters. The AGB reports that although such groups have existed in only a handful of states (Hawaii, Massachusetts, Minnesota, North Dakota, and Virginia) and are now moribund in several of these states, they generally appear to improve the quality of the individuals who populate public college and university governing boards.[17] More than one governor, however, has chosen to ignore the recommendations of his or her state's screening board or refused to reappoint outstanding board members when they are members of the other political party.

Nevertheless, a multitude of reasons exist for establishing a nonpartisan group that generates suggestions for appointment. First, public colleges and universities are large economic enterprises that deserve attention. Not every citizen is qualified to serve on the boards of these substantial institutions. Second, as we have noted, campus operations are distinctive and call for trustees who have the background, the time, and the ability to contribute. Third, public institutions of higher education are shaping the future of our society, and as we have seen, many have not been doing so in a fashion that emphasizes access and affordability. This is a "we-can-do-better" area.

The identification of highly qualified individuals who have the talent and time to give to a trustee position ought to be a front-burner issue. In the long term, the presence of productive public colleges and universities is directly connected to the economic growth of states.[18]

Contributions to a political campaign should not be a disqualifier to membership on a governing board but ordinarily should not carry major weight in board appointments and elections. Political sophistication and connections can be useful and should not be ignored. Optimally, however, competence and commitment should be valued above all else.

How does this work in the real world? The University of Virginia (UVA) provides a representative example. Over the past decade, UVA has been the scene of several board squabbles and an aborted sacking of a sitting president. Thus, board membership has been demanding. The UVA campus student newspaper reported that ten of twelve voting members of the UVA board who were Virginians had made financial contributions to the political party of the governor, while only three had contributed to the other party.[19] This is the way of the world and describes nearly every state, irrespective of which political party is in power.

Whatever the means of their selection, the first-order obligations of governing board members are to ensure that the institution has an appropriate mission, is financially sound, and is efficiently operated. As they satisfy these fundamental tasks, however, board members should view themselves as fiduciaries who have an obligation to citizens, taxpayers, students, and families in addition to the institution to whose board they have been appointed. Their university is a creature of the state and exists to benefit the state and its citizens (some of whom are students). This means the fiduciary responsibilities of trustees extend beyond the confines of the campus and include representing, promoting, and protecting the interests of the public at large.

The fiduciary challenge for board members arises when the best interests of the campus diverge from those of the citizenry. Trustees must occasionally be willing to incur the wrath of faculty and administrators in order to exercise their fiduciary duties. Yet it also is true that the best interests of the citizenry should not be defined by who received the most votes in the most recent election. On occasion, therefore, board members must also be willing to swim against that tide, especially if that tide would politicize campuses.[20] Careful, reasoned, logical assessment is the order of the day for board members when they exercise their fiduciary responsibilities.

A Need to Improve the Orientation and Training of Board Members

An AGB document identifies the challenge: "Most people selected for governing boards are bright and well-intentioned, but they may lack a clear understanding of what is expected of them."[21] Further, many trustees do not know what they do not know. They need to be oriented and trained.

However, the AGB reported in 2017 that only five states (Arkansas, Oklahoma, Texas, Virginia, and West Virginia) mandate the orientation and training of new board members.[22] Nearly all of the remaining forty-five states provide orientation and training sessions, but new and reappointed board members can usually serve even if they do not attend the sessions. Both the AGB and the American Council of Trustees and Alumni (ACTA) offer training materials and sessions for public campus board members. ACTA places a greater emphasis upon trustees' rocking the boat of higher education by asking challenging questions and controlling costs than the AGB, but it also is more identified with conservative political positions.

Higher education coordinating and governing boards often provide orientation and training, and both our own experience and AGB evidence suggest these are valuable experiences, especially for new board members. Nevertheless, only sometimes do these sessions give much attention either to access and affordability issues or to material relating to social and economic mobility. "Too touchy" is how one New England state higher education official described these subjects to us. He went on to say, "We have lots of other material to cover, and these topics are likely to generate arguments."

This is an unfortunate conclusion because it usually is possible to separate "what is" (factual presentations) from "what ought to be" (preferred policies). Board members should be familiar with the factual pricing, debt, and mobility data presented in chapters 1 and 2 of this book. Each then can reach his or her own conclusions about the implications of these data. We present our views in this book, but the parable of the elephant should remind us that not everyone is going to see things the same way.

Board member orientation and training should also focus on topics such as the legal responsibilities and potential liability of trustees, the impact of technological developments on campuses, demographic trends, teaching loads, space usage, sources of research funding, mission creep, the role of foundations and fund-raising, intercollegiate athletics, auxiliary enterprises, demographics, the roles that incentives play on campus, retention and graduation rates, the measurement of institutional impact, and so forth.

The list of topics worthy of coverage may seem almost endless, and perhaps it is. It is obvious that not all of these topics can be covered in a single session. Some can be dealt with by the equivalent of TED Talks—ten- to fifteen-minute forays into specific topics such as intercollegiate athletics. Board members can tackle these topics at their leisure, but if they fail to do so, they should not be allowed to serve. It is appropriate for governing boards to assign a specific TED Talk and then allot time to discuss it at the next board meeting.

The higher education environment changes rapidly, and therefore existing board members should not be ignored. They may bridle at being asked to "learn" about their campus and higher education when they have already served a term, but some topics on the preceding list (probably including our chapter 1 and 2 material) are likely not familiar to them. Targeted sessions can alleviate such problems.

Ultimately, however, even though public governing board members are volunteers, if they do not complete appropriate orientation and training, they should not be allowed to vote in board meetings. The stakes are too high to permit unknowledgeable individuals to make critical decisions.

We intentionally stir the waters by stating our support for providing at least symbolic compensation to public college governing board members. Not only should they be reimbursed for any legitimate expenses they incur as trustees, but they should also receive at least modest compensation that gratefully acknowledges their time and service.

Members of corporate boards are compensated, but with that compensation comes the firm expectation that they will show up prepared for committee and board meetings. The same logic should apply to public college trustees. The easiest way to get this practice started is to have the state legislature make a lump-sum appropriation to each institution for this purpose. Say that board member receives $500 per full board meeting and $250 per committee meeting. If the board meets four times a year and each board member attends four committee meetings annually, it would cost $36,000 a year to compensate a twelve-member board. This is small change in most legislative sessions in most states.

Should there exist certification curricula or processes for trustees that states could use to orient and train their board members? Partners for College Affordability and Public Trust, a higher education advocacy foundation, has bandied this notion about but has not produced materials or resources that would accomplish the task. Even if one could obtain agreement on a curriculum, the higher education circumstances of individual states vary substantially, and states would thus likely want to supplement national orientation and training with their own. The time and expense of doing so would be significant. So far these considerations have deterred the Partners for College Affordability and other seemingly interested organizations, such as the Association of Governing Boards, from moving forward.

Why should the legislature make such an appropriation? For two reasons. First, it places legislators in the position of acknowledging that some hard but socially valuable work is required of those who serve. A board appointment should not be considered a lark. It is serious business. Second, compensation puts board members on notice that they are expected to attend meetings (and will not be paid if they do not) and that they should come prepared. The dual symbolism behind the payments is important.

A Need to Reform Accreditation

Institutional and program accreditation processes are usually expensive and tend to push all participants into a common mold. At the programmatic level, accrediting bodies such as the Accreditation Council for Pharmacy Education and the National Association of Schools of Music bludgeon institutions into spending more by setting standards for student-faculty ratios, faculty teaching loads, required space, specific equipment and internet needs, and of course faculty salaries. At the institutional level, regional accreditors threaten the accreditation of institutions for matters that have little or nothing to do with the quality of education and much more to do with who is exercising control or which institutions are being threatened by innovation.

The rationale behind accreditation—to maintain and improve quality—is a noble one, but relatively few programs or institutions can truthfully say that accreditation achieves this aim even when it forces their institution or even their state to pony up more resources. More commonly, departments and institutions learn that it can be risky to innovate or break the mold because such steps might displease accreditors.

Many accrediting bodies seemingly heed the famous Japanese adage "The nail that sticks out gets hammered down." As a consequence, institutions and programs often rigidly adhere to metrics that count faculty publications, measure teaching loads, and the like. It has become increasingly common for institutions and their academic subdivisions, such as schools of medicine, business, and nursing, to hire consultants from institutions that have just achieved accreditation or recently had it renewed. The hiring institutions then follow the models provided by these just-reaccredited institutions, sometimes copying pages of material verbatim for submission. Indeed, this practice likely increases their probability of accreditation success. Such processes discourage innovation, tend to become mechanical, and usually ignore fiduciary responsibilities.

Wise governing boards will advocate accreditation reform so that the process focuses more on the quality of educational outputs rather than upon the quantity of educational inputs or methods of delivery. This kind of attention to educational outputs is good for a campus even if it is not going through accreditation. We urge board members not to limit their purview to conventional output measures such as graduation rates because such metrics are highly predictable if one knows students' entering standardized test scores and parental incomes. Trustees should instead broaden their outlook to value-added measures of learning (What did our institution add? What innovations did they adopt?), indicators of the postgraduate success of their students, measures of the extent to which a program or a campus enhances income and social mobility, and the subsequent civic lives of their graduates. They should be wary of measures that do little more than repackage and rescale standardized entrance test scores and parental incomes.

As Susan Phillips and Kevin Kinser have pointed out,[23] oversight of American higher education has traditionally had three major participants: the federal government, which has focused primarily on oversight of

Quis custodiet ipsos custodes? (Who will guard the guardians?) The US Department of Education is responsible for monitoring college accreditation agencies, but the time and attention it pays to this task have been limited. Hence, accrediting agencies usually can do their own thing without much scrutiny. Individual institutions and governing boards shrink from questioning or opposing accrediting agencies actions because they "fear retribution" (the words of a president to us).

See Antoinette Flores, "The Unwatched Watchdogs," Center for American Progress, September 19, 2019, www.americanprogress.org/issues/education-postsecondary/reports/2019/09/19/474492/the-unwatched-watchdogs.

financial matters, including student financial aid; states, which have been concerned with financial support and sometimes consumer protection; and accreditors, who have been concerned with educational quality. The three activities are interconnected and have some overlap. The federal government, for example, uses regional accreditation as a necessary condition for an institution to participate in federal student loan programs.

Board members need to understand this three-legged stool, which exhibits some Rube Goldberg qualities. All three major participants should act as fiduciaries on behalf of students in particular, but the federal government does relatively little of this in the financial aid arena. Unless smacked in the face with scandal, the feds usually ignore matters such as the amount of debt students incur and institutions' role in determining this. Rare is the state whose funding mechanism rewards institutions that perform well on the economic mobility scale. And accrediting bodies seem to believe that issues of access and affordability are none of their business. When is the last time a regional accrediting body criticized a campus for the income stratification of its student body, its low mobility index, or for tuition and fee increases far in excess of reductions in state support?

Ideally, all three bodies should give more attention to these issues. Accreditation procedures should be sensitive to them lest they implicitly begin to measure how societal wealth and income are translated into outcomes rather than measuring the contributions of the institution.

Realistically speaking, no single governing board can do much more than advocate for sensible change in this arena. Nevertheless, board members need to understand that accreditation processes are imperfect, and they should not conclude that accreditation will necessarily provide them with the information that they as fiduciaries should want. Accreditations and reaccreditations are officious processes that frequently provide members of governing boards with little of substance. This is a lesson that often disappoints board members, but it is an important one because accreditation only indirectly signals that a governing board has been behaving as a fiduciary.

The Need for Board Members to Avoid Being Co-Opted

The notion that many members of the boards of public institutions of higher education may end up being co-opted is minimized by some, not least because they find it difficult to admit that it does occur, perhaps even on their own campuses. Co-opted by whom? Nearly always, the college president. Let's delve into this phenomenon, which is related to presidential and administrative charisma, expertise, and the ability to determine agendas.

Albert Speer, the German architect who fell under the sway of Adolf Hitler in Germany in the 1930s and 1940s, ended up running the German wartime economy. Speer was cultured, urbane, and well educated. Yet even as the Third Reich was folding like an accordion in April 1945, he felt a primal need to visit Hitler one last time in surrounded Berlin. Although presumably debilitated physically and about to die, the Führer remained a magnetic, charismatic personality to Speer and many others.

Decades later, after serving twenty years in prison, Speer commented to a biographer that charisma "is the most dangerous quality there is" because of the ways it can be used for ill purpose or outright evil.[24] While we would vouch that few if any college presidents are evil, many are charismatic figures who have the ability to sway audiences by word and deed and thereby convince all who listen to "join their team." Indeed, many college and university presidents having this charismatic dimension are effectively endowed with a capacity to stimulate herding behavior, creating social pressure to conform.[25]

Writers dating back to Max Weber[26] have noted that one of the practical operational impacts of charisma on individuals and audiences is the creation of emotional bonds. Attracted or smitten individuals lose their bearings and consequently overlook or ignore important data and signals. On campuses, they uncritically assume that the charismatic individual they admire (often the president) is doing good things and has the best interests of the campus at heart; hence her proposals are likely good ideas. In the case of board members, they come to believe that while they may need to do some refining of the president's proposals—perhaps for a new building or a tuition and fee increase—if this president whom they trust says these initiatives are necessary, then this quite likely to be true, and hence her ideas deserve support.

Charisma is a tricky concept because it can be used for good or ill. When used wisely, it can open ears, hasten progress, and seal deals. US presidents Theodore Roosevelt, Franklin D. Roosevelt, John F. Kennedy, and Barack Obama oozed charisma and mobilized it to pursue their own concept and vision of the public good. In the academic realm, the legendary Father Theodore Hesburgh did so for Notre Dame and once was called "the most powerful unelected official this nation has ever seen."[27] At the other end of the spectrum, individuals such as Adolf Hitler, Joseph Stalin, Mao Zedong, and Charles Manson wielded their charisma to pursue and accomplish evil ends.

Today, leaders such as Michael Crow of Arizona State University, recently retired Diana Natalicio of the University of Texas at El Paso, Mitch Daniels of Purdue University, Waded Cruzado of Montana State University, and Freeman Hrabowski III of the University of Maryland, Baltimore County, evince charismatic abilities. It is not that each doesn't have some naysayers. Rather, it is that their analyses, words, and endorsements carry immense weight both on and off campus, and this influence typically makes a decisive difference.

Our normative view is that society generally is better off because many university presidents wield charismatic influence. However, even though most college presidents use their charisma to accomplish mostly good things, the same charismatic qualities also enable them gradually to co-opt the members of their governing boards. Trustees are wined and dined when they come to campus; they receive choice football and basketball tickets along with great seats for lectures, performances, and other university events that pique their interest; they do not have to worry about parking tickets. They are made to feel they are vital cogs in an important phenomenon and are pleased when their successful president asks them what they think and on occasion implements their ideas. Skillful presidents orchestrate this scenario, whether or not they acknowledge doing so.

As time passes, satisfied trustees less often challenge ideas coming from the president's office and less frequently check their institution's dashboard indicators because they have gained confidence in what is occurring. Most trustees buy into the president's narrative about what the institution is, how it is ranked, and what it is attempting to accomplish. No doubt the institution's preferred "story" contains many elements of truth. Seldom, however, does it provide a complete or candid picture.

Gradually, many board members evolve into partisans for their institution and president. Their fiduciary roles correspondingly recede, and they think not in terms of what is good for citizens, taxpayers, and students, but rather what is good for the corporate concept of the university as it has been defined for them by their charismatic president. They offer highly attractive compensation packages to their institution's president because "we can't afford to lose her."

As William G. Bowen, a former president of Princeton University once noted, collegiate governance can evolve such that the board effectively ends up working for the president rather than vice versa.[28] Depending upon the values, energy, and foresight of the president, this can lead to excellent results, though it also has the potential to produce disastrous outcomes, primarily because the responsible parties—board members—have lost their way and have stopped doing their jobs. Consequently, co-opted trustees do not sense problems looming on the horizon until they are slapped in the face by reality. Board members "need to be sensitive to signs that problems may be developing," and a telltale sign of such problems is when board members are "not having their questions answered quickly and completely"[29]

Presidents deserve great attention and respect because they usually know more about the institution than anyone else. Further, the president is the only individual connected to the institution who can see its corpus in totality rather than through the lens of a specific constituency or administrative area. That said, presidents are not infallible. As we will see, they are typically ambitious individuals who respond to the goals and incentives placed in front them. The problem is their responses may not always be the ones governing board members had in mind.

Just as charisma can be used for good or bad ends, the superb knowledge and perspective that presidents possess can be a positive or negative factor. Presidents who know the nooks and crannies of their institutions can be extremely productive leaders because, among other things, they have the ability to call upon the breadth of the institution to accomplish worthy goals. They understand its strengths and weaknesses. But this knowledge likely means they also have the ability hide or suppress vital information, selectively release supportive data and reports, use foundations and public-private partnerships to skirt board and legislative directives, and intimidate those who seek to question or investigate.

By no means do we suggest that most presidents do potentially counterproductive things most of the time. We do argue, however, that all but a few presidents do *some* of these things *some* of the time. When this occurs, they may rationalize their behavior by saying to themselves that they had the greater good of their campus in mind. Nevertheless, this is not always so, and counterproductive behaviors are especially common at mediocre, faltering, and failing institutions. Such scenarios arise because inattentive board members are ignorant of the true state of their campus.

"Good boards ask good questions," is how Peter Eckel and Cathy Trower put it.[30] Eckel and Trower, authors of a useful and practical guide to college and university governing boards, note that the work of college and university boards can become routine over time, leading board members to become complacent and disengage. They propose a variety of means to increase board engagement and stimulate legitimate curiosity by and among trustees.

These specific proposals may be worthy of attention:

- *Break routines.* Eckel and Trower observe that "routines are the enemy of curiosity."[31] Don't structure all meetings the same way, and don't always meet in the same place at the same time. The Association of Governing Boards agrees.
- *Commit sufficient time.* Don't overload agendas with topics that deserve attention but that will not receive it because of a lack of time. Well-chosen consent agendas can be helpful ways to preserve time for the most important issues.
- *Relabel some challenges as puzzles and pose them as questions.* Issues that are framed as problems or that appear to put someone on the spot typically provoke defensive behavior rather than problem solving. Instead, where and when possible, promote topical discussions that are more likely to lead to more free-wheeling thought processes, better questions, and a sense of achievement. On occasion, finger pointing and blame assessment are required, but wherever possible, boards should design their discussions of challenges and problems to lead to greater understanding and solutions rather than takedowns of individuals or offices. The latter may be necessary, but a board meeting seldom is the best forum within which to do so.
- *Strive to develop a culture of curiosity.* On any board, it should on occasion be possible for a trustee to act as the devil's advocate or to broach new ways of thinking about issues. Make it possible for board members to do so without being ostracized. Encourage board members to walk in someone else's shoes—students, parents, faculty, staff, alumni, and so forth.

Dealing with Board Members Who Don't Agree

Board members who are doing their jobs are not micromanagers, but they do ask questions and look for answers. This can be bothersome to some. Decades ago, Mark Bailey noted that some trustees end up being labeled "troublesome" because they disrupt or reduce the productivity of board meetings. But he also sagely observed that the existence of a troublesome

Robert Reich, prolific author, professor, savant, and former US secretary of labor, when reportedly asked about his impressions of his service as a governing board trustee at his alma mater, Dartmouth College, tellingly said, "We ate well." Many boards of trustees do not come to grips with vital institutional issues.

board member may be evidence of a destructive board culture and counterproductive board agendas and procedures. That is, it is possible that the board is at fault, not the putative troublemaker.[32] If, for example, a board member is deemed problematic because she questions the validity of the institutional narrative ("we have the best teacher education program on the West Coast") or does not immediately accept an administrative explanation, it is possible that she is doing what board members should do as well as being correct.

Whether or not nonconforming board members are virtuous, they are often urged by their colleagues to offer support for the institution and to "show respect." Public unanimity is encouraged at most board meetings; contrary trustees usually are advised to air their grievances in private and not to "disrupt" board meetings. If they still feel they must opine in opposition, then they are urged to state their case succinctly, avoid grandstanding, and not spend time fueling the media with what is perceived to be negative coverage. In truth, these suggestions may be good advice for any board member, but the spirit with which this message is delivered is the key.

With respect to an alleged troublemaker, one former trustee lamented to us that "she thinks our board meeting is the House of Commons and this gives her the right to heckle and interrupt speakers." Trustees whose conduct is palpably unwelcome will likely end up being counseled by the board chair and senior board members; this is appropriate. Deft conversations with the disrupter by senior board members that incorporate a generous amount of listening and perhaps some problem solving may be useful. However, the result may be the opposite of what is intended. The disruptor may feel either pressured or silenced inappropriately, and therefore even gentle counseling may harden her attitudes and behavior. Nevertheless, it is important to try.

When nonconforming trustees are elected members of the board and have their own awakened set of supporters willing to challenge prevailing powers, they may wield considerable power and garner substantial media coverage. Board members are forewarned that elected officials are notorious for detecting which direction a parade is traveling and then sprinting to the front of the parade to lead it (or at least appear to lead it). This is another reason why boards must be judicious in responding to what they perceive to be provocations by individual board members. Once again, the best advice to board members is "Keep your eyes on the prize." Remember that the fiduciary responsibilities of the board should transcend personalities.

Our experience reveals that board members who fail to conform are often isolated and omitted from key conversations. Where they sit at meetings may change as well as whether the chair even recognizes them to speak. Time limits may be placed on their speeches and presentations. Additional counseling may occur, and key external figures may be asked to intervene. Nevertheless, once truly disruptive trustees have acquired a platform, however, they will be difficult to silence if they really wish to vent. These dynamics provide an additional reason for us to favor the use of nominating committees that provide governors with the names of suggested board members.

Ultimately, the worth and value of the interjections and objections of a nonconforming board member are judged historically. Did he turn out to be accurate and on target with respect to the facts? Was she prescient in anticipating future developments in higher education and society? All things considered, did he advocate for principled positions that appear to have increased the welfare of the citizenry? Was she acting as a fiduciary? If the answer to one or more of these questions is "yes," then his nonconforming, even disruptive, behavior may be judged favorably by the public and the media as time passes. If the answer is "no," then his activities will be judged harshly.

The uncanny thing about the semi-disciplinary scenarios we are describing with respect to nonconforming board members is that it is the

A description of the elusive ideal: "The admiration that these board members have for each other and the president who brought them to the board seems to have a positive impact on the board's work. Attendance at most meetings verges on 100 percent. Members report that there is vigorous debate during meetings. 'Because there is a high level of trust, we can speak our minds, work our way through tough issues.'"

Helen Ouellette and Barbara Wheeler, "Two Patterns of Good Governance," *In Trust,* Spring 2015, www.intrust.org/Magazine/Issues/Spring-2015/Two-patterns-of-good-governance.

members of the board and not the president who usually exercise this discipline. This highlights another talent of a charismatic leader; she has the ability to convince others to perform less attractive tasks. The wise president wields this influence carefully, however.

Given the charismatic nature of many presidents, the inability of some board members to get their hands around complicated issues, and the disciplinary dynamic we have just described, it is unsurprising that 99 percent of college trustees go with the flow and vote in favor of cost-increasing proposals placed in front of them.

We also should not be shocked to learn that despite the requirements of open meeting laws, much of the business of public higher education is carried out behind closed doors and is only afterward formally ratified at open board meetings. Constituencies such as students and families who might object to cost increases or unhappy landowners who protest eminent domain property seizures are seldom represented at the meetings before the meetings. They may receive the opportunity to speak to a board committee or even at a full board meeting, but by that time they are likely standing in front of a locomotive that is already steaming ahead. It usually takes a meeting room stuffed with protestors and surrounded by pickets to deter boards from their predetermined actions.

To cement charismatic relationships, many effective college presidents or their senior vice presidents visit personally with each board member before board meetings and carefully explain the initiatives that will come before the board, as well as answer questions on those or any other topics. These meetings are time-consuming but can be extremely useful—presidents can get a sense of the board member's receptivity, and board members can ask challenging questions or broach topics that might not be welcome in a full board meeting. Nevertheless, in these pre-board meetings (in some states, no more than two board members can be present at such meetings because of open meetings laws), the three Cs of charisma, confidence, and competence reign supreme. Such meetings reduce the probability that open disagreements will be aired when the board meets formally. A downside is that these tête-à-têtes also keep from the public eye interesting discussions and vital topics that ideally should be heard in open session.

Trustees should understand that formal board meetings are thoroughly orchestrated by effective presidents.[33] Skillful presidents ensure that the board and the public will meet the all-conference basketball player who is also in the university's honors program, the student who went to India to work with Mother Teresa, the veteran thirty-year staff member who leads the local Habitat for Humanity chapter, the theater company that just returned from a well-received statewide tour, and the faculty member who just received a huge research grant from the National Institutes of Health. Only rarely will board members hear from single mothers who are struggling to pay rising tuition and fees, former students who have dropped out, or parents who have accumulated $40,000 or more in debt to be able to send their child to State U. If the members of the popular theater company end up working as long-term baristas in local coffee houses after graduation, that is also unlikely to be brought to the board's attention by the president. Given this milieu, it cannot be regarded as astonishing that many board members know little about the cost increases and income mobility data presented in earlier chapters of this book. Their eyes are focused on other metrics, and their ears ring with testimonials from the success stories paraded in front of them.

Paul Levy, a former member of the governing board of the University of Pennsylvania who resigned because of his disapproval of how the university treated a professor, commented piercingly that "the board is large and its formal meetings are entirely show and tell, with discussion severely limited and vote outcomes never in doubt. . . . The corporate world offers a parallel to trustees' abdication of their fiduciary duties."[34] This, in a nutshell, describes many board meetings on many campuses.

Individuals of goodwill may differ about whether a specific institutional policy that is good for their university is also in the best interest of the state, but it is important that possible conflicts between the two be identified, discussed, and evaluated. For example, is it really in the best interest of the state to support an institution of higher education that is heavily stratified on the basis of family incomes? To charge students $60 per credit hour to support the institution's intercollegiate athletic teams? To enable students to earn a baccalaureate degree without ever having taken a course either in history or in a laboratory science? These are of course debatable questions, but ones that deserve attention at board meetings—ideally preceded by meetings or retreats that cogently explore the details and complications of such issues. Absent an emergency, there should be no rush to judgment, but rather considered discussion and evaluation of policy alternatives.

The salient point is that board members should not interpret their governance task in a parochial fashion through the lens of their institution. Instead, they should act jointly as representatives of the citizenry at large as well as individuals concerned about a specific institution. However tempting it might be to act as an advocate of a particular campus, in their roles as board members, trustees should see a larger statewide canvas and balance their local duties with their statewide obligations.

Admittedly, this enlightened, broader view of a board member's fiduciary duties is not enshrined in law in most states, but it is a vital step toward tempering college cost inflation. It is worth noting that United States senators and representatives often face similar tensions. Should they vote only for what they perceive to be in their state's (or district's) best interest, or should they consider the welfare of the nation as a whole? It will suffice to observe that those regarded as the great legislators of our time have often transcended local considerations and jealousies and instead have perceived larger societal values and then advocated and voted accordingly.

In most states legislation is required to reorient the responsibilities and thinking of board members. Our experience suggests that sub rosa many public colleges and universities will attempt to torpedo such legislation because they perceive it as threatening the power of campus administrators and perhaps entire campuses. Privately, many presidents will confess that they do not want their board members to act as fiduciaries for the citizenry; instead (surprise, surprise!) they want well-heeled, generous institutional partisans.

Still, if we expect to dampen the upward spiral in the costs being imposed upon students attending our public colleges and universities, and if we expect to improve the extent to which campuses generate economic and social mobility, then a fiduciary point of view by board members is a virtual requirement.

The Need to Refashion Campus and Board Incentives, Goals, and Assessment

In their popular undergraduate textbook, *Modern Principles of Economics*, Tyler Cowen and Alex Tabarrok put it simply: "Incentives matter."[35] By incentives, they mean both rewards and penalties that are designed to influence behavior. Finding the right combination of incentives, however, is not an easy task on a campus. What incentivizes one individual may turn off another because of differences in their tastes and preferences. One college president may be motivated primarily by the size of her paycheck while another might revel if she is the center of attention. Still others may value walking into the football locker room or counting aloud the number of Rhodes Scholars the institution has produced.

With respect to incentives and goals, Cowen and Tabarrok also point out that the most successful and enduring social institutions are those that align the self-interest of individuals with the broader interests of society as a whole. In such cases, individual achievements benefit the many rather than just a few, but individual achievers do not feel damaged because they too are rewarded. Such circumstances do not arise automatically on campuses.

A persistent problem in modern American colleges and universities is that the interests of public college presidents and senior administrators

In 2015, the University of Maryland euphemistically labeled its new discipline-specific tuition surcharges on students in business, engineering, and computer science "Affordable Flagship Excellence, Access and State Economic Growth." This phraseology, however, could not disguise that the change would produce winners and losers and that costs were going to increase for a large number of students. Regardless, the surcharges were approved by the university's Board of Regents, demonstrating that misalignment can also exist between governing boards and students.

University of Maryland, Office of the President, "Proposal for Affordable Excellence, Access and Economic Growth," Press Release, May 1, 2015.

(and faculty and staff, for that matter) do not necessarily align with those of students, families of students, and citizen taxpayers. For example, most students prefer low tuition and fees, and more students are likely to enroll as tuition and fees decline. But administrators and faculty understand that reduced tuition collections may not generate sufficient revenue for them to accomplish their priorities (salaries, teaching loads, library resources, programmatic breadth, computer support, etc.). This constitutes a "misalignment" in the parlance of Cowen and Tabarrok because the interests of students and administrators diverge. As one veteran administrator put it to us, "We're not all singing from the same hymnal." Cowan and Tabarrok use both theory and empirical evidence to show that this leads to problems.

Furthermore, what is good for a representative campus may not be good for the state itself because the same dollar cannot be spent in two places. When State U's budget increases, there may be fewer dollars to repair potholes on highways or to subsidize school lunches for lower-income first graders. Such is fiscal reality.

Governing boards provide a variety of incentives to campus employees, but especially to presidents. Problems can arise in this regard. Suppose a governing board decides to bestow a financial reward on its college president because enrollment has increased beyond a preselected target number. This reward may seem well deserved, but trade-offs and unanticipated side effects might accompany such a decision. To begin, no one should conclude that the president was solely responsible for the enrollment increase. If anything, it was the product of a team effort involving numerous people on and off campus. But how does one meaningfully reward a team that numbers dozens or even hundreds of individuals?

Let's further complicate matters. Suppose the president is a conniving gent who lowered his institution's admissions standards in order to pump up student enrollment. In addition, what if the existence of this incentive caused him to transfer money from the library to the admissions office so that he could exceed the goal placed in front of him? There are other possibilities, but the point here is that incentives and penalties sometimes set in motion a series of actions and reactions that are not at all what those providing the incentives had in mind.

The situation we just have described exemplifies what has become known as a "principal-agent" problem. How can the people we label "principals" (analogous to the stockholders of a corporation) get their "agents" (the managers and employees of the corporation) to do what the principals want them to do? Principal-agent problems arise in higher education when the goals and desires of citizens and taxpayers (the principals in this case) differ from those of their agents (trustees, presidents, faculty, and others at colleges and universities).

In a for-profit situation, the primary interest of stockholders is likely the price of the shares of stock they own and the size of the any dividends they receive. CEOs, managers, and employees, however, may be more interested in the size of their own salaries and benefits, the number of people who report to them, the splendor of their offices, how many vacation days they receive, and under what circumstances they can retire.

The traditional way to solve such a misalignment of interests between owners and managers has involved giving the managers shares of stock—that is, to make them owners/stakeholders so that they too would prosper if the agents (stockholders) did. This would create a coincidence of interests. Typically, however, the shares would be granted only if the price of the corporation's stock exceeded a specified level (say, $75 per share) on a certain date.

Astute managers soon realized that they could game this incentive system by pumping up the price of the firm's stock at the critical points in time. They would deftly choose when to report sales or profits, emphasize short-run expenditures at the expense of longer-term needs such as research and development, or even reduce the number of outstanding shares of the corporation's stock.

How does this apply to governing boards and presidents? The potential for principal-agent misalignment in higher education is substantial. There are many different hymnals from which campus constituencies might sing. Like corporate CEOs, college presidents may not have the same goals as the governing board or the public. Rankings, ratings, and the size of their own salary may loom large in their estimation. Further, whatever goals presidents are given by their boards, one should not underestimate how their fertile imaginations can over time render numeric goals meaningless. Figuratively, college presidents begin to imitate K-12 schoolteachers who often "teach to the test" when their work is evaluated in terms of how well their students perform on a standardized examination.

These circumstances illustrate "Campbell's Law"—namely, "The more any quantitative indicator is used for social decision-making, the more subject it will be to corruption pressures and the more likely it will be to distort and corrupt the social processes it is intended to monitor."[36] As applied to college presidents and governing boards, this implies that over time, college presidents (and others on campus) tend to find ways to use to their personal advantage any metrics that governing boards impose upon them.

Presumably, most individuals would agree that it is essential for governing boards to measure presidential performance and properly incentivize presidential behavior. Campbell's Law, however, predicts that many presidents will become adept at finding ways to turn on their heads the incentives, rules, and restrictions that governing boards, governors, and legislators impose on them.[37]

Acknowledging potential problems with incentive structures, however, does not mean it is a hopeless task to use rewards, penalties, and

Reacting to complaints about college costs, legislators in a southern state froze general tuition and fees for in-state undergraduate students only to find that wily administrators extracted more revenue from students anyway by establishing discipline-specific charges (for example, for students in engineering and nursing), increasing course laboratory fees, and charging more for services that had previously been gratis, including sought-after seats at football games. Further, several institutions increased their non-resident enrollments because the prices they charged these students were not frozen. The end result? Fewer in-state students, who ended up paying higher prices.

The Association of Governing Boards (AGB) says that "boards are accountable to the mission and heritage of their institutions, to the transcendent values that guide and shape higher education (self-regulation, shared governance, educational quality, fiscal integrity and academic freedom), to the public interest and public trust, and to the legitimate and relevant interest that various internal and external constituencies represent." This is a lofty statement but omits mention of the fiduciary relationship board members should have with the citizenry, or of any need for accessibility and affordability, though these might be considered transcendent values. If so, then boards on dozens of four-year public campuses would appear to give them little weight.

Richard Novak, "State Policies and Practices to Improve Board Governance," *Trusteeship Magazine,* September/October 2012.

rules to influence campus behavior. Rather, board members must be aware of potential problems, understanding that in most decision-making and assessment circumstances, both benefits and costs attach to any choice they or their campus makes. "There are no freebies," a president of a flagship institution observed to us.

Interestingly, there are cases when campuses readily recognize that actions generate both costs and benefits. Consider the case of a basketball coach who populates the school's basketball team with individuals whose academic credentials are suspect. Virtually everyone understands that if the coach's contract contains a clause that rewards him or her for winning games and making postseason tournaments, this situation is likely to occur.

Discerning governing boards discard the notion that their administrative, faculty, and staff agents always act in the best interests of their institutions. These agents will do so if campus incentives can be aligned correctly, but they may go astray if this is not the case. Acknowledging this reality does not relegate these campus keystones to a moral trash heap but instead recognizes the powerful albeit complex role that incentives and disincentives play in influencing behavior on campus.

Richard Vedder of Ohio University, a persistent but perceptive critic of higher education, once wrote an opinion piece in *Forbes Magazine* entitled "Would You Buy a Used Car from a University President?" In it, Vedder argued that "college presidents these days are increasingly considered to be somewhat shifty individuals, the kind [of] whom you would be suspicious [if you were] buying a used car."[38] Although Vedder's rhetoric is harsh, many associated with academe, including board members, prefer to assume that presidents, provosts, and deans are exempt from self-serving behaviors. Unfortunately, depending upon the incentives placed in front of them, they may not be.

Although any decision ordinarily carries both costs and benefits, some choices can be clearly recognized as superior to others. Some alternatives clearly dominate others because they confer more benefits at the same or lower costs than available alternatives. Rigorous assessment may be required to quantify these benefits and costs, but some parties on campuses have turned against such assessment because past evaluations have relied on questionable criteria and demanded excessive time. William Bowen and Eugene Tobin, in their perceptive 2015 book, *Locus of Authority*, observe that even though assessments that focus on the cost-effectiveness of academic programs and teaching methodologies have acquired a bad reputation in some academic precincts, they are necessary and should be regarded as an exercise in common sense because it is essential to know how well institutions perform their most fundamental activities.[39]

There are several lessons to be drawn here. First, it is essential that administrators and boards make continual efforts to evaluate what the

Wise boards engage experienced, knowledgeable consultants to help them fashion incentives that are paid out over time and to which conditions are attached. The passage of time enables evaluators to see if any unintended side effects emerge. In the case of the college president who was rewarded for increasing enrollment but lowered admissions standards and diverted funds to achieve this goal, conditions might have been attached relating to the quality of students attracted, the size of the admissions budget, and the transfer of funds. Optimally, governing boards establish provisional compensation accounts for those being incentivized and pay the incentives into this account, which should draw interest. At scheduled dates in the future, the proceeds of this account can be paid out to the individual being incentivized if none of the side constraints have been violated. The "no immediate payout" procedure also helps organizations avoid embarrassment, as when a basketball coach receives an incentive payment for winning the conference tournament but is later terminated when an NCAA investigation produces evidence of major violations. Boards that do not bother with these alignment safeguards should recognize that they are engaging in risky behavior.

institution is doing. These assessments can address questions as basic as "Are our students really learning?" or "How well do we use the space we have available?" or "Are our graduates finding gainful employment?"

Second, governing boards must be humble enough to recognize that many performance metrics they might develop to measure their president's performance (or that of the institution) can potentially be gamed and therefore distort his or her subsequent behavior. Incentives influence behavior, but unless care is taken, incentives may encourage behavior that is unproductive or irrelevant. An incentive may appeal to board members because of its simplicity (increase enrollment by 10 percent and you will be paid a $100,000 bonus), but also turn out to be the easiest for an administrator to game. A president or vice president can reallocate resources away from other important activities in order to meet the enrollment goal, and board members may never learn this has occurred. In the same vein, beware the president who agrees to cap in-state undergraduate tuition and fees because he knows he can make up for this by increasing out-of-state student enrollment.

Suppose classroom and laboratory space appear to be in short supply. Would it be less expensive to schedule more eight o'clock classes (and thereby make use of unused space) or to erect a new building? The seemingly obvious answer might be to teach more eight o'clock classes, and this might well be the optimal decision, but the wise decision-maker does not stop there. There may be reactions to this new world of eight o'clock classes, including a tendency for these early classes to be taught by graduate assistants and adjunct faculty rather than regular faculty and for the students in these classes to be freshmen. Astute, realistic weighing of benefits, costs, and alternatives is required. Board members must always ask themselves (and administrators) what side effects might arise when regulations change or incentives are altered.

Third, the gaming of metrics and standards declines when boards find ways to make the good of the individuals entrusted with decision-making synonymous with the well-being of the overall organization. This confluence is not easy to accomplish, but it is critical if one wants presidents, faculty, staff, and even members of the governing board to behave in ways that benefit the institution and society writ large. One need not be Bernard de Mandeville or Adam Smith to understand that in many situations the pursuit of private gain can be harnessed to produce public virtue.[40]

Fourth, if we view these matters from 30,000 feet, it is clear that governing boards, governors, legislators, and campus personalities ranging from presidents to secretaries should be continually urged to align their activities with those of the broader citizenry that has established and supports public colleges and universities. In the case of governing boards, they must give special care to the metrics used to evaluate institutional success and individual performance, especially those that apply to their presidents. Here is where the board's fiduciary responsibilities come into play. Boards should not incentivize and reward growth, size, rankings, and NCAA basketball tournament appearances if their most important objectives are actually the number and quality of educational opportunities offered to students, the amount of learning that occurs, the subsequent contributions of students to society, and the impact of the institution on the quality of the life of citizens.

Governing boards must unmistakably identify what is most important (the "transcendent values," mentioned by the Association of Governing Boards). If admitting and graduating students coming from a wider swath of the citizenry is more important than moving up in college rankings or reducing teaching loads, then trustees must say so and skew campus incentives accordingly. Supportive behavior, if recognized and wisely rewarded, will likely follow.

Many books have been written about presidential assessment, and we will not duplicate those discussions here. It is enough to note that best practice involves an annual general assessment of a president by the board itself, based on jointly agreed-upon goals and objectives, and every three years or so a much more thorough assessment, for which the board invites several reputable, experienced external individuals to evaluate both the institution and the president.

After several years of service, it is difficult to separate the performance of the president from that of the institution, and these triennial assessments work better on campus if they are labeled institutional assessments rather than presidential assessments. Some campus constituents inevitably interpret the announcement of an upcoming presidential assessment as a signal that the governing board is preparing to dump the president. To avoid this scenario, boards should speak in terms of institutional assessments rather than presidential evaluations.

Experienced evaluators, if encouraged to do so, can help a board identify misalignment of campus objectives and highlight the unintended side effects of improperly specified goals and incentives. They can help specify incentive structures for the campus that are less likely to be gamed and that are consistent with the board's fiduciary role. Yes, there is expense involved in doing so, but refusing to incur such expenses falls into the "penny wise, pound foolish" category. Boards should remember that most public colleges and universities are highly complex operations, and it takes knowledgeable, experienced hands to understand their activities.

The Need to Increase the Clout of Statewide Higher Education Governing Boards

The empirical results presented in chapter 4 carry several messages with respect to tuition and fee increases. Holding many relevant variables constant, we found the following:

- Tuition and fee increases are lower in states that have statewide coordinating or governing boards. Statewide control and inspection bring with them moderation in the cost increases that affect students.
- Tuition and fee increases are lower in governance situations where institutions do not have their own board but instead share a board with other campuses.

The implication of these findings is that governance supervision beyond the campus makes a difference. "Own" boards (that is, governing board that deals with one institution and no others) are by nature more receptive to tuition and fee increase proposals from administrators. Indeed, our chapter 4 regression analysis found that between 2003–04 and 2016–17, net real tuition and fee increases per full-time equivalent (FTE) student were $1,148 higher at own-board institutions than at institutions subject to a statewide governing board.

Why is this so? Own-board members are more likely to be co-opted by senior administrators, especially the institution's president. If they were not already, they more readily become advocates for their institution rather than acting as fiduciaries. One reason is that board members learn to rely upon senior administrators for information. When board members have a question, they find they can usually receive a prompt answer from the president or other senior administrators. They gain confidence in these individuals and therefore are inclined to trust their data and their recommendations. Over the years, we have watched this process unfold on numerous campuses. It is a predictable organizational phenomenon whose application is not limited to higher education. Unless a corporation is losing money or market share, harried members of its board usually rely upon the firm's senior vice presidents to prepare them for meetings and provide them with data.

It isn't that key campus personnel (including the president) deliberately supply trustees with false information. Rather, the difficulty relates to the way in which they frame issues and the data they choose to provide. Consider the case of a flagship state university whose administrators can legitimately brag that the 51 percent of the students who come to its campus from the bottom quintile of the income distribution subsequently rise to the top income quintile after graduation (Harvard University Opportunity Insights data). If this is the only piece of information one knows or hears, then it surely seems as if the campus is serving as a major springboard for societal economic mobility. But what if only 2.8 percent of the institution's student body comes to it from the lowest income quintile? As a consequence, the campus has a Harvard University Opportunity Insights mobility index of only 1.46, which is below the flagship average of 1.66, and substantially less than the 2.06 average posted by our entire sample of institutions. Are the members of this institution's governing board aware of this information?

We have deliberately not supplied the name of the institution described in this example because we don't know how its administrators present these and similar data to the university's governing board, if they do so at all. Rather, we provide this example to give readers a taste of how information is often conveyed on campuses. Members of governing boards are likely to receive distilled versions of relevant data, or, if they receive less flattering data, these numbers may be hidden inside a hefty three-ring binder.

More experienced or perceptive board members learn how to ask the right questions in order to receive appropriate data. They understand what is required to place issues in context. Relatively few trustees advance to this stage, however, because doing so requires a commitment of time and exceptional devotion to the task, in addition to personal inquisitiveness and intelligence. Further, in some situations, it might be difficult for a board member to assume this role without being regarded as a nettlesome disrupter or agenda breaker.

In the case of statewide governing boards, it is more difficult for campus administrators to co-opt board members and staff because these latter individuals are more accustomed to placing campus issues in context. They do this constantly. In addition, statewide governing board staff (who often have great influence) are usually located physically distant in a state capital. Attitudinally, they usually are more distant as well. Statewide governing board members and their staff must deal with multiple institutions, and many take pains to show that they don't play favorites. This attitude changes the tone of conversations concerning institutional appropriations requests, capital projects and program proposals, and costs and affordability.

An important means by which statewide boards can restrain costs is through their control of institutional missions and programs. Mission and program creep drives costs and exerts upward pressure on tuition and fees. Often energized by their faculty, regional institutions in particular seek to offer master's and doctoral degrees and to establish themselves as research institutions. Community colleges clamor to offer baccalaureate degrees, and in states such as Florida they are now doing so and being referred to as "state colleges." Seemingly every campus wants to emulate the institutions it perceives to be above it in the academic hierarchy. This behavior is often reactive and competitive. "State U has begun to offer a bachelor's degree in cyber security, and we're falling behind." Or "Metro U has a spiffy fitness center that makes ours look like somebody's backyard garage. And we're losing students to them because of it."

The issue here is not whether these academic requests are based upon reality or have any demonstrated connection to producing superior graduates. They may. Instead, the key nugget is that competitive processes and perceptions of campus personnel drive requests that eventually must be paid for by taxpayers and students. It is easier to convince one's own board members (as opposed to statewide board members and their staff) of the virtue of a request by giving them a well-orchestrated tour of "deficient" facilities or by sensitizing them to the "superior" academic programs or facilities already in place at brother and sister institutions.

We have seen this scenario unfold numerous times at individual institutions both before and during their governing board meetings. Board or committee meetings often feature the appearance of special interest representatives ("experts") who might include representatives from the institution's athletic conference, off-campus housing providers and developers, auditors, the Urban League, the local mayor or city manager, accrediting association personnel, alumni, or donors. They are the equivalent of friendly witnesses who take the stand in a courtroom.

Such scenarios are not so easy to construct with members of statewide boards and their staff, who may feel less obligated to take care of a specific institution because of the precedent it would set. Yes, one can invite statewide personnel to attend a football game or major concert, but their attendance is likely to be spotty, especially if it is a regional institution offering the invitation. By all odds, it is easier for members and staff of statewide boards to say no than it is for own-board personnel to do so.

Lest readers conclude that we believe all expansions of mission are bad, we hasten to note that institutional missions and offerings should indeed change in response to changing economic, social, and demographic factors. The evolution of Boise State College into the 24,000-student Boise State University illustrates a change in mission that responded productively to the economic expansion and population explosion of the Boise metropolitan area as well as to the geographic remoteness of the state's two flagship institutions—the University of Idaho and Idaho State University—from this action. Indeed, the most logical and defensible mission changes for four-year public institutions of higher education have often occurred in larger metropolitan areas not already inhabited by a flagship. In Florida, the emergence of Florida Atlantic University, Florida International University, the University of Central Florida, and the University of South Florida illustrate this evolution. In Virginia, the rise of George Mason University, Old Dominion University, and Virginia Commonwealth University likewise falls into this category. In Texas, a host of well-regarded public institutions have arisen in its major metropolitan areas. In general, it is easier to make the case for mission change and expansion for a metro leader institution than it is for a classic regional institution founded as a teachers' college in a rural location.

Likely there is interaction between the size of tuition and fee increases and the size of state appropriations for higher education. It is reasonable to assume that cuts in state appropriations stimulate tuition and fee increases. But it also is possible that in some cases tuition and fee increases subsequently influence state appropriations. If campuses can generate funds by charging higher tuition and fees to students (especially those from out of state), then some legislators might conclude that those institutions do not need as much state support.

Recognition of the dynamics between tuition and fees and state appropriations influenced our empirical work in two ways. First, it militated in favor of considering tuition and fee revenue and state appropriations together, as we did in chapter 4. Second, we can avoid most of the problems associated with potential lags in the relationship between tuition and fees and state appropriations by examining changes in these magnitudes over an extended period of time. Thus we chose to consider a fourteen-year time period—from 2003-04 to 2016-17—rather than single years.

The bottom line, however, is that cost containment is more likely to occur when a statewide governance board exists and has the authority to analyze and approve or reject proposals that exert upward pressure on tuition and fees. Hence, a partial solution to the escalation in college costs is to grant more authority to statewide boards to judge institutional budget, curriculum, and capital requests. This requires that these boards be adequately staffed. Statewide governance is not free. We already have noted that former California governor Jerry Brown concluded that statewide governance was a waste of money. Further, there is the possibility statewide boards will hamper innovation and experimentation.[41]

We acknowledge these costs and possibilities, but we believe the benefits to students and citizens identified in chapter 4 justify moving in the direction of meaningful statewide governance in every state. This is not to say that statewide boards should become involved in the daily operations of a campus or its curricula. Our recommendations relate only to the determination of institutional missions, programmatic approvals, budgetary and capital requests, tuition and fee levels, and statewide assessments of educational effectiveness and use of space. Statewide boards should have nothing to say about to who gets tenure in the Department of Sociology, what constitutes a theater major, or how many athletic teams a university fields.

The Benefits of Additional Transparency

Sunshine, as the saying goes, is a marvelous disinfectant. In the context of colleges and universities, sunshine (transparency) enables all parties to make more informed decisions, improves outcomes, and exposes misaligned incentives.

Let's begin at the beginning, when students and their parents are considering higher education alternatives. Nobel Prize-winning economist George Stigler established that accurate information in the hands of both producers and consumers improves the functioning of markets and makes them more efficient.[42] More individuals end up better off in their own eyes when they have access to accurate information concerning the prices, quality, and performance of goods and services. Their searches bear more fruit when they can easily access reliable information and do so at low cost to them.

We understand the value of up-to-date, accurate information when we are shopping for a new automobile and find a website that allows us to compare makes, models, and prices. Unfortunately, Stigler's ideal does not describe much of higher education today. Often information is hard to find and its reliability is in doubt. Fortunately, these are problems governing boards can rectify if they choose to do so.

Students and parents would clearly benefit from knowing the net price they are likely to pay at a specific institution, the amount of debt they are likely to incur, and what will be required for them to pay off this anticipated debt. The answers to these questions are likely to depend upon a variety of factors including the student's choice of major, whether they attend part time or full time, whether they work, and so forth. But, once these factors are specified, it is entirely possible for every institution to work out a plan that commits both the institution and the student to a firm strategy for funding the student's education and a schedule for repaying any debt incurred. More than one plan might be developed to reflect different circumstances for each student. The relevant point is that students and parents need to know the likely consequences of their actions. Governing boards must ensure that they have this opportunity.

The plans developed for students should include an option for debt repayment based upon the student's subsequent expected income. There is much to be said in favor of income share agreements, in which students sell a claim to their future earnings in exchange for funding for their college educations.[43] Purdue University's innovative income-based "Back a Boiler" debt repayment plan demonstrates one way this can be accomplished.[44]

Given that many institutions do not possess endowments large enough to allow them to mount their own income-based debt repayment plans, one could argue that states and the federal government should develop new programs or refine existing ones. In response to this constraint, as well as the weakness in current federal government income-based debt repayment programs, Jason Delisle of the American Enterprise Institute has proposed a federal income-sharing program that would enable each student to draw on a $50,000 line of credit from the federal government to finance her higher education. Subsequently, income-tax withholding would be used as the debt repayment mechanism for the borrowing student. Debt repayments would not exceed, say, 5 percent of a borrower's income, payment would last no longer than twenty-five years, and total debt repayments could not exceed 1.75 times the amount borrowed.[45]

Our task here is not to evaluate income share programs in detail but rather to stress the transparency that should accompany these and any similar student-debt agreements. Who can disagree that graduating students and their parents should not discover on commencement day that they owe far more in loans than they thought, or that some of their loans had been accumulating interest while the student was studying? Who will argue with the idea that graduating students and their parents ought to know how they will repay their accumulated college-related debts? Who will make the case that it doesn't matter if students are surprised after graduating when they are unable to find a job related to their major or earn more than minimum wage? Factual transparency on these issues, combined with timely financial advising by institutions, is highly beneficial to students, who are in a vulnerable position.

Ideally, institutions ought to supply continually updated alumni income data by department or discipline so that students can intelligently evaluate their options. Each institution's website is an excellent location for these data to be published, but colleges and universities should also be required to send this information to the US Department of Education, where it can be added to the already useful College Navigator website.

Many institutions conspicuously fail to clearly outline how much debt entering students are likely to incur, and even more decline to explain the either the consequences of this debt or the magnitude of financial commitment required for the debt to be repaid. Many campuses apparently view this as someone else's job. They in effect extract tuition and fees from students and parents and then cast them out on their own. Nor do many institutions actively counsel students about the economic consequences of defaulting on federal student debts. Student debt is non-dischargeable in most bankruptcies, meaning one cannot escape it by declaring bankruptcy. Student debt follows one forever. Hence, it must be taken seriously.

Institutions can be transparent about their costs, student debt, and graduates' incomes if they wish to be—or if they are required to do so. In Leibniz's "best of all possible worlds,"[46] institutions would happily and voluntarily provide the requisite information and related financial and educational-choice counseling to create better-functioning marketplaces. We intuitively know that most do not do so and will probably never do so unless mandated by law because they likely perceive the costs of moving in this direction as outweighing the benefits accruing to them. Hence, like so many other federal dicta that have developed incrementally in higher education, provision of this information in a specified timely, easy-to-access fashion may have to be made a requirement for an institution to participate in the federal student loan program.

Collegiate transparency needs, however, are not limited to net prices, student debt, and repayment plans. Each public institution's budget and transactions ought to be open, available, and accessible on its own website and on a statewide website so that comparisons can be more efficiently made. It should be made an easy task for any individual to find State U's budget on State U's website as well as to find all State U's transactions as they are posted against this budget within thirty days of the transaction. In a nutshell, public colleges and universities must establish and maintain transparency in their financial operations.

The typical public institution of higher education in our sample operates in a financially complicated world that involves many streams of income other than state appropriations and tuition and fee revenue and a variety of expenditures on items not directly related to instruction, research, and public service. All these income sources and expenditures should be accessible on the institution's website.

Further, some flagships have as many as fifty related foundations designed to support institutional initiatives. These foundations, as well as public-private partnerships, may act to camouflage if not hide transactions that might prove to be embarrassing if exposed to the public. We understand the need to maintain confidentiality in the identity of some donors, although such cases should be few and far between. Expenditures, however, are another matter. Every expenditure of every institution-related foundation or public-private partnership should become part of the public domain within six months of the transaction, including activities that involve a series of transactions extended over months or even years. Exceptions (such as, perhaps, those involving real estate matters or intellectual property developments) that would hide transactions from public view should require an affirmative order from a state court before they can be exercised.

In addition to state-related and foundation transactions, institutions are often involved in public-private partnerships. A city housing and redevelopment corporation, for example, might undertake real estate transactions on behalf of an institution and then sell a package of properties acquired through eminent domain to the institution or to one of its foundations.

These transactions ought to be transparent so that important strategic moves on the part of a campus are not hidden from public view. The six-month provision suggested above should apply. If it can be demonstrated that public notice might jeopardize a transaction and that the costs outweigh the benefits of public knowledge about the institution's activities, then the institution would need to seek a court order authorizing an exception. Institutions should not be allowed enter into agreements with external bodies that do not include transparency provisions, albeit with the modifying provisions just cited.

Another class of valuable data should be posted on institutional and state websites: measures of university operations and performance. Included here are credit hours generated by department and program; costs per credit hour generated by department and program; administrative, faculty, and staff salaries; research funding and overhead cost-recovery dollars; space utilization; salaries earned by students after they graduate; student retention and graduation rates; standardized and learning achievement test score results, including Graduate Record Examination scores, nursing board examination results, and the like; income distribution data for students; mobility rate data; and the number of administrative positions by classification. Five past years of data should be required initially, with incremental years added successively thereafter.

Some campuses and statewide coordinating and governing boards already post some of these data, and all of them should be required to exhibit this transparency, which will incrementally redound to the benefit of many different parties: members of governing boards, students, parents, faculty, legislators, governors, the media, and even, eventually, administrators. When there are fewer secrets, misalignment of objectives and private game playing on campuses and between campuses will recede. Further, over time, the reputation of public higher education for being mysterious and somewhat impenetrable will decline, and public confidence in public higher education will increase when it is widely acknowledged that anyone who wishes to spend a bit of time can learn what is going on.

Institutions will likely argue that these transparency requirements will impose additional costs on them, and here they are correct.[47] We believe the benefits, however, clearly exceed the costs, and those benefits are widely and generously distributed across many different segments of society. As George Stigler argued, many individuals and groups will make better decisions if they have better information to support their decision-making. What we propose here is a common-sense, good government initiative that should have been implemented many years ago.

Mobilize Parents?

At first glance, it seems as if the financial self-interest of the parents of college students should lead them to actively lobby in favor of moderation in increases in college costs. Yet for the most part it has never occurred—despite the fact that in 2018, for example, parents were on the financial hook for more than $90 billion of federal Parent PLUS Loans they had taken out on behalf of their children.[48]

Hence, while the Consumers Union actively represents consumers and numerous organizations represent those who purchase and use steel, United Airlines tickets, beer, Apple products, Lexus automobiles, and dozens of other products, no national interest group has ever emerged on behalf of the parents and families of college students.

Why? The most expensive four-year public college and universities are typically those with elite and flagship status. Most undergraduates know that living on the campus of an elite or flagship institution will likely be more expensive than staying home and commuting to a regional or metro leader institution. It seems plausible that the prestige attached to gaining admission to one of these higher-priced institutions may cause some families to treat such an event like one would the purchase of a new BMW or Mercedes automobile. It is a sign of distinction, a signal that one has arrived, and therefore it is a bit gauche to carp about the price.

It also is true, however, that only about one-half of all college students today are financially dependent on their parents or family (this percentage is higher if we look only at undergraduates and eliminate from consideration for-profit institutions).[49] This situation reduces the motivation of many parents to show concern over college costs. This is their kids' problem, not theirs.

Nevertheless, the most important reason there is no higher education parental equivalent of the Consumers Union is that students, parents, and families are transients. A conventional undergraduate student may attend an institution for four to six years, and during that time the interest of the student's parents in tuition and fees may be high. Once this student leaves the institution, however, this concern dissipates because they no longer are paying the bills. They become more interested in their former dependent's job, marriage, and family. Tuition and fees? They are now someone else's problem.

As often is true in higher education, there is a bit of irony attached to this situation. Rather than facing a united group of students and parents complaining about the prices they must pay, universities skillfully swivel any consideration 180 degrees and convince these individuals not only not to complain, but also to boast about the quality of their experience and to start sending their alma mater financial gifts. Corporations such as the Ford Motor Company or Delta Airlines can only dream of living in such a world.

Final Thoughts

Higher education is a peculiar enterprise with distinctive traits. The Old Dominion Freight Line, Inc. (ranked 689th on *Fortune Magazine's* list of the 1,000 largest firms in the United States in 2018)[50] and Old Dominion University may have similar names and be of similar financial size, but they are very different creatures.

One difference between campuses and businesses is how they price their products. Institutions of higher education consistently sell many of their products (for example, a bachelor's degree in nursing) at prices well below the cost of producing that product. This is a recipe for financial disaster in the business world and, if pursued at Old Dominion Freight, would lead it into bankruptcy. What English Department pulls its own weight financially? Whereas the Old Dominion Freights of the world cast off services and routes that lose money, conditions must be *in extremis* in higher education before administrators will criticize, much less close, an academic program for being a fiscal drag.

Identifiable differences such as these between the business world and academe may prove difficult for some members of governing boards to accept or fully understand because they instinctively feel their business acumen should apply. Some of it does, but not all.

In addition, some newly appointed members of public university boards are taken aback when they find that the notion of shared governance prevailing on most public university campuses means that they are bound by previous agreements that long ago dispensed the board's powers to other groups on the campus, especially faculty. "We may have had legal authority," opined a board member to us, "but we gave it away." The acerbic observation that "this is like turning over the asylum to the inmates" is not treated as a joke by some board members.

They also learn that even the president of the institution has limited authority to *require* faculty to do as he wishes. Presidents prosper not when they are order givers, but rather when they are charismatic, skilled, persuasive negotiators who can convince members of their academic community to follow their lead and actively support their initiatives.

In short, many new members of governing boards arrive on campus not quite so well prepared for their duties as they may have anticipated. A 2016 Virginia legislative commission report revealed that nearly one-third of board members in Virginia's public colleges and universities reported they understood higher education operations or public finance only "somewhat," slightly," or "not at all."[51] The same study also found that about half of the members of the state's public college boards believed they had "only a limited ability to influence decisions about institutional efficiency or non-academic spending."[52] Further, as already noted, many do not know what they do not know, a circumstance whose impact should not be underestimated.

The Virginia report underlines the need for board members to learn the peculiar folkways and mores of public higher education so that they can become effective board members. This does not mean they should assume that current ways of doing things on campuses have stood the test of time and therefore must be efficient. Rather, respectful probing and analysis, leading to suggested improvements, should be the order of the day. Even if the Virginia report's sobering survey results accurately reflect the state of collegiate governance throughout the United States (and they may in some instances), this should not prevent legitimate inquiry by board members. Trustees are, we argue, fiduciaries who hold a public trust and therefore must assess whether the things they observe and the proposals presented to them are in the public interest.

Board members should take their fiduciary duties seriously even when their overall conclusion is that things are running well at their institution. They can do this without becoming micromanagers. Trustees should become respectful interrogators who pose interesting questions, ask for clarifications and evidence, and request relevant data. They should not be afraid to ask "Why?" and should be willing to vote "no" if a campus proposal collides with their fiduciary responsibilities.

These developments in American public higher education are much more likely to occur if we firmly establish as a bedrock principle that board members are fiduciaries for students and the public. But we also need to change the manner in which most board members are selected, expand and improve their training and orientation, and provide them with some financial compensation.

Board members at colleges and universities also will do a better job if institutions clarify and hone their missions. In addition, as we have seen, they must pay closer attention to the incentives and goals they place in front of campus personnel, especially their president, lest they generate unwanted side effects.

The performance of board members will improve if state legislatures and the federal government mandate increased transparency on the part of institutions. In the case of trustees, improved transparency with respect to institutions' activities will enhance their ability to interpret what is happening on their campuses. Disclosure is also likely to reduce counterproductive game playing on campuses because selfish actions not in the best interest of the institution usually shrivel in sunlight. The major beneficiaries of enhanced disclosure, however, will be students and their parents, who are particularly vulnerable when institutions make it difficult for them to obtain essential information.

The always quotable Winston Churchill once commented, "To improve is to change; to be perfect is to change often."[53] We believe we have made the case that it is time for change in public higher education. Perfection, of course, is not on the horizon, but there is no more productive place to start the process of transformation and improvement than with public college and university governing boards, who occupy commanding positions of authority and influence in the realm of higher education. Practically speaking, governing boards have greater potential to incentivize and implement change than any group except college and university presidents, and the presidents report to governing boards.

Members of governing boards, however, must deal with what at times may seem to be an *Alice in Wonderland* world; the usual rules do not seem to apply. All the more reason for governing boards to keep their eyes on the prize—that is, recognizing the foundational reasons why their institutions exist and fulfilling their fiduciary responsibilities.

We are neither asking nor expecting governing boards, governors, state legislators, and the professoriate to clean the Augean stables. Our proposed action agenda is much more focused and plausible. But the first step is to recognize and acknowledge the existing situation. Only then can wise changes be implemented. Our hope is that this volume will serve as a productive catalyst.

6 We Can Do Better II
Looking Inside Our Public Colleges and Universities

> Each institution raises all the money it can. Each institution spends all it raises.
>
> Howard R. Bowen, *The Costs of Higher Education* (1980)

> You must be the change you wish to see in the world.
>
> Attributed to Mahatma Gandhi

In a probably apocryphal story about higher education, a tenured faculty member is talking to a legislator at a reception. The legislator asks the prof, "What's your teaching load?" Prof replies, "Nine hours." Legislator responds, "That's a good day's work. Keep it up."

The story aptly illustrates the cognitive disconnect that can exist between higher education and the larger society from which it springs. Many citizens confess they do not really understand what colleges and universities do or exactly how they do it.[1] They can readily identify some academic outputs, such as the number of students who earn degrees, and many keep track of a university's football or basketball team. Most citizens are a bit puzzled, however, should the conversation veer into topics such as shared governance, affirmative action, general education programs, peer evaluations, free speech zones, overhead cost recovery, the need for journal articles written about Chaucer, and the like. These topics have an "inside baseball" flavor to them.

Public puzzlement substantially disappears, however, when the subject switches to whether America's colleges and universities are operating efficiently or are priced appropriately. Most adults believe that campuses are bureaucratic, over-administered, inefficient, and too expensive.[2] They believe there is considerable room for institutions to reduce costs and increase their effectiveness by reorganizing and refocusing their efforts. While they largely agree that a college degree is the portal to a good job and economic prosperity, they also think that there must be better ways for colleges to operate. The discussions surrounding the financial cuts imposed upon the University of Alaska in 2019 exposed these views for all to see.[3]

Our task in this chapter is to evaluate the initiatives that colleges and universities might undertake on their own campuses to help dampen cost increases. This is Robert Frost's "The Road Not Taken" transplanted to academe, with the fork in this road being defined by access, affordability, and mobility. In the end, we are told Frost's traveler chose the road "less traveled by and that . . . made all the difference"[4]—a circumstance we believe should apply to more campuses and their governing boards today insofar as student costs are concerned.

Some of the innovations we propose will require the explicit approval of governing boards; all would benefit from trustee knowledge and endorsement.

Eschew Ranking Competitions; Increase Emphasis on Access, Affordability, and Mobility

In the early 1980s, *U.S. News and World Report* took a flier and began to rank America's colleges and universities. This turned out to be a propitious move, and *U.S. News*'s annual rankings of what it considers to be the best institutions are still taken seriously nearly forty years later. Predictably, the success of *U.S. News* attracted competition, and in 2019 Willard Dix identified an unlucky total of thirteen ranking systems that focused on American higher education.[5]

To the extent that ranking metrics provide useful information, they can be advantageous to a variety of parties, but especially to students and their parents. Nevertheless, the very popularity of the rankings set into motion a competition among institutions desirous of improving their rankings. This was underlined by Monks and Ehrenberg, who found that at least among elite private institutions, incremental improvement in rankings generated additional student applications, resulted in higher standardized student admissions test scores, and even resulted in upper-income student bodies that required less financial aid. Falling rankings motivated the opposite—fewer applicants, lower student test scores, and greater demands for financial aid.[6]

Whether the focus is on *U.S. News*'s rankings or popular alternatives published by *Forbes Magazine,* the *Princeton Review,* and the *Wall Street Journal,* an institution's final ordinal ranking, mathematically speaking, is a weighted sum of its rankings in a dozen or more subcategories. The subcategories reflect variables such as standardized student test scores, faculty salaries, graduation rates, student debt, incomes earned by graduates, campus atmosphere, and, on occasion, affordability.

Of course, everything in a ranking depends upon the factors selected and the weight attached to each factor. Access and affordability do not merit so much as a mention in some ranking systems and are seldom accorded a substantial weight if they are included. *CollegeAtlas.org* is one of the few ranking systems that includes these factors explicitly. The notion of institutions functioning as engines of student mobility is foreign to most ranking systems; the architects of ranking systems do not seem to care whether an institution excels at moving individuals up the economic scale.

While those producing the ranking systems argue they are acting in the best interests of students and their families, the reality is that they have created a competitive system revolving around their rankings that motivates presidents and governing boards to abandon their fiduciary responsibilities, at least to some degree. Presidents can be counted upon to brag when their institution moves up a few spots in a ranking and do so for good reason; board members typically reward them as a result, and they become attractive candidates for presidencies at more prestigious institutions.

But there are a number of costs attached to achieving enhanced rankings. First, it may cost tens of millions of dollars for an already well-ranked campus to improve its ranking in the area of faculty salaries or to discount the institution's tuition fees sufficiently to attract more students with elevated standardized test scores. Second, an upward movement in an institution's ranking also usually means that the institution is less interested in enrolling academically promising lower-income students, who tend to have lower standardized test scores and greater financial need.

These dynamics tend to propel public institutions of higher education toward stratification on the basis of social and economic classes. Upward income mobility of enrolled students declines. But until Chetty et al. began to generate mobility indexes for individual campuses, who was counting?[7]

A portion of the trend on campuses toward greater stratification and reduced mobility may reflect the broader evolution of American society. Income stratification and inequality have edged upward in the United States.[8] Nevertheless, a root of the problem insofar as campuses are concerned is the incentive systems that most governing boards have devised for their presidents. Presidents tend to do what they are paid to do. If moving upward in an external ranking is incentivized but the economic mobility of students is neglected, then presidents and campuses will behave in utterly predictable ways. If fielding a Top 25 football team is rewarded, but little or no attention is given to the amount of money a lower-income student must borrow in order to attend, this sends a strong signal to the campus concerning what is really valued and what will be rewarded.

We offer only tough love here as a way to remedy this situation. An essential beginning step toward improving access, affordability, and mobility is for governing boards to distance themselves from the ratings game and to do this publicly. Put differently, members of governing boards must exercise their responsibilities as fiduciaries and make it clear that external ranking systems will not determine the university's priorities and resource allocations. As we noted in chapter 5, this will require that governing boards retool the incentives they place in front of their president and the campus. Otherwise, their initiative is likely to result in lofty rhetoric, but no progress.

Increase Transparency

We will not replicate our earlier discussion of the virtues of transparency and how transparency can assist the board in fulfilling its fiduciary responsibilities. The critical point is that this evolution likely must start with the governing board. Not only must boards be transparent in their own

There are costs attached to reducing income and social stratification on campuses. On average, students coming from lower-income households will bring with them lower SAT and ACT test scores and have reduced probabilities of retention and graduation. Consequently, campuses that admit more lower-income students may see their rankings decline. Further, lower-income students may require special services and programs focused on them if they are to stay and succeed. Such programs are not free.

activities, but they must also mandate that their campuses operate on the same basis. On most campuses, this will require that the board adopt new transparency policies and that the campus website be developed and cultivated as an easy-to-access source where any interested party can obtain vital budgetary, personnel, and expenditure information.

The transparency responsibilities of board members do not stop here, however. Additionally, trustees must ensure that prospective and current students and their families can easily access information about cost, the burden of any debt they may assume, what it will take to repay this debt, what it will likely mean if they drop out and do not graduate, and what employment prospects for graduates are, program by program and major by major, so that students can make more rational decisions.[9]

None of these innovations will be free, and they will require the reallocation of resources inside the institution. As fiduciaries, board members should charge their president with ensuring that the necessary support is provided and subsequently audit the performance of these efforts.

Why are these initiatives so important? We already have catalogued the negative impact that student debt has upon home and auto purchases. Furthermore, unwieldy student debt relative to income can lead to personal bankruptcy. The challenge is for institutions to find ways to impart critical financial information to students and parents and to devise a reasonable plan for each student and family that speaks to both the amount of debt the student can assume and what it will take to pay it back. Too many campuses take a pass in this regard. Governing boards need grab the bull by the horns to change this.

In general, transparency reduces strategic game playing by individuals and campus constituencies and diminishes the probability that individual and institutional goals will be in conflict. It thus saves money and improves performance. Transparency about how student debts eventually must be repaid usually reduces the average amounts that students choose to borrow and is likely to reduce the proportion of individuals who later default on those debts. To fiduciaries (including especially trustees), these should be important developments.

Prune the Curriculum

College and university catalogs once were dense, lengthy bound-paper documents weighing several pounds. Now most catalogs are published online, where they can be constantly updated. This means one can no longer apply what one former president labeled "the scales test"—weighing the catalog to see how much material it contained. Heavier catalogs signified more programs, centers, majors, minors, and courses. This former university president wasn't necessarily against the beefing up of catalogs, whether or not online, but knew well that curricular and programmatic faculty, space, and numerous other initiatives required additional funding.

Presidents, provosts, deans, and members of governing boards should be wary of curricular proposals that to come them with the suggestion or assurance that "this won't cost anything." This is seldom true. Decisions to expand curricula that are not matched by comparable reductions will likely lead to a series of inefficiencies, including higher unit costs, reduced class sizes, inefficient use of space, and a variety of augmented specialized expenditures (such as for library materials). It isn't that such developments are bad *per se*. Rather, it is that they are expensive, and each carries an opportunity cost because the resources could be used elsewhere.

When presented with proposals for new departments and new academic majors and minors, governing boards must rely upon the judgments of the president and academic officers. Board members should not attempt to decide what constitutes the right curriculum in physics or who deserves promotion and tenure in art. But this does not mean that they should not ask questions. What is the concrete evidence of student or societal demand for what is being proposed? Where will the money come from? When will the new program be evaluated to see if the current forecasts hold water? Is this program conducive to distance learning? Can it be shared with other institutions? Ideally, board members will have the opportunity to float these questions before the meeting when firm decisions will be made. If this opportunity is not provided, the board should be willing, except in unusual cases, to table the proposal until its legitimate questions are addressed.

Why should the board exhibit these concerns? Because incremental cost increases on campus exert upward pressure on tuition and fees. Although the causal chain isn't precisely linear, it is nonetheless quite real. State appropriations now fund only a fraction of institutional expenditures (less than 10 percent at some flagships). The rest of the funding must come from students and a variety of other sources. Hence, it is almost inevitable that students in general (although perhaps not those in a specific discipline) will be required to pay for curricular innovations. Awareness of this reality should not bring a halt to such innovations; however, it should bring discipline to administrative proposals, especially if presidents and senior administrators know that such items are not automatically going to become part of a consent agenda at board meetings.

Control Amenities

Let's face it—students like amenities, and there is evidence that many are willing to pay for upgrades to their college experience.[10] Thus, elaborate fitness facilities, water parks, ski runs, food deliveries, marble countertops in living facilities, the ability to choose among 100+ food entrées and eat as much as one wants, a tavern in the student union, a shuttle bus that picks up students at local bars and brings them back to campus, intramural athletic programs, state-of-the-art game rooms, intercollegiate athletic teams—these are among the ways institutions differentiate themselves.

Many student amenities are paid for by specific fees, which Kelchen reports have been growing more rapidly than tuition.[11] Whether or not supported by specific student fees, amenities place upward pressure on the cost of higher education. Administrators must be prudent in this regard, and faculty must not be blasé and say it is none of their business. It is their business if they are fiduciaries and looking out for the long-run best interests of their students.

The authors recently talked to a young woman who upon graduation found herself saddled with such a high level of student debt that she was forced to set aside her career plans (which focused on a public service occupation) and drive a truck. She did so intensively for three years and was able to get her student debt under control. She commented that she had "loved" her college experience and provided us with a litany of great amenities she had enjoyed on her campus. "I never really understood," she told us, "that there would come a time when I had to pay for all of that."

Governing boards therefore should be judicious in responding to requests that additional amenities be supplied. They should remember that City College of New York produced ten Nobel laureates and a raft of notable graduates on a campus remarkably free of amenities. In the end, amenities are usually enticing add-ons, not necessities.

Administrators, faculty, staff, students, and board members also need to acknowledge that there also are equity concerns attached to many campus amenities. Only some students use the amenities, and other students (because of their residence or work commitments) cannot access them even if they want to do so. Is it fair to tax all students to satisfy only a proportion of them? We cannot supply the answer to this question because so much depends upon the circumstances and needs of each campus. What we say definitively, however, is that fiduciaries should not ignore these questions.

Rather than supplying "free" amenities, a more refined approach for administrators and governing boards is to attach user fees to specific amenities. This ensures that no student will end up paying for another student's fun and games and also makes it possible to assess whether students really want the amenities in question. The general principle is straightforward: whenever possible and sensible, trustees should avoid mandatory fees that support specific amenities that only some students will use. This an obvious but often-ignored way to help control costs. Still, its cost-reducing effects must be weighed against the possibility that this approach could come down hardest on students whose ability to pay is limited.

Monitor Enrollments and Class Sizes

While college and university ratings systems such as those published by *U.S. News and World Report* provide information such as student-faculty ratios and the percentage of classes on campuses that enroll fewer than twenty students, these data are not always useful to trustees because they are averages and may well disguise particular departments and programs whose classes are at the extremes. Thus, the 21:1 student faculty ratio listed for the University Nebraska-Lincoln[12] does not tell trustees anything about what average class sizes are in, say, the institution's French major, or how many students enroll for French 388, Body Language: Love, Politics and Self in French Literature, how often this course is offered, or how much variation there is in class sizes.[13]

Our point is *not* that institutions such as the University of Nebraska should cast an evil eye on their undergraduate French degree programs or upon specific courses inside French majors. Instead, our interest is much more general: to point out that faculty time, classroom space, and laboratories devoted to the support of one major tend to be discipline-specific and often are not transferrable to students in other majors and disciplines. This is especially true at the graduate level. Veritable barriers exist between departments, disciplines, and course sequences. The end result is that dramatic differences can arise between and among academic disciplines and programs in terms of how intensively resources are used in each.

Administrators cannot avoid making choices concerning the amount of support given each program. As Bowen noted above, the number of good things that could be accomplished with additional funds is almost unlimited, but funding is not. Hence, decisions must be made.

Governing boards should not presume to make allocation decisions concerning departments and programs. They would be wise, however, to monitor overall administrative choices. As they do so, their focus should be much less on what is happening in a particular department or major and much more on institutionwide patterns. Does the institution offer majors and degree programs that have little or no enrollment, confer few degrees, and are not central to the institution's mission? How expensive are these programs? What other valuable undertakings could be supported if funds were transferred from these programs? Trustees should ask these questions, inspect the answers, and support administrators who make rational choices that keep the welfare of the entire institution in mind.

A specific example is instructive. A 2018 *Chronicle of Higher Education* article entitled "What We Hire in Now: English by the Grim Numbers" and subsequent coverage in *Inside Higher Education* detailed the precipitous fall in the number of open English faculty positions being advertised at the meetings of the Modern Language Association.[14] The *Chronicle* also reported in summer 2019 that Columbia University had failed to place any of its PhD candidates into a tenure-line university position.[15] Despite the long-term deterioration in the market for English faculty, English departments (including at Columbia) continue to churn out increasing numbers of PhD recipients. Our conclusion is not that doctoral programs in English should be axed (though perhaps some should be), but rather that governing boards need to hold the feet of administrators to the fire and ask them to allocate their limited resources wisely and efficiently, given the institution's mission. Administrators and trustees must think in terms of alternatives—that is, opportunity costs—and recognize that the same dollar cannot be spent in two places.

Suppose the fully allocated cost of a PhD program in English is $500,000 annually. What other things could be accomplished elsewhere in the institution with this $500,000? For example, could the same funds be used to increase freshman-to-sophomore retention? If so, how could this be accomplished, and how much improvement would result? How central to the institution's mission is the PhD program in English (or any other program under scrutiny)?

We don't pretend that that this type of decision-making is easy. It may be distasteful and perhaps even end a few friendships. Nonetheless, we argue that it is a necessary feature of modern academic life, which is dynamic rather than static. Trustees must ensure that their administrators do not shirk from making allocational judgments, that administrators are well armed with appropriate information when they do so, and that they respect the institution's mission in the process.

To what end should boards do these things? Biting the allocation bullet is a practical exercise of the board's fiduciary responsibilities. It enables institutions to do more with less and represents one avenue to moderating the rising spiral of higher education costs.

Control Administrative Expenditures

Between 2003-04 and 2016-17, the 275 institutions in our sample increased the proportion of their budgets that they spent on administration relative to instruction. In real, inflation-adjusted terms, this shift amounted to an average of about $180 per full-time equivalent (FTE) student. At an institution of 20,000 FTE students, this change amounted to an additional $3.6 million in administrative expenditures annually. This is not an earth-shaking result, but it does lend mild support to those who argue that administrative expenditures have been growing unnecessarily. However, institutions can legitimately argue that federal and state regulatory requirements (for example, those relating to human subjects research, student financial aid, and Title IX) are at least partially responsible for their increased administrative expenditures.

Ordinarily, governing boards should not get involved in questions about how many administrators are needed in student affairs or how much the institution's financial controller should be paid. These are matters for the president to decide. It is legitimate, however, for trustees to keep their eyes on the growth of administrative posts and expenditures overall compared with other institutional activities, especially instruction. Since many aspects of administration are personnel intensive, this inspection must include the salaries paid to administrators.

In chapter 4 we noted that HBCUs spend far more on administration per FTE student than institutions in any of our other five classifications. This should be a matter of concern for members of HBCU governing boards because some of these dollars could be used for other purposes.

Hence, one of the performance expectations for their presidents might well be a reduction in their institution's administrative expenditures or administrative positions. The enrollment bonus example we supplied earlier, however, should inspire caution among trustees in terms of how such goals are to be devised and measured. A simple relabeling or reclassification of existing positions might make it appear that administrative expenditures have decreased when in reality they have not.

We hasten to note that the possibilities we have just outlined are not the exclusive province of HBCUs. Virtually any clever president and administration can game a simple administrative metric if they put their mind to it. Hence, trustees are well advised to use experienced individuals to help them establish goals and measure performance. Best of all, however, they need to hire a president who is a fiduciary and shares their values.

Price Scarce Resources

We have already discussed the virtues attached to pricing scarce campus resources. Here, the relevant point relates to the role governing boards should play in this process. Trustees should support intelligently chosen administrative plans that place prices on scarce resources and where possible bring an end to the common campus charade that vital resources are somehow free to the institution and to those who use them.

If administrators do not present pricing proposals, then trustees should ask why. It is not unreasonable for the board to use a president's success in pricing scarce campus resources as one criterion in evaluating her.

As we noted previously, it does not pay for the campus to place prices on every scarce resource because the gains from pricing might be exceeded by the costs of operating the system. Still, some institutional resources (notably space) are obvious candidates for pricing.

Consider Alternative Instructional Modes

One of the messages of the parable of the blind men and the elephant is that board members must strive to see the university as a whole rather than only its parts. This attitude applies especially to the institution's support for and participation in alternative modes of instruction, including distance learning. What does not capture the interest of a specific faculty member of a department may nonetheless be in the best interests of the institution as a whole.

Board and administrative interest in innovative approaches to higher education may be necessary because the Beethoven string quartet simile has always had great currency on campuses. Many, perhaps most, faculty members think this way. These attitudes aren't genetic; they are experiential. Some version of the string quartet often describes how faculty members were trained in graduate school and how they came to know their disciplines. They often seek to transplant these models to their current situations.

This area provides an additional example of the misalignment of interests on some campuses. A typical faculty member may receive praise and some additional salary for developing new distance-learning courses or for finding more efficient ways for students to learn. But such efforts are usually not the avenue to achieving promotion and tenure. It isn't that these things are considered unworthy but rather that they are typically accorded less importance in committees where promotion and tenure are decided. What counts more? On a typical four-year public campus, refereed publications and external grants received.

In other words, the behaviors rewarded by academic departments and schools often diverge from those that reflect the interests of the university as a whole. Trustees need to appreciate this possibility, and they should both encourage and support administrative proposals that overcome this inertia.

One more caveat: board members cannot and should not write promotion and tenure regulations or proposals that focus on distance learning and other innovations. They can, however, incentivize their president to push forward in these areas as financial and market conditions permit.

The economics of high-quality distance learning can make it expensive, but substantial economies of scale usually exist. Substantial initial investments must often be made in equipment and personnel. As a result institutions will initially experience high unit costs, but as their programs serve more students, their unit costs will decline. Getting to that lower unit cost point can be problematic, however, and some campuses have little or no realistic chance of getting there. Consequently, for many campuses, distance learning may be too expensive to pursue on their own, and they are better advised to develop productive partnerships with private sector providers or other universities.[16] Such partnerships help individual campuses avoid the need to make large-scale fixed-cost investments upfront in order to become a player and provide institutions with ways to enrich their curricula without having to mount an entirely new program.

Yet distance-learning ventures do not always go well. In 2018, the University of Virginia announced the layoffs of thirty-eight staff members owing to low enrollments in its online courses.[17] Enthusiasm, commitment, and, yes, incentives count, as well as the magnitude of resources devoted.

Governing board members should be alert to these realities and opportunities because distance learning is not going to go away. Instead, it is already threatening the existence of some small, regional institutions and changing how campuses provide a variety of programs and services. If campus administrators are not already paying attention to developments in this arena, board members must prod them to do so.

Measure and Evaluate

We made the case in the previous chapter that measuring what institutions do (or say they are doing) can be highly beneficial. Although not all things can be measured with confidence or accuracy, productive fiduciary boards need to know if students are learning, how efficiently space is being used, how well their campus prepares its graduates for the job world, how student retention rates vary by discipline and demographic category, how many students their faculty teach compared with similar faculty at other comparable institutions, and so forth.

Some of these metrics can be used to incentivize and evaluate the president, although our enrollment story should inspire some degree of caution. Ultimately, however, the measurement and evaluation situation come down to this: board members are less likely to make good decisions and less likely to be able to act as fiduciaries if they are unable to measure and assess the most important things happening on their campuses. Thus, the order of the day for board members is continuously measure, assess, and evaluate, but to do so with prudence and with the participation and leadership of their president and her senior administrators.

Final Thoughts

Because the focus of this chapter is on initiatives that can be taken inside colleges and universities to improve access, affordability, and mobility, the role of governing boards in this regard is both differentiated and limited. Except under emergency conditions, the primary duties of fiduciary governing boards are to clarify the institution's mission; secure its financial stability; assess its performance; appoint, incentivize, assess, and reward its president; and adopt policies that promote these ends.

Boards, even those that are appropriately inquisitive, should not become involved in the daily operations of their institutions and should only with the greatest care substitute their judgment on academic matters for that of the president and faculty. They should avoid the temptation to micromanage. By no means, however, does this imply that trustees should become rubber stamps for administrative and faculty proposals. It is entirely appropriate for them to ask questions, require evidence, and weigh whether a proposal (including the budget of the institution) is consistent with their fiduciary responsibilities to students, families, and citizens.

As necessary, boards can and should nudge administrators, faculty, and staff (and occasionally students) to deal with important issues or to confront reality. It is appropriate for the board to charge its president to work with the campus to develop proposals on specific topics or to ask the campus for its best thinking on a specific issue. For example, trustees might charge their president to work with the campus to develop proposed policies and procedures to ensure that individual students and parents become aware of the financial mathematics associated with student debt, how it will be repaid, and the consequences of default. Further, a reasonable deadline (perhaps the end of a semester or academic year) might be attached to this request.

Ordinarily, a governing board should not threaten to proceed on its own if its campus does not act in a timely fashion, but this consequence should be implicit in such requests, and their president should understand this. It should also be clear that the board requests proposals, not decisions. Boards must not forfeit their fiduciary responsibilities to any campus constituency, although they should be open to other views and listen earnestly to campus advice.

Wise boards will require that their president be the conduit for all proposals coming from the campus and that they have in hand the president's recommendation in every instance. Boards that enable campus constituencies to make an end run around their president should not later be surprised when they learn that her authority, leadership ability, and charisma have been damaged.

Governing boards have the ability to set the institutional tone—why the campus exists, what it values, what it is attempting to accomplish, and how best it can achieve its goals. Boards have much to do with establishing the campus culture. They can make a major difference.

In chapter 4, we relied upon regression analysis to examine why some campuses consistently exceed statistical expectations in terms of their six-year graduation rates while others fall woefully short. Many of the observed differences appear to depend upon what campuses value and how campus constituencies approach their jobs. Governing boards and trustees occupy ground zero in this regard. They, along with the president, are primarily responsible for institutional values, direction, and attitude. If trustees show that access, affordability, and mobility are important considerations and incentivize their president accordingly, then over time their campus is much more likely to reflect these concerns.

Establishing campus climate is a responsibility all board members must take seriously. It is not something that can be accomplished overnight. It requires a sympathetic president, a willingness to candidly establish goals, the ability to assess progress, and, let us add, patience. Relatively few members of governing boards serve long enough to see the results, which helps account for the reluctance or inability of many trustees to focus on such matters. It is much easier for them to devote their attention to the new engineering building being planned, or which intercollegiate athletic conference best fits their institution, or the overhead cost-recovery percentage earned by the institution on federal research grants. These are worthy topics and deserving of attention, but they are not central to the board's fiduciary role.

7 A Proposed Action Agenda for Governing Boards

> These administrators are like cookie monsters searching for cookies. They seek out all the resources that they can get their hands on and then devour them.
>
> Ronald G. Ehrenberg, *Tuition Rising: Why College Costs So Much* (2000)

"Well, it's not all that bad," a highly placed higher education executive told us recently when we were talking with him about the costs of higher education. In support of his premise, he opined that the United States boasts the best university system in the world. The strongest evidence of this, he said, was the millions of international students who annually come to this country to study: "They willingly pay high prices to come here and study because they know it's worth it."

His assertions contain both truth and an element of de facto deception. He was correct in his observation that American colleges and universities exert a magnetic pull that attracts students from around the globe. It is also true that a significant proportion of these incoming students pay non-resident tuition and fees that usually are two to three times as high as those assessed in-state residents. This is market-based evidence of their esteem for American higher education.

As we talked more, however, we could discern that the influx of international students he cited was functioning as a prop for a larger point the executive really wanted to make. Implicitly, he was inviting us to take a leap of faith and agree that the international student value proposition also applied to the more than 12 million American undergraduate students who pay in-state tuition and fees at public institutions of higher learning. He wanted us to accept the notion that the elevated prices Americans pay to attend their own state's public colleges and universities are reasonable and indeed appropriate. Tacitly, he was also assuming that most American college students either have the ability to pay elevated costs of attending college or are fully capable of assuming and servicing the debt required to do so.

Empirical evidence, however, undermines the validity of these inferences. First, student enrollment is down. In the fall of 2018, American colleges and universities enrolled 19.92 million students, compared with 21.02 million in 2010.[1] Indeed, enrollment has fallen for eight consecutive years.

Second, student loan debt is up. The Federal Reserve Bank of New York reported that in the first quarter of 2019 the total student loan debt of American households was a gargantuan $1.49 trillion. The figure rose by $79 billion in 2018 alone.[2] Let's provide some context for this figure. In 2018 student debt rose by an average of more than $3,900 per headcount student. More than one million student loan borrowers go into default each year, and one-quarter of all student debtors find themselves in default within four years after leaving school.[3] Students who graduated in 2010 (at the end of the Great Recession) had repaid only 5 percent of their debt balances five years later.[4]

Third, the price of college is rising faster than average inflation. Between July 1998 and July 2019, as the Consumer Price Index rose 57.21 percent, published college tuition and fees rose 181.02 percent (fig. 7.1). This was more than 75 percent faster than the average price of medical care (an outlay about which many complain) and about 70 percent faster than average energy prices. In contrast, some things became less expensive during this period—the average price paid by consumers for computers and peripheral equipment declined more than 70 percent.

Some might quibble with figure 7.1 by pointing out that a majority of undergraduate students do not actually end up paying the full published tuition and fee charges presented in the graph; they pay a lower "net price" that reflects the value of any grants the students have received. This is true, but as we observed in chapter 1, the *net* prices have also soared—almost exactly 100 percent in real terms between 1998-99 and 2018-19—according to the College Board.[5] We also found in chapter 1 that it required the typical American worker 244 hours of work to pay inflation-

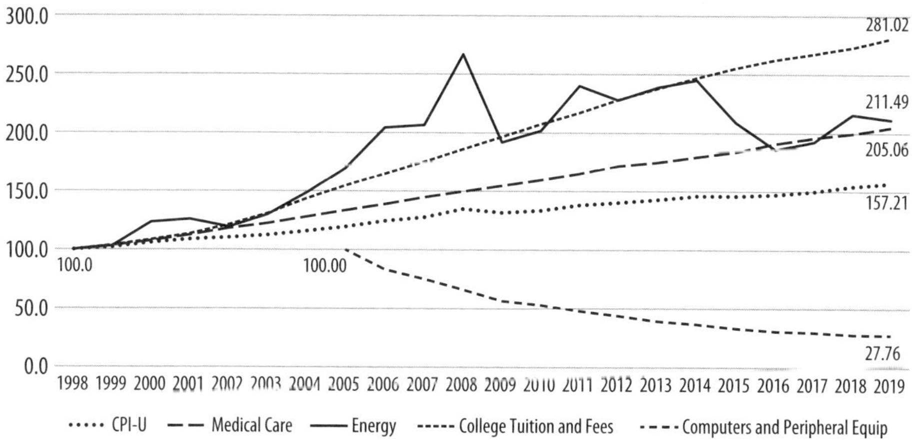

Figure 7.1. Index of Changes in Prices of Selected Items, July 1998–July 2019. *Source:* US Bureau of Labor Statistics, Consumer Price Index, www.bls.gov.

adjusted net tuition and fees at the average public university in the year 2000, but it took an eye-opening 447 hours to do the same in 2018.

What Do Governing Boards Need to Understand about the Causes of Tuition and Fee Inflation?

Figure 7.1 sends a strong message. If we were in a legal proceeding, both sides would likely now stipulate—that is, agree—to the facts presented. Tuition and fees have risen rapidly; net prices have risen rapidly; both have risen far more rapidly than either the Consumer Price Index or median household income. What would not be stipulated to, however, are the reasons for these observed rapid increases in tuition and fees.

What do board members need to know about the root causes of tuition and fee inflation? Let's briefly sketch and evaluate the major hypotheses that purport to explain tuition and fee inflation.

Reductions in State Support

In chapter 4, we documented that overall state financial support for four-year public higher education—adjusted for inflation as well as for the number of full-time equivalent (FTE) students—has declined over the past twenty-five years. Respected sources such as the College Board and the State Higher Education Executive Officers Association (SHEEO) support this inference, although in nineteen of the fifty states, real funding per FTE student did increase over our study period. Nevertheless, between 1992-93 and 2016-17, the typical public institution's state funding fell in real terms by $371 per FTE student. We also found in chapter 4 that when we looked at tuition and fee increases and state funding changes together, the typical four-year public campus ended the 1992-93 to 2016-17 period with $3,753 more to spend in real terms per FTE student.

However, major differences exist among the states and even among institutions within the same state. Wyoming, for example, ended this twenty-five-year period $6,221 per FTE student better off in real terms, but Missouri ended up $186 worse off. Institutions in our elite group ended the period $2,882 better off per FTE student in real terms, but the comparable number at HBCUs was only $537. Among institutions, the University of Kentucky ended the period $1,011 worse off, while the University of Cincinnati was $2,136 better off.

Thus, the landscape for state funding of four-year public higher education has been highly varied across the United States. What holds true, say, for the University of North Dakota (where state funding was up by $2,004 per student FTE in real terms) has little to do with the situation at California State University, Fresno (where the comparable number was down by $2,753).

At the end of the day, however, reductions in state funding cannot account for the magnitude of tuition and fee increases we have observed in recent decades in four-year public higher education. Simply put, despite the focus that colleges, universities, and national higher education organizations place on dwindling state appropriations, there are additional causes for the tuition and fee increases that institutions and their governing boards have imposed.

Archibald and Feldman

Many governing board members and college presidents cite the work of Robert B. Archibald and David H. Feldman[6] to justify, or at least explain, the rapid increases in the costs of higher education. Archibald and Feldman put forward multiple plausible arguments, one of which is that the nature of higher education makes it difficult for college and universities to increase their productivity in the same fashion as many private sector firms.

This perspective on higher education is an application of the famous "cost disease" hypothesis—now most associated with economist William Baumol—and his simile involving a four-musician string quartet that performs Beethoven masterpieces. If one wanted to increase the productivity of the musicians in the performing quartet, how could this be accomplished? Have them play faster? No, this would ruin the music. Eliminate one or two of the musicians? No, again, because our ears would tell us that the performance is not the same. There is a reason why string quartets have two violins, a viola, and a cello. By implication, therefore, it is difficult or impossible to increase the productivity per person-hour of a string quartet.

Further, the music that string quartets typically play is not conducive to standardization. In contrast to personal computers or cell phones, which can be difficult to tell apart, each of Beethoven's string quartets is distinctive and cannot be commoditized. By extension, academic courses and majors resist standardization because they are distinctive and resist mass production techniques that might generate cost economies of scale.

The same might be said of students. They are not identical peas in a pod, but instead unique individuals with distinctive learning styles and career needs. One size does not fit all students, and only highly discerning faculty members have the ability to respond to these individual needs. But these are time-consuming processes and have little in common with productivity-enhancing assembly lines.

Archibald and Feldman contend that higher education's productivity and pricing challenges are not unusual and point out that roughly similar circumstances exist in other markets for specialized services—for example, lawyers and legal services, some physicians and health services, and perhaps even auto repair and hair salons. In economic jargon, fixed production coefficients exist in these situations, and their production processes cannot be altered without fatally injuring their products.

There is some empirical evidence to support the presence of the cost disease at public colleges and universities. This is an important reason why colleges and universities rely so heavily on the string quartet simile to justify the absence of productivity increases in higher education and the inevitability of rising tuition and fees. Most higher education associations go a step further and argue, although less persuasively, that the cost disease also justifies higher than average inflation rates in higher education.

Archibald and Feldman additionally rely upon what we will term an "input mix" argument to make their case. They contend that colleges and universities are victimized by having to purchase higher than usual proportions of expensive inputs in order to operate. Examples of these expensive inputs include information technology personnel, engineering faculty, and research equipment. The prices of these items have been rising much faster than prices in general. Hence, the argument goes, it is inappropriate to measure the costs colleges must pay by the run-of-the-mill Consumer Price Index (CPI). Instead, alternatives such as the Higher Education Price Index (HEPI) or the Higher Education Cost Adjustment (HECA) must be employed to obtain an accurate reading of higher education cost inflation. The HEPI and the HECA consistently generate higher estimates of the costs that colleges must pay than the humble CPI.

The problem is that the propositions just described do not apply to all institutions and in any case have only partial empirical validity. They provide anything but a complete explanation of the observed escalation in tuition and fees. In recent decades, for example, real net tuition and fees have risen faster than either the HEPI or the HECA. Consequently, arguments based upon cost disease provide only limited cover for the pricing behavior of the four-year public institutions that one can see in figure 7.1.

It is true that the "production" of higher education is dissimilar to the production of a wide range of items ranging from Caterpillar tractors to computers to fast food and aluminum. Michigan State University is not General Motors. Even so, it does not follow that time-honored modes of providing higher education cannot be tweaked to change a campus's cost structure or that technology cannot be used on occasion to alter and accelerate how students learn. Production coefficients in higher education (describing the relationship between inputs such as faculty and outputs such as credit hours generated and learning) are only semi-fixed; just ask departments whose faculty ranks are increasingly filled with adjunct rather than full-time, tenure-line appointments or whose faculty now habitually teach courses online.

Institutions have the ability to vary who teaches a course, the manner in which it is presented, and how many students are in the class. Yes, many on campus say, one can do these things, but quality will suffer. This is not a response grounded in hard empirical evidence. There is little rigorous evidence that quality (however measured) deteriorates when things are done differently in classrooms. Indeed, "no significant difference" has become almost the standard result when different instructional modes are compared.[7]

In fact, reality has proved to be somewhat different from these assertions of quality. Recent empirical evidence questions whether conventional modes of college and university instruction have produced much additional value added in the form of student learning or have equipped students to think more logically or critically.[8]

We acknowledge that disciplinary accrediting agencies, faculty handbooks, and faculty union contracts are among the forces that may limit the extent to which changes in time-honored higher education practices can be implemented. Nevertheless, our experience tells us that more often than not, it is attitudes among faculty and administrators that constitute the most enduring impediments to change, not inflexible rules and standards. It is commonplace for faculty and administrators to shelter themselves behind accrediting agencies, handbooks, and contracts in order to frustrate changes in the way their worlds operate. They are comfortable as they are and do not wish to be disturbed. There is a bit of irony attached to this circumstance. Campus personnel who consistently vote for change agents in their local, state, and national elections often become profoundly conservative when it is their own domains that might be altered.

Individuals who argue that higher education is what it is because of factors largely beyond its own control and that it therefore cannot escape

If we cannot demonstrate that the typical college graduate has learned a great deal while in college, then why has the financial value of a college degree increased in recent years? The usual economic explanation is "signaling"—graduation from college signals that individuals have a certain level of native intelligence, some capacity to follow directions, an ability to complete at least some tasks, some level of ambition, and perhaps some social and team skills as well. In his 2018 book *The Case against Education*, Bryan Caplan argues that signaling accounts for at least half of the earnings differential between college graduates and high school graduates. We believe this share varies dramatically between disciplines as well as between institutions.

an unavoidable economic fate seem unaware of numerous places where educational innovations have been implemented successfully. Among many, consider the successful retooling of large enrollment courses on many campuses (Virginia Tech's effective Math Emporium does so for 8,000 students taking basic-level mathematics courses).

Strategies such as flipping classrooms that make students more active learners also have become more common. In a flipped classroom, many course materials are introduced outside of class time, while in-class time is reserved for questions, applications, and assessments. Readings, prerecorded lectures, and internet-based exercises are among the ways students encounter course materials outside of conventional classrooms in this model.

Lurking constantly in the background is the growing influence of distance learning. More than 6.3 million students registered for at least one distance-learning course in 2016. One out of every seven American college students now takes *only* distance-learning courses.[9] Whatever one's view of the validity and effectiveness of distance learning, it is clear that we no longer live in the world of fixed proportions that is the foundation stone of the string quartet simile.

It is appropriate to acknowledge that distance-learning modes do not fit the learning styles and needs of every student. However, the reverse also is true: full-time residential college attendance is out of the question for millions of those currently taking college courses. Many models of higher education exist, and it is inaccurate to assume that the Beethoven simile describes the length and breadth of higher education. It simply isn't so.

Bowen's Rule

Another hypothesis related to rising student costs with some empirical validity is Bowen's Rule, named after Howard R. Bowen (not William G. Bowen, whom we met in chapter 5), who served as president of Grinnell College, the University of Iowa, and Claremont Graduate College. Bowen famously listed five propositions that collectively have become known as Bowen's Law:

1. The dominant goals of institutions are excellence, prestige, and influence.
2. There is virtually no limit to the amount of money that an institution could spend for seemingly fruitful educational ends.
3. Each institution raises all the money it can.
4. Each institution spends all its raises.
5. The cumulative effect of the preceding four laws is toward ever-increasing expenditure.[10]

Anyone who has spent much time on an American campus will recognize some of these behaviors, including "institutional pursuit of rankings, the waging of seemingly perpetual capital campaigns, the construction of new facilities, new study and research centers, upgraded campus food, climbing walls, lazy rivers, expanded student services and entertainment, extra layers of administration—all of which eventually are paid for partially or wholly by students or those who fund students."[11] Cornell's Ronald Ehrenberg scenically observed that colleges are cookie monsters that "seek out all the resources that they can get their hands on and devour them."[12] This is quintessential bureaucratic behavior, as expounded decades earlier by economists Mancur Olson, William Niskanen, and others[13] and as assiduously practiced for centuries by public officials.

There is credible, large-sample evidence to support Bowen's Law and, to a lesser extent, Baumol's cost disease.[14] Martin and Hill's seminal 2014 study of university costs included 133 public universities and examined changes in average total expenditures per student by these institutions in two periods between 1987 and 2011. They found that Bowen's Law caused a 29 to 51 percent increase in total costs at these institutions, depending upon a variety of factors such as institutional type. Their estimate of the impact of Baumol's cost disease was smaller (a 23 to 32 percent increase in total cost). Together Baumol's cost disease and Bowen's Law accounted for 61 to 74 percent of the change in total per student public university costs between 1987 and 2011.

Does the typical trustee understand the impacts of Bowen's Law and Baumol's cost disease on their institution? Only somewhat, we believe, based on our own experience and their actions. Intellectually, board members may understand that Bowen's and Baumol's dynamics are working in the background, but once they buy into the institution's narrative, perhaps become co-opted by the president, and cease to act as fiduciaries for society at large, the record reveals that they consistently vote in favor of the tuition and fee increases placed before them. In so doing, they give empirical validity to the predictions of Bowen and Baumol. However, let us be clear: our claim is not that trustees are evil, but rather that many are ill informed and have become distracted from their real responsibilities.

A fair takeaway from the evidence is that many institutions have increased tuition and fees not because they needed to do so, but rather because they could. Between 2003–04 and 2016–17, no one forced Arizona State to increase its real, after-inflation tuition and fees by an average of 6.27 percent annually.[15] Yes, ASU's real state appropriation per FTE student fell from $8,627 to $5,856 during this period expressed in constant dollars (2016 prices), but this translated to only a 3.16 percent annual rate of decline.[16] By our estimate, ASU ended this fourteen-year period about $180 million better off in real terms, and this is after taking its rising student population into account.

Choices made on the ASU campus and by the ASU administration (and the Arizona Board of Regents) likely produced a litany of benefits resulting from these additional funds. Although we don't doubt that ASU accomplished some good things with these dollars, we believe it is difficult to argue that decisions involving cost increases of this magnitude were in the best interests of students, their families, and Arizona citizens. What is "good" for a campus or even a specific academic program may not be so good for students, parents, and citizens.

The simple reality is that the price-making power of elite and flagship institutions is considerable, and most of them are not shy about exercising this power. Their ability to extract higher prices from their student bodies is constrained by only two factors—possible adverse public reactions and a limit on the size of increase their governing boards are willing to approve. Well-informed, inquisitive governing boards must inspect these situations closely, bearing in mind all the interests they should be representing and not simply those of certain well-established campus constituencies.

Federal Student Loan Programs

Those who rally to the defense of current higher education pricing schemes often ignore or downplay recent research suggesting that federal student financial aid has in its own way contributed to tuition and fee price inflation. This is a complicated issue, but credible sources such as the Federal Reserve Bank of New York have concluded that federal student aid has stoked tuition and fee increases.[17] In essence, federal financial aid validates institutions' cost increases because that aid is based upon individual institutional costs, which colleges and universities now have less reason to restrain.

Some of individuals' unwillingness to accept these findings stems from their fear that doing so might lead to a contraction in the federal government's student loan activities. This they do not wish to see. We agree that federal student loans serve as a vital source of funding and mobility to millions of individuals. The problem is not the aim of federal student loan programs but how they are administered. Because institutions have no financial skin in the federal student loan game, they have little or no incentive to counsel students to borrow only what they need or to worry about their ability to repay what they borrow. Indeed, the opposite might be true; if keeping a student in school and paying tuition requires loading her up with debt, then these institutions have an incentive to do just that. This behavior appears to be especially common at for-profit institutions of higher education.

Increasingly, one hears the argument that institutions ought to bear some financial responsibility when their students default on their student debts. This, some believe, will cause institutions to be more prudent. We agree in principle but note that loan default rates vary significantly among institutional types. Many HBCUs, for example, would be severely tested if they were held responsible for the loan repayment performance of their former students.

A Variety of Causes

Finally, board members should become educated on the evidence presented in chapter 4. These data tell us that no single hypothesis concerning the causes of tuition and fee inflation is capable of explaining the diversity of tuition and fee scenarios observed among the 275 institutions in our fifty-state sample. A variety of reasons exist for the pricing and financial aid behavior we have documented. While we believe states should assume a much greater responsibility for funding public higher education than they currently do, their laggard funding performance cannot explain the bulk of the tuition and fee increase behavior seen since the turn of the century. This is a telling lesson that members of the public college and university governing boards should not ignore.

Practicalities: On-Campus Changes That Governing Boards Should Undertake, Incentivize, or Mandate

We commend the following actions and developments to governing boards.

Act as Fiduciaries

This step is all-important and will often require a major reorientation in the thinking of the members of governing boards. In most states, changes in the law will be required to establish that members of governing boards have a fiduciary responsibility to citizens, students, and students' parents as well as to the institutions they govern. Even absent such laws, there is nothing to prevent governing boards from adopting this course of action immediately and putting it into their policy manual. This is most urgent on elite and flagship campuses, where cost inflation has been the most pronounced and burdensome to students and their families.

Clarify the Institution's Mission

A proportion of the increased costs of higher education have been generated by institutions' attempts to do too much. To parrot an oft-used but accurate phrase, institutions should not attempt to be all things to all people, and this dictum applies even to the flagship campuses that dominate their states. Most would agree that not every flagship institution needs a program in nuclear engineering—or, for that matter, a medical school or a law school—to be academically respectable. Governing boards must resist the blandishments of administrators and faculty who urge them to support the academic equivalent of keeping up with the Joneses. Sometimes the Joneses are an exemplar worthy of emulation, but in other cases following the Joneses will dilute quality and force students to bear higher costs.

We acknowledge that trustees may require both a degree of discernment and some bravery to ascertain which requests placed before them are of sufficiently high priority that they justify asking students and parents to pay more. Board members should apply much more than a de minimis standard, however, when they contemplate increasing tuition and fees. It is also legitimate to ask precisely how a proposed change would benefit students and citizens.

Train and Retrain Board Members

We believe many members of the governing boards of four-year public colleges and universities are not fully aware of the issues we have presented in the previous chapters. To improve this situation, legislators should mandate continual training experiences, even for existing board members. Further, board members should be at least modestly compensated for this training, as well as for their attendance at full board and committee meetings.[18] This compensation will help underscore the importance of their service and incentivize trustees to take their responsibilities seriously. Should state legislatures, for whatever reason, choose not to mandate training, individual governing boards should move ahead with their own training programs and, as noted earlier, use TED Talks and similar devices as occasional vehicles to do so.

Ensure Transparency

The notion that students and families will make better decisions about higher education if they are better informed is almost unassailable. Students and families are highly vulnerable when they make their higher education decisions, and institutions can improve this decision-making by giving these parties access to more and better information about costs, student debt, the means of paying off student debt, class sizes, employment prospects, incomes earned by alumni, and the like. The same logic applies to trustees. Governing board members will make superior decisions when they have access to more and better information.

Each campus's website is an ideal place for conveying valued additional information, although we also advocate that states bring this information together in a statewide website so that trustees, students, and parents alike can readily compare and contrast. Information is more valuable to decision-makers and analysts when it is timely. Therefore, boards should ensure that comprehensive line item budgets, as well as all debits and credits against these budgets, are posted on these websites within thirty days of any transaction. In our ideal world, legislators will mandate this transparency.

Be Appropriately Inquisitive

There is a critical difference between trustees who are appropriately inquisitive and those who are instinctively suspicious and perhaps even disruptive. It is the job of fiduciary trustees to ask why, to wish to see the evidence, and to be interested in alternatives. It is their responsibility to look backward and forward at the same time—to understand what has occurred as well as to anticipate the future.

Members of governing boards should accord campus presidents great respect but understand nevertheless that the flow of information from the president and the campus will be filtered. Hence, when they want to know certain things, they must probably ask. Asking the right questions, however, requires understanding the big picture and the ability to perceive what is most important and then prioritize. For many board members, this is an acquired skill; most do not come to their board membership with a command of the salient issues they will face.

We have highlighted one set of issues relating to access, affordability, and mobility that have largely eluded many trustees nationally. They are ill informed in this arena and will likely need to ask questions to become better informed. If board members are not aware of matters such as the income distribution of the student body, the average amount of debt assumed by students, the incomes they subsequently earn, and their institution's performance on the Harvard University Opportunity Insights mobility index, then they need to acquire this information.

Yet board members' inquisitive spirit should not be confined to issues relating to accessibility, affordability, and mobility. Fiduciary trustees also should want to know whether students are really learning and whether they graduate with the ability to think analytically and critically; whether specific campus services work; whether the institution's investments in non-academic activities such as student services and intercollegiate athletics are productive uses of funds; how faculty teaching loads stack up against those at comparable institutions; how well the institution's space is being used; where the institution's foundations are spending their money and what it costs to raise money; and how much subsidy the institution provides for faculty research and outside grants. The list goes on. There is much to be inquisitive about, and much can be accomplished if board members keep their eyes on the prize by bearing in mind their obligations to students, parents, and citizens.

Wise board members avoid inquisitions reminiscent of the Mueller report congressional hearings and find ways to request data and information in non-threatening, non-confrontational ways and, where possible, with generous advance notice. Their aim ought to be to create an atmosphere in which a team of individuals connected to the institution (including members of the board) explores critical topics and develops alternative courses of action. But these forays into good governance usually must start with a thoughtful, well-placed question, such as, Why do we do things this way? What is the effect of this policy on students? How do other comparable institutions handle this issue? From this process should come new policies, refined incentives, and improved performance. A successful team effort is attainable.

Measure Performance

We are not logical positivists who believe that if one cannot measure something, it either doesn't exist or doesn't matter. But we do believe that governing boards should support attempts to measure what it is that public colleges and universities do. We've already noted that measurement sometimes strikes a discordant note in some campus precincts because of the feeling that some things academics do can't be usefully or easily measured and that attempts to measure fritter away resources that could be used for other purposes. Both of these concerns are legitimate, but they should not deter board members from seeking to measure institutional performance.

Institutional research offices on campuses ought to be doing far more than simply toting up numbers of student majors in various disciplines or credit hours generated (although these are necessary functions). They should be attempting to provide answers to the myriad questions we posed in the previous section, beginning with, Are students learning?

Tackling some of questions we posed and developing a culture of measurement will require that resources be devoted to this purpose. Board members may need to nudge administrators to move in this direction. Doing so is appropriate because without appropriate information board members and administrators are driving in the dark without headlights.

Update and Improve Incentives

We again assert that incentives (and disincentives) really make a difference. When incentives are misaligned, or improperly implemented, campus performance falters. Boards need always ask, What behavior (virtuous or not) might we expect from an individual who is confronted with this set of incentives?

Boards should not assume that their president and key campus administrators will automatically default to the behavior trustees prefer. Reality may be very different. The principle-agent problem may arise between boards and presidents. This is one of the reasons why incentives must be chosen carefully and with an eye to the potential ways they can be gamed as well as the side effects they may induce. Our example of the presidential incentive tied to enrollment illustrated potential problems. It also showed why many boards would benefit from the assistance of experts in defining the incentives they place in front of campus constituents, especially the president.

Wise boards make incentive payments conditional and do not let them mature immediately. Whenever possible, boards should take a long view, in essence adopting a wait-and-see posture. We advocate what might be termed a deferred, conditional annuity. These financial instruments are not complicated and can be managed by the institution's foundations. They must, however, be under the control of the board.

Incentives should not apply only to administrators and staff. Faculty must be incentivized wisely as well. Meritorious performance, promotion, and tenure should be recognized and rewarded. This means that governing boards should ordinarily be supporters of merit pay systems rather than across-the-board salary structures. If necessary, they should firmly push administrators in this direction.

However, administrators and trustees should not ignore non-monetary forms of recognition—titles, status, ceremonies, awards, listings, featured articles in campus publications, and so forth. Handwritten thank-you notes and recognition ceremonies for jobs well done can be effective in creating loyalty and a sense of community. We remember well a board chair who became famous for writing notes to faculty, staff, and students when they achieved excellence. No matter that this board chair received the names of the deserving from the campus president; she wanted to let the members of the campus community know that their toil (and often extra effort) were noticed and appreciated. This practice paid dividends when the campus hit hard times. Her word and her views were accorded respect even though her messages (and those of the board) frequently contained tough medicine.

In sum, rare is the campus individual who does not appreciate being recognized for his excellent work, and administrators and boards must jointly develop campus traditions that do so. This will turn out to be cost-minimizing behavior if members of the campus community become more productive. Indeed, recognition in any of a number of forms could easily mitigate salary aspirations of faculty and others on the campus.

Broaden Trustees' Access to Campus

Under the pressure of limited time and full agendas, typical board members economize by visiting various parts of the campus less often and by inviting fewer members of campus constituencies to talk with them. In addition, when these visits or contacts do occur, they tend to be arranged and orchestrated by senior administrators, who may by intent or happenstance arrange this contact in a fashion that ends up showing the board member what the administrator wanted her to see rather than what she should see. This is understandable behavior by both parties, but it is often suboptimal if the board wants to obtain a better feel for the institution and its people. It is risky for board members to make decisions without some knowledge of the people affected by those decisions.

Many presidents are loath to put trustees in close contact with individuals they cannot control (a description that applies to many faculty as well as certain students and staff), but to some extent such contact is a necessity if board members are to perform their jobs appropriately. In particular, if a governing board has a fiduciary relationship to the institution's students, then there is no substitute for talking frequently with wide cross sections of the student body (which, we note, is not synonymous with student government). How else can they truly understand the impact that rising costs and student debt have upon the lives of students and their families?

Boards on occasion should schedule open public forums outside of regular board meeting hours where they can listen to and interact with members of the campus community. They should understand that a non-random sample of individuals is likely to show up at such gatherings, and they may hear odd tales that cannot be generalized, but these meetings nevertheless can produce vital information and understandings. If something big is happening on campus, they'll soon learn about it. There is nothing wrong with senior administrators organizing and backstopping these forums, and administrators should attend because they will inevitably be needed to respond to certain queries. But they should not be able to control the sessions.

Boards and the administration should also jointly sponsor the appearance of individuals who will speak to critical academic issues, including access and affordability. Other speakers might be brought in to converse with board members on targeted topics such as the viability of distance learning, student internships, intercollegiate athletics, and liberal versus job-oriented education. Bringing in speakers with contrasting points of view to participate in roundtables is especially informative.

The activities we describe are time-intensive, and it is not realistic to expect all trustees to attend all events. The central point, however, is that a governing board needs to avoid situations where the only information it receives is what comes to it filtered through the president and senior administrators. We again stress that presidents typically know more about their institution than anyone else, and their views, interpretations, and proposals should be accorded great respect. Absent a full-blown crisis, board members must work through (and not around) their president to implement change and deal with circumstances that arise. Still, administrators are not the only parties to whom board members should listen.

Place Prices on Scarce Resources

Scarcity is an undeniable feature of life. Resources that have value are not unlimited in amount and availability; hence, both individuals and institutions must make choices about which resources they will use (and not use). It is perhaps trite to observe that the same dollar cannot be spent two places, and there are only twenty-four hours in a day. But these truisms remind us that we live in a world in which choices must be made.

Ordinarily, people make better choices when they are aware of the opportunity cost (most attractive forgone alternative) attached to their decisions. If we spend money on new computer software, then we can't spend the same dollars on student help. If we subdivide a classroom into graduate student offices, then the same space cannot be used to teach classes. What is the least efficient thing we can sacrifice in order to be able to make a more efficient expenditure? This is the attitude board members should cultivate.

Prices provide decision-makers with information about the alternatives being sacrificed to achieve a specific goal. Placing a price on the use of an automobile from the university's motor pool enables individuals to gauge what they are giving up in order to use that automobile. Placing a price on a seat behind the university's bench at a basketball game against a major rival does the same thing.

Most academics understand and agree when a price is placed on the use of a university's motor pool automobiles or its prime basketball seats. However, many campus constituents bridle at placing prices on scarce academic resources even though zero-priced resources often end up being used unwisely. If a department doesn't have to pay for the individuals who fix its computers, or for its use of the university's investment team, or for its use of motor pool vehicles, then it tends to become careless in its use of these resources.

Typically, the most badly used (and underused) resource on a college campus is space. Professors, departments, and schools all seemingly covet as much space as they can get, provided they don't have to pay for its use. When names and ownership rights are placed on space, however, it often sits idle. If another department wants to use empty space, it is likely out of luck because it doesn't "own" it and the "owners" often get into the habit of locking the doors to the rooms they "own." If, however, the putative owners were charged a fee for using that space, their attitudes might be very different. They might even seek to rent the space to the other department.

We've seen this dynamic in action. At one university, the lights at the football stadium frequently burned late into the night and were not turned off until hours after all stadium users had gone home.[19] When the athletic director was quizzed about this behavior, he grinned and noted that he did not have to pay the electric bill—the university paid it. This problem was resolved when the athletic director was given a budget to pay for the electricity he used at the stadium and billed for it monthly. Magically, the lights began to be turned out much earlier. To use the terminology we developed above, placing a price on stadium electricity eliminated a misalignment of objectives and addressed a waste of resources.

Boards should think of prices as incentives (and disincentives) designed to encourage intelligent behavior. Prices usually diminish stupid, profligate behavior, whether the focus is use of space, the university's motor pool, information technology personnel, or library-related services. Just as budgets discipline spending, prices also have a leavening influence on academic behavior.

We must, however, issue a caveat. It makes no sense to implement a pricing system that costs more to operate than it saves. Even though some resources (perhaps ballpoint pens and manila folders) might be wasted if they are not priced, placing a price on each professor's use of them likely would be more bureaucratic and expensive to implement than any savings achieved. Hence, administrators must choose carefully what resources they price. The role of governing board members is to support intelligently designed campus pricing systems and to raise the idea of such systems if their campus acts as if everything is free.

Minimize Amenities Competition

In chapter 5, we pointed out that the fee portion of tuition and fees has been growing more rapidly than the tuition segment. Compulsory fees frequently are the way campuses choose to pay for campus amenities. But we also saw that amenities carry distributional concerns—all students may pay for an amenity that only a few students use or enjoy. Hence, in many cases, user fees are an appropriate way to finance additional amenities.

Trustees must weigh these matters wisely and recognize that students tend to have high rates of discount. This is economic jargon that says students often place a high value on their current consumption and enjoyment and a lower value on their still undefined future. Students often do not cope well with deferred gratification.[20] For example, more than a few students go into debt in order to "really enjoy themselves" (the words of an undergraduate) during their campus years. This means that governing boards on occasion must function *in loco parentis* and do what they perceive to be best for students rather than what students might prefer.

Most board members have no problem with their *in loco parentis* role on matters of curriculum and agree that students cannot be given complete freedom over the content of their major courses of study. Many board members shy away from dictating amenities, however, and are inclined to favor nearly any amenity that students like because the amenity is deemed to be helpful in the competition for students.

Some campus administrators, especially those in admissions and student affairs, almost surely will argue that their institution must provide certain new or enhanced amenities or risk being left behind when students make admissions decisions. They will produce students who say they are quite willing to pay for the popular new amenity of the moment. Dare we say "fad"?

Because of the incentives placed before them, many admissions directors resemble football coaches and athletic directors. More is seldom enough. Admissions personnel are rewarded on the basis of their ability to attract applications and enroll students of a certain quality, not on the basis of how much debt these students subsequently assume, whether they graduate, or whether they can find a job related to what they have studied. This is another example of how individual objectives are misaligned with institutional objectives.

Trustees must be sensitive to these issues, recognize the roles that incentives can play, assert their fiduciary duties, and, as Patrick Callan has noted, be willing to say no.[21] Costs increases can be moderated if the members of governing boards do not confuse private residence hall bathrooms with the quality of education or educational essentials.

Keep an Eye on Research Funding and Subsidies

Presidents revel in announcing that their campus has just set a new record for externally funded research. The notion that State U is actively involved in pushing back the frontier of knowledge is highly attractive, particularly when it is accompanied by a story or two demonstrating how this new knowledge moves out of the laboratories and research centers into salable products and usable techniques ("tech transfer"). In 2016, the most profitable patent at a public university was the University of Minnesota's Ziagen, an HIV drug that generated more than $450 million in revenues that year. In second place was the University of Florida's better-known Gatorade, which reaped $288 million. Between 1992 and 2014, the University of California system earned $2.31 billion in patent license income, followed by the University of Washington, with $962.1 million.[22]

But most institutions' technology transfer offices (73 percent) actually lose money, and those institutions end up heavily subsidizing their research and development activities rather than the other way around.[23] The major form of this subsidy is reduced faculty teaching responsibilities. Say that Professor Smith in the Department of Geology, who earns $150,000 per academic year, would ordinarily teach six courses, but her teaching responsibilities are reduced to three courses so she can pursue her research. The cost of this subsidy is $75,000 plus the value of her fringe benefits, which probably increase the cost to about $100,000.

Some of Professor Smith's teaching responsibilities now will be fulfilled by adjunct and part-time faculty; graduate students will also take their turns in the classroom. Further, to the extent that Professor Smith's experience and training make her a superior teacher, the quality of instruction that students receive from her replacements may decline.

Only about 35 percent of all classroom sections in higher education are currently taught by tenured or tenure-track faculty; about three-quarters of all faculty by number are not tenured or tenure-track.[24] One would think that the impact of these hiring practices upon student learning, retention, and graduation would be well documented, as would any effects upon each institution's overall resource allocation. However, the number of rigorous studies treating these issues is small. Most suggest that the use of adjunct and part-time faculty has had some negative impacts on student learning, retention, and graduation,[25] but one study supported by the reputable National Bureau of Economic Research found that students learned more when they were taught by adjuncts rather than tenured or tenure-track faculty.[26]

Adjunct and part-time faculty are much less expensive to retain than tenured or tenure-track faculty, and employing them therefore frees up some funds. A large sample study using data from the Integrated Postsecondary Education Data System (IPEDS) and the Delta Cost Study found that when four-year public institutions hire these less expensive faculty inputs, they spend the savings on other tasks, including maintenance, administration, recruiting, admissions, counseling, student organizations, and athletics.[27] In other words, the freed-up dollars are not spent on instruction.

Back to our geology faculty member, Professor Smith. If she has received an extramural grant to fund her research, then some or all of this expense may be met by the grant. Funding, however, seldom comes from outside unless the faculty member's expertise resides in one of the sciences, engineering, or health-related disciplines. The reality is that institutions, not grants, pay most faculty members to undertake their research, and this is especially true in the arts, humanities, education, law, and many of the social sciences. Published research in refereed outlets is an expectation facing many faculty, and it is the institutions themselves that pay a majority of faculty members to do this publishing.

Most federal research grants are accompanied by overhead or indirect cost recovery funds designed to reimburse institutions for the many things they provide the researchers working on the grant—space, equipment, computer support, research assistants, and so forth. These funds typically account for 50 percent or more of the value of an award. Administrators value these overhead dollars highly because these funds can usually be used more flexibly than state-appropriated funds. That is, some of these dollars can be parceled out to support the things the administrators most value.[28] Their targets may have something to do with undergraduate education, access, affordability, and mobility, but in our experience this is usually not the case. There is little prestige or romance attached to funding additional Pell Grant students, but enhanced rankings, and perhaps even higher administrative salaries, connected to the opening of a new research center devoted to the study of global warming or to the disclosing of a new set of patents reaps publicity benefits that presidents and other high-ranking administrators cherish.

This discussion should not be interpreted to mean we are anti-research. Far from it. We both have extensive records as published scholars, grant recipients, and consultants and, outside of our administrative positions, have benefited from reduced teaching loads so that we could pursue our research interests. The salient lesson here is that most research and scholarly activity at four-year institutions is subsidized, often heavily so, when faculty release time for scholarly activity is included. This is a phenomenon that administrators should track closely because it usually involves a huge resource commitment.

Board members need to familiarize them with this scenario and avoid being hypnotized by grand announcements concerning research and development triumphs. If necessary, they must prod administrators into action. Trustees should focus on three areas: (1) ascertaining who is actually paying for the research activities of faculty, (2) identifying the adjustments in faculty hiring and related expenditures their institution is making as a consequence, and (3) assessing the collective impact of these activities on student learning, retention, graduation, and subsequent success.

The New York Times has editorialized that current trends in this general arena constitute a crisis.[29] Perhaps. What we can say is that many trustees understand the strength and importance of the trends we have noted here and by all odds should become better informed. As necessary, trustees should remind administrators of their fiduciary responsibilities and hold them accountable accordingly.

Recognize the Importance of Room and Board Costs

On a typical four-year public campus today, in-state tuition and on-campus room and board charges are roughly the same. Thus, governing boards have ample reason to pay attention to room and board charges because they are a significant cost driver.

The College Board's 2018 report on college pricing tells us that between 1990–91 (when the Board began to keep track of net tuition and fees) and

2017–18, inflation-adjusted net tuition and fees at four-year public institutions on average rose 2.15 percent annually. Meanwhile, over the same period, inflation-adjusted campus room and board charges rose an average of 2.25 percent annually.[30] These percentages reflect cost increases *in excess of* increases in the Consumer Price Index.

It is legitimate for governing board members to ask why campus room and board charges should be rising 2.25 percent more rapidly on an annual basis than the Consumer Price Index. It isn't because food costs and rental costs were skyrocketing. Both costs roughly tracked the Consumer Price Index between 1990–91 and 2017–18.[31]

We believe an important reason why campus room and board charges have increased so rapidly is that institutions have been constructing (or refurbishing) ever more splendid residence halls—replete with private bathrooms, marble counter tops, upscale exercise facilities, adjacent recreation centers, and much more expansive and expensive food services. While we understand the competitive pressures that cause institutions to move in this direction, this is not a trend that board members should encourage. Indeed, they should at the very least ensure that a healthy proportion of campus residence halls offer less ostentatious, less expensive choices.

Pay Attention to Retention and Graduation Rates

In terms of tuition and fee revenues, one student who is retained for four years and graduates is the rough financial equivalent of four students who last only a single year. One obvious reason for this is that it is costly to have to recruit additional students. Further, students who leave before graduating and have accumulated debt are 28 percent more likely to default on those debts than those who graduate.[32] One can easily argue that some proportion of the financial subsidy that states provide their public campuses has gone to waste when students drop out. Thus, whether one takes the view of an individual student or that of society, there are good reasons for institutions to focus on improving their retention and graduation rates.

Trustees must acknowledge that an important—indeed, perhaps the most important—reason students drop out of an institution before graduation is that they can no longer afford to attend. Put differently, unmet financial needs loom large as a reason why students drop out of four-year public colleges and universities. This situation reflects the fact that the *net* price of attending the typical four-year public institution of higher education increased 3.08 percent faster than the annual percentage growth in the Consumer Price Index between the 2001–02 and 2017–18 academic years. Meanwhile, inflation-adjusted median household income rose at the rate of only 0.29 percent annually.[33]

The reality imparted by these numbers is difficult to escape. Most campuses have been guilty of exacerbating the affordability situation rather than improving it. As David Kirp expressed it in a challenging *Chronicle of Higher Education* op-ed, "We have met the enemy and he is us. Pogo's immortal line is dead on."[34] The enemy, unfortunately, all too often turns out to be individual campuses and their governing boards.

The challenge confronting members of governing boards is to falsify Pogo—that is, to prove his observation wrong by energetically containing costs and supporting institutional resource allocations that promote student retention and graduation. Trustees should become familiar with campuses that are using technology to give greater attention to individual students and to respond to their particular circumstances. Atlanta's Georgia State University (GSU), an ethnically diverse 34,000-student institution, supplies an excellent example. Between 2003 and 2017, GSU increased its six-year graduation rate by 22 percent, and technology played an important role in this success.[35]

Because campuses evolve in distinctive ways, what works on one campus may not have relevance on another. Even so, data sets exist that compare each institution's predicted retention and graduation rates to its actual rates.[36] Some institutions consistently exceed expectations. It is appropriate for board members to ask administrators to identify such institutions and to distill the lessons that can be learned from them.

Don't Hesitate to Use Outsiders

Fresh sets of eyes often can be helpful to board members. It is a mistake for trustees to assume they know and understand all that is before them.

Although few things in higher education are more irritating than outside evaluators and experts who are brought to a campus to share their insights but turn out to be profoundly ignorant or disrespectful of local conditions and needs, governing boards are well advised to use seasoned outside evaluators to provide them with a fresh perspective on issues and individuals. This is particularly true when it is time to evaluate their president, as we pointed out earlier.

The challenge is usually to find outside evaluators and consultants who have experience and track records—that is, people who are capable of viewing the academic enterprise knowledgeably because they themselves have large experience sets. Nevertheless, boards should not shy away from seeking the occasional advice of less-established individuals who seek to upset established academic applecarts. Those institutions that took the time twenty years ago to listen to distance-learning savants are happy today they did so.

The outside individuals we reference here are not to be confused with the corporate consultants dispatched by large national consulting firms. These individuals are usually expensive and frequently produce visually attractive reports that say little and could fit many different institutions. Our experience is that consultants' reports are often not their most valuable output. Instead, it is the conversations they have with campus personnel and board members that generate the most useful ideas and innovations.

One often finds the optimal consultant by noting the people who have been successful and innovative in their positions and by reading their past reports. National higher education associations may be the place to start this search, but talking to members of other boards and other presidents can also be fruitful. Boards should have someone search the literature on a subject to define the issues and to see who is writing or speaking about these issues. The *Chronicle of Higher Education* and *Inside Higher Education* are good places to start.

Overall, a useful consulting exercise should produce information, materials, conversations, and advice that will assist the board in performing its fiduciary duties.

Final Thoughts

Words such as "crisis" and "scandal" are often used to describe conditions in higher education today. Merely saying something is a problem does not attract much attention. Something must be labeled a crisis or a scandal in order to command the eyes and ears of a public saturated with messaging.

We too talk of crisis (though less of scandal) and argue that the societal predicament we have outlined is very real and that its solution is vitally important to the future of American democracy. In our view, states engage in risky behavior if their campuses de facto serve only some segments of society and thereby pit one group of individuals against another. If not countered, the deterioration in college access, affordability, and mobility we have described will accentuate centrifugal forces that will eventually tear apart our society.

Social and economic mobility has been declining in the United States, and the usual ladders of opportunity that Americans could climb to better themselves have become fewer in number with rungs that are farther apart. An increasing proportion of individuals with talent and promise either have no access to a ladder or have no hope of climbing one even if they find it.

We do not argue that higher education is the only cause of the distressing societal developments we have witnessed in recent decades. Fundamental changes in the world economy, including the rise of China, the internet revolution, artificial intelligence, automation, increasing urbanization, the aging of American society, challenging immigration circumstances, and even the disappearance of the American frontier, deserve mention. Nevertheless, we believe the evidence is clear—public higher education has become part of the problem rather than a reliable, significant part of the solution.

Traditionally, higher education was widely perceived as a vital link in the fulfillment of the American Dream because it provided opportunity to motivated individuals and did so at prices that ordinary Americans, even first-generation Americans, could reasonably afford. Institutions such as City College in New York City became legendary for the upward economic and social thrusts they provided to ambitious but often almost penniless individuals.

Alas, this no longer holds true on a majority of campuses. All too often public higher education now acts as an engine that promotes inequality and tightly rations opportunities, especially at its premier institutions.[37] To those who pay attention to data, this change in role and function is now visible at flagship state universities in all but a few states. When a flagship institution enrolls only 15 percent of its undergraduate student body from the bottom 60 percent of the American income distribution (as at the University of Virginia), or when African Americans constitute only 7 percent of enrollment (as at Georgia Tech, even though 30 percent of Georgians are African Americans), then one can sense societal mobility and opportunity slipping away.

Many of the prime opportunities for social and economic mobility today are to be found in jobs related to science, technology, engineering, and math (STEM). Highly visible employers such as Google and Amazon exemplify such opportunities, but many STEM-related positions can also found in more conventional engineering, statistical, and health sciences organizations as well as in government. Therefore, one might well inquire, What better way to prepare for such positions than to attend an elite, STEM-oriented flagship institution such as Clemson, Georgia Tech, Purdue, Texas A&M, or Virginia Tech? This sounds like a viable plan until one learns that only 3.2 percent of the student bodies at the first four institutions on the list come from the bottom quintile of the income distribution, while at Virginia Tech the comparable number is only 2.8 percent.[38] Opportunities exist in theory, but they may be largely illusory.

Presiding over this evolution have been public college and university governing boards. With few exceptions, trustees on these boards must approve all increases in the cost of attending the public institutions they govern. As a result, and regardless of whether or not governing boards recognize their power, they in fact serve a function similar to that of the Transportation Security Administration at an airport. To a large extent they decide who can access a seat on the higher education airplane, who cannot, and under what terms.

The record shows that governing board members have placed their stamp of approval on increases in real net tuition and fees in public higher education that have more than compensated institutions for the loss in public funding that most endured. As we have seen, the typical four-year public campus ended the 2003-04 to 2016-17 period $1,605 per FTE student better off than when it started, while the typical flagship ended up $2,711 better off.

This scenario occurred because the typical institution invoked substantial increases in tuition and fees that it did not match with comparable expansions in financial aid. Consequently, the real net prices paid by students climbed. As time passed, this pattern priced an increasing number of students out of the market for higher education and progressively altered the mix of students attending specific institutions. This change did not occur in a single year or even in a single decade. It was the result of an evolution over at least the past quarter century.

Through decision and inattention, governing boards have contributed to the stratification of individual campuses and American society. Only in a few instances do we believe this strategy to have been deliberate. But deliberate or not, the end result has been significant—stratification on the basis of income, vastly increased student debt, and reductions in social and economic mobility. This is a recipe for institutional and societal failure.

Can we reverse this course of affairs? Of course, but it will require action on the part of many different individuals and groups. Standing at the head of the line are college governing boards and their member trustees. Throughout this book, and especially in this chapter, we have outlined a variety of ways that board members can enhance their knowledge and effectiveness to better fulfill their duties as fiduciaries. More than any other group in society, governing board trustees have the ability to repair the current situation. They are centrally located and legally responsible. There is no better time for them to start than today. They need and merit support as they move in new directions. American society will be better and far more durable for it.

Notes

Chapter 1. Their Answer Is Always Yes

1. Jeffrey J. Selingo, "Americans Love Higher Education, Just Not Their Universities," *Washington Post,* July 17, 2017, www.washingtonpost.com/news/grade point/wp/2017/07/18/americans-love-higher-education-just-not-their-universities/?utm_term=.cdf09e084415.

2. Critiques from the right include Charles J. Sykes, *Fail U: The False Promise of Higher Education* (New York: St. Martin's Press, 2016) and Warren Treadgold, *The University We Need: Reforming America's Higher Education* (New York: Encounter Books, 2018), and from the left, Jennifer Washburn, *University, Inc.: The Corporate Corruption of Higher Education* (New York: Basic Books, 2005). Also see a summary of left-of-center works in Jeffrey J. Williams, "Deconstructing Academe: The Birth of Critical University Studies," *Chronicle of Higher Education,* February 19, 2012, www.chronicle.com/article/An-Emerging-Field-Deconstructs/130791. Other critiques come from a college president, Mitch Daniels, "Annual Open Letter to the People of Purdue from Mitch Daniels" (January 2018), https://www.purdue.edu/president/messages/annual-open-letters/1901-med-openletter-full.php; and from a businessman, Max Nisen, "America's Higher Education System Is Spectacularly Inefficient," *Business Insider,* October 1, 2013, https://www.businessinsider.com/most-inefficient-education-systems-2013-10.

3. Viet Thanh Nguyen, "College Admissions Are Corrupt Because Universities Are. Here's How to Fix Them," *Washington Post,* March 19, 2019, www.washingtonpost.com/outlook/2019/03/19/college-admissions-are-corrupt-because-universities-are-heres-how-fix-them/?utm_term=.f54cfaf1758e.

4. The Gallup data are summarized in Scott Jaschik, "Why Republicans Don't Trust Higher Ed," *Inside Higher Ed,* August 17, 2017, www.insidehighered.com/news/2017/08/17/new-data-explain-republican-loss-confidence-higher-education.

5. "*Consumer Reports* Partners with Reveal to Investigate the Nation's $1.3 Trillion Student Debt Crisis—What Caused It and What People Can Do about It," *Consumer Reports,* June 28, 2016, www.consumerreports.org/media-room/press-releases/2016/06/cr-survey-finds-45-of-people-who-have-left-college-with-student-loan-debt-say-college-was-not-worth-the-cost-more-than-half.

6. Moody's study and data are summarized in Kellie Woodhouse, "Closures to Triple," *Inside Higher Ed,* September 28, 2015, www.insidehighered.com/news/2015/09/28/moodys-predicts-college-closures-triple-2017.

7. Wage rates are from US Bureau of Labor Statistics, "Employment, Hours, and Earnings from the Current Employment Statistics Survey (National)," Series CES0500000008, https://data.bls.gov/timeseries/CES0500000008. Tuition and fees are from College Board, *Trends in College Pricing 2018* (New York: College Board, 2018), Table 2, https://trends.collegeboard.org/college-pricing/figures-tables/tuition-fees-room-and-board-over-time.

8. College Board, *Trends in College Pricing 2018,* Table 2. The time period here is 1992–93 through 2017–18.

9. Center for Microeconomic Data, Federal Reserve Bank of New York, "Non-Housing Debt Balance," accessed May 7, 2019, www.newyorkfed.org/microeconomics/hhdc.html.

10. Center for Microeconomic Data, Federal Reserve Bank of New York, "A Snapshot of Household Debt and Credit," accessed May 7, 2019, www.newyorkfed.org/microeconomics/hhdc/background.html.

11. Paul Fain, "College Enrollment Declines Continue," *Inside Higher Education,* May 30, 2019, www.insidehighered.com/quicktakes/2019/05/30/college-enrollment-declines-continue.

12. "Some Colleges Have More Students from the Top 1 Percent Than the Bottom 60. Find Yours," *New York Times,* January 18, 2017, www.nytimes.com/interactive/2017/01/18/upshot/some-colleges-have-more-students-from-the-top-1-percent-than-the-bottom-60.html.

13. Lest we forget, one-half of Wayne State University's governing board sued the other half in 2019 in a battle for board control. David Jesse, "Half of Wayne State University Board Sues Other Half," *Detroit Free Press,* June 27, 2019, www.freep.com/story/news/education/2019/06/27/wayne-state-university-board-lawsuit/1586495001.

14. Melissa Korn and Rachel Bachman, "When Scandals Hit Campus, College Boards Rarely Get Hurt," *Wall Street Journal,* November 9, 2018, www.wsj.com/articles/when-scandals-hit-campus-college-boards-rarely-get-hurt-1541768400.

15. Reuters, "Michigan State to Pay Out at Least $500 Million to Nassar Victims," May 16, 2018, www.reuters.com/article/us-michiganstate-nassar/michigan-state-to-pay-out-at-least-500-million-to-nassar-victims-idUSKCN1IH2WI.

16. *Chronicle of Higher Education,* "Tuition and Fees, 1998–99 through 2018–19," December 31, 2018, www.chronicle.com/interactives/tuition-and-fees?cid=wcontentgrid.

17. Net tuition here means after institutional grants have been deducted.

18. These funding data come from State Higher Education Executive Officers Association (SHEEO), *State Higher Education Finance (SHEF): FY 2018* (Boulder,

CO, 2019), https://sheeo.org/wp-content/uploads/2019/04/SHEEO_SHEF_FY18_Report.pdf.

19. American Council of Trustees and Alumni, *How Much Is Too Much?* (Washington, DC, 2017), www.goacta.org/images/download/controlling-administrative-costs.pdf. The council relied on data from the US Department of Education's Integrated Postsecondary Education Data System (IPEDS) for its estimates. All American institutions of higher education that receive federal financial support are required to make copious submissions of data to IPEDS on an annual basis. Institutions have some discretion, however, over whether they report an expenditure as instruction rather than administration.

20. Declaration of Independence, "America's Founding Documents," National Archives, www.archives.gov/founding-docs/declaration transcript. If one Googles "disappearance of the American Dream," hundreds of links pop up, each providing a distinctive view of changing conditions in American society.

21. Jeffrey Selingo, "Public University Governing Boards Oversee Multi-Billion-Dollar Operations. They Should Start Acting Like It," *Washington Post,* November 2, 2018, www.washingtonpost.com/education/2018/11/02/public-university-governing-boards-oversee-multibillion-dollar-operations-they-should-start-acting-like-it/?utm_term=.fc1b369b3225.

22. US Census, "Population and Housing Unit Estimates," www.census.gov/programs-surveys/popest.html.

23. Minnesota Office of Higher Education, "Educational Attainment Data," 2017, www.ohe.state.mn.us/spages/educ_attain.cfm.

24. SHEEO, *SHEF: FY 2018*.

25. The SHEEO does not use the Consumer Price Index for All Urban Consumers (CPI-U) to measure price changes on the grounds that the collection of goods and services purchased by colleges and universities is distinctive. Instead, it uses the Higher Education Cost Adjustment (HECA), which typically records rates of inflation that are 15 to 25 percent higher than those of the CPI-U. The HECA has received strong criticism from Andrew Gillen and Jonathan Robe, *Stop Misusing Higher Education-Specific Price Indices* (Washington, DC: Center for College Affordability and Productivity, 2011), https://files.eric.ed.gov/fulltext/ED536149.pdf.

26. Federal Reserve Bank of St. Louis (FRED), "Real Median Household Income in Minnesota," series MEHOINUSMNA672N, https://fred.stlouisfed.org/series/MEHOINUSMNA672N.

27. *Chronicle of Higher Education,* "Tuition and Fees, 1998–99 through 2018–19."

28. SHEEO, *SHEF: FY 2018*. Note, however, that SHEEO uses the Higher Education Cost Adjustment (HECA) rather than the CPI-U to compute real prices. See note 25.

29. President Blackhurst was quoted in Josh Verges, "Minnesota State University Presidents Say Tuition Freezes Aren't Working," *St. Paul Pioneer*

Press, April 17, 2018. *Chronicle of Higher Education* data do not reveal either a freeze or a reduction in tuition and fees at MSUM in recent years, except for the 2014–15 academic year, when in-state tuition and fees were reduced 5.6 percent. MSUM's sticker price tuition and fees rose 154.0 percent between the 2000–01 and 2016–17 academic years (82.4 percent in real terms). MSUM's tuition and fee increase for the 2017–18 academic year, for example, was 4.6 percent even though the state's inflation-adjusted support per FTE student for public higher education increased 0.3 percent between 2015–16 and 2016–17, and 26.3 percent over the previous five years. For funding data, see SHEEO, *SHEF: FY 2018*. For tuition and fee data, see *Chronicle of Higher Education*, "Tuition and Fees, 1998–99 through 2018–19."

30. James V. Koch, *The Impoverishment of the American College Student* (Washington, DC: Brookings Institution Press, 2019).

31. Regarding the extent and significance of geographic living-cost differentials, see Richard J. Cebula, "The Analysis of Geographic Living-Cost Differentials: A Brief Empirical Note," *Land Economics* 65 (February 1989): 64–67.

Chapter 2. Governing Boards and Economic Mobility

1. Raj Chetty, John Friedman, Emmanuel Saez, Nicholas Turner, and Danny Yagan, "Mobility Report Cards: The Role of Colleges in Intergenerational Mobility," NBER Working Paper 23618 (Cambridge, MA: National Bureau of Economic Research, 2017), www.nber.org/papers/w23618. The work of this group is now most accessible at the Opportunity Insights website, https://opportunityinsights.org/education.

2. Harvard economist Raj Chetty was one of the members of the team that published the NBER study. He directs the university's Opportunity Insights research center (https://opportunityinsights.org), which continues to look at access, affordability, and mobility issues in higher education as part of its broader focus on finding ways to move individuals and families out of poverty.

3. One should not, however, ignore the racial implications of the economic segregation of college student bodies. Consider that the Harvard University Opportunity Insights project found that almost 75 percent of the student bodies of HBCUs emanate from the lowest 60 percent of the income distribution.

4. Partners for College Affordability and Public Trust, "Trustee Votes Project—Virginia" accessed May 30, 2019, https://www.pcapt.org/initiatives/trustee-vote.

5. Harvard University Opportunity Insights, "Data: Mobility Report Cards, Table 2: Baseline Cross-Sectional Estimates of Child and Parent Income Distributions by College," https://opportunityinsights.org/data/.

6. Chetty et al., "Mobility Report Cards," NBER.

7. Lindsey Reichlin Cruse, Eleanor Eckerson, and Barbara Gault, "Understanding the New College Majority: The Demographic and Financial Character-

istics of Independent Students and Their Postsecondary Outcomes" (Washington, DC: Institute for Women's Policy Research, 2018), https://iwpr.org/publications/independent-students-new-college-majority.

8. Paul Fain, "College Completion Rates Decline More Rapidly," *Inside Higher Education*, November 17, 2015, www.insidehighered.com/quicktakes/2015/11/17/college-completion-rates-decline-more-rapidly.

9. National Center for Education Statistics, College Navigator, https://nces.ed.gov/collegenavigator/.

10. *2009 Barron's Profiles of American Colleges* (Hauppauge, NY: Barron's Educational Services, 2009).

11. Non-campus-based public institutions such as the University of Maryland Global Campus (84,000 students) also occupy this space.

12. As of 2019, Truman State University had been ranked the number-one regional state college in the Midwest twenty-two years in a row by *U.S. News and World Report.*

13. *Chronicle of Higher Education*, "Tuition and Fees, 1998–99 through 2018–19," accessed May 17, 2019, www.chronicle.com/interactives/tuition-and-fees?cid=wcontentgrid.

14. State Higher Education Executive Officers Association (SHEEO), *State Higher Education Finance (SHEF): FY 2018* (Boulder, CO, 2019), Table 4, https://sheeo.org/wp-content/uploads/2019/04/SHEEO_SHEF_FY18_Report.pdf.

15. SHEEO, *SHEF: FY 2018*, Table 8.

16. SHEEO, *SHEF: FY 2018*, Figure 3.

17. College Board, *Trends in College Pricing 2018* (New York, 2018), Figure 9, https://research.collegeboard.org/pdf/trends-college-pricing-2018-full-report.pdf. Note, however, that some argue that these cost estimates "may be wildly off base." See Ben Myers, "How Colleges Give Students a Flawed Sense of Living Costs," *Chronicle of Higher Education*, July 10, 2017, www.chronicle.com/interactives/cost-of-living.

18. Jennifer Ma and Sandy Baum, *Trends in Community Colleges: Enrollment, Prices, Student Debt, and Completion* (New York: College Board, 2016), https://trends.collegeboard.org/sites/default/files/trends-in-community-colleges-research-brief.pdf.

19. These are authors' calculations. Published work by the SHEEO reveals that between 1993 and 2018, the average real state educational appropriation per FTE student declined from $8,200 to $7,853, while average net real tuition and fee collections increased from $3,657 to $6,788. Hence, the typical institution ended up $2,584 per FTE student better off in price-adjusted terms at the end of this twenty-five-year period than it was at the beginning. SHEEO, *SHEF: FY 2018.*

20. Scholarships.com, "Federal Grants," www.scholarships.com/financial-aid/grants/federal-grants.

21. College Navigator.

22. See, for example, Catherine Jones, "How Tuition Pricing at Colleges Deepens Class Divides," *New York Times Magazine,* September 10, 2019, www.nytimes.com/interactive/2019/09/10/magazine/college-admissions-paul-tough.html?action=click&module=News&pgtype=Homepage.

Chapter 3. Who's in Charge and Does It Make Any Difference?

1. Wikipedia, s.v. "California Postsecondary Education Commission," accessed January 20, 2019, https://en.wikipedia.org/wiki/California_Postsecondary_Education_Commission.

2. Eric Kelderman, "When California Eliminated Its Higher-Ed Commission, Little Was Lost, Speaker Says," *Chronicle of Higher Education,* August 5, 2015, www.chronicle.com/article/When-California-Eliminated-Its/232165.

3. Education Commission of the States, "50-State Comparison: State Postsecondary Governance Structures," March 5, 2019, www.ecs.org/50-state-comparison-postsecondary-governance-structures.

4. Robert C. Lowry, "Governmental Structure, Trustee Selection, and Public University Prices and Spending: Multiple Means to Similar Ends," *American Journal of Political Science* 45 (October 2001): 845–61.

5. Michael K. McLendon, James C. Hearn, and Christine Mokher, "Partisans, Professionals and Power: The Role of Political Factors in State Higher Education Funding," *Journal of Higher Education* 80 (November/December 2009): 686–713; David Tandberg, Jacob T. Fowles, and Michael K. McLendon, "The Governor and State Higher Education Executive Officer: How the Relationship Shapes Support for Higher Education," *Journal of Higher Education* 88, no. 1 (2017): 110–34.

6. This is one reason why some board members find it difficult to evaluate the efficacy of tuition and fee increase proposals that have been presented to them.

7. National Center for Education Statistics, College Navigator, https://nces.ed.gov/collegenavigator.

8. A sociological perspective on the organization and operation of public higher education may be found in Mitchell L. Stevens, Elizabeth A. Armstrong, and Richard Arum, "Sieve, Incubator, Temple, Hub: Empirical and Theoretical Advances in the Sociology of Higher Education," *Annual Review of Sociology* 34 (August 2008): 127–51; and Mitchell L. Stevens and Ben Gebre-Medhin, "Association, Service, Market: Higher Education in American Political Development," *Annual Review of Sociology* 42 (July 2016): 121–42.

9. Richard Novak, "State Policies and Practices to Improve Board Governance," *Trusteeship Magazine,* September/October 2012, 34.

10. In 2018 the *Detroit Free Press* documented extensive alleged conflicts of interest involving investment practices at the University of Michigan (UM). See Matthew Dolan and Davide Jesse, "University of Michigan Pours Billions into

Funds Run by Contributors' Firms," *Detroit Free Press,* September 13, 2018, www.freep.com/story/news/local/michigan/2018/02/01/university-michigan-endowment-donor-funds/1066143001. UM invested more than $400 million in funds managed by alumni who simultaneously advised UM how to invest its money. UM has essentially shrugged off these revelations. While these well-documented episodes did not involve members of UM's elected governing board, they demonstrated the tensions that can exist when any university has business dealings with influential donors. One of the authors has been employed as a consultant by almost fifty governing boards and in the process has observed a half-dozen analogous circumstances involving governing board members. Each circumstance was acknowledged by institutional leaders, but only two led to any action by the institutions and all went unreported.

11. College Navigator.

12. State Higher Education Executive Officers Association (SHEEO), *State Higher Education Finance (SHEF): FY 2018* (Boulder, CO, 2019), Table 4, https://sheeo.org/wp-content/uploads/2019/04/SHEEO_SHEF_FY18_Report.pdf.

13. Robert A. Scott, *How University Boards Work* (Baltimore, MD: Johns Hopkins University Press, 2018).

14. This is the definition used by the National Center for Education Statistics in its oft-cited Integrated Postsecondary Education Data System, usually referred to as IPEDS. All institutions of higher education that receive federal financial aid must send copious data to IPEDS annually. These data have some quirks and should not be confused with tablets handed down from Mount Sinai. See, for example, the challenges that IPEDS has encountered in dealing with distance education: Carl Straumshein, "An Insufficient Census," *Inside Higher Education,* September 26, 2014, www.insidehighered.com/news/2014/09/26/ipeds-survey-misses-thousands-online-students-often-counts-too-many. The data, however, are widely relied upon and generally viewed as usable.

15. College Navigator.

16. See A. C. Pigou, *The Economics of Welfare* (London: Macmillan, 1932); Bruce Yandle, "Monopoly-Induced Third-Degree Price Discrimination," *Quarterly Review of Economics and Business* 11 (Spring 1971): 71–75; and Richard J. Cebula, "Market Independence and Third-Degree Price Discrimination: Comment," *Quarterly Review of Economics and Business* 20 (Summer 1980): 106–09.

17. SHEEO, *SHEF: FY 2018.*

18. Jeffrey Selingo, "Who Is to Blame for Rising Tuition Prices at Public Colleges?" *Washington Post,* October 20, 2017, https://www.washingtonpost.com/news/grade-point/wp/2017/10/20/who-is-to-blame-for-rising-tuition-prices-at-public-colleges/?utm_term=.7b3b5e70a81e.

Chapter 4. Tuition and Fees, Governing Boards, and State Financial Support

1. Jon Marcus, "Most Americans Don't Realize State Funding for Higher Ed Fell by Billions," *Hechinger Report,* February 26, 2019, www.pbs.org/newshour/education/most-americans-dont-realize-state-funding-for-higher-ed-fell-by-billions.

2. The SHEEO reports that FTE students totaled 10,205,097 in 2008 and 10,929,357 in 2018. It also reports that real state support for public higher education per FTE student fell from $8,848 to $7,853 during the same period. The mathematics are (10,205,097 × $8,848)—(10,929,357 × $7,853) = $4.446 billion. State Higher Education Executive Officers Association (SHEEO), *State Higher Education Finance (SHEF): FY 2018* (Boulder, CO, 2019), Tables 3 and 4, https://sheeo.org/wp-content/uploads/2019/04/SHEEO_SHEF_FY18_Report.pdf.

3. We use the July value of the Consumer Price Index for All Urban Consumers (CPI-U) for all of these twenty-five years.

4. The SHEEO typically makes two additional adjustments to its state funding numbers. First, it adjusts state funding to reflect the level of instruction, the argument being that one instructional mix can be more expensive than another. Second, it uses another index that reflects the average cost of living in each state. The intent of these two adjustments is to make dollars comparable across time periods and state lines. It is not clear, however, that the three SHEEO adjustments taken in sum achieve this goal. The SHEEO adjusts for price inflation using not the CPI-U, but the Higher Education Cost Adjustment (HECA), which consistently reports much higher rates of inflation for campuses than the CPI-U or the oft-cited Higher Education Price Index (HEPI). The HECA has taken heavy criticism (see Rick Seltzer, "How to Count Higher Education Costs," *Inside Higher Education,* June 28, 2016, www.insidehighered.com/news/2016/06/28/higher-education-cost-adjustment-under-fire-again), and we do not use it in the work presented in this book. Nor do we adjust for levels of instruction because such an adjustment implicitly assumes that the labor-intensive instructional model institutions currently use is optimal. This assertion is a variation of the string quartet simile, which Baumol originally popularized as at least a partial explanation for why productivity increases were so minimal in service-oriented industries, including higher education. For a more detailed discussion of this hypothesis, see chapter 7 and James V. Koch, *The Impoverishment of the American College Student* (Washington, DC: Brookings Institution Press, 2019).

5. See, for example, Peter Arcidiacono, "Ability Sorting and the Returns to College Major," *Journal of Econometrics* 121, nos. 1–2 (2004): 343–75.

6. William F. Blankenau, "Public Schooling, College Subsidies and Growth," *Journal of Economic Dynamics and Control* 29, no. 3 (March 2005): 487–507.

7. A brief but excellent summary of this evidence is contained in Kristin Blagg and Erica Blom, "Evaluating the Return to Investment in Higher Educa-

tion" (Washington, DC: Urban Institute, 2018), www.urban.org/sites/default/files/publication/99078/evaluating_the_return_on_investment_in_higher_education.pdf.

8. A recent example relating to Pell Grants is Jeffrey T. Denning, Benjamin M. Marx, and Lesley J. Turner, "Propelled: The Effects of Grants on Graduation, Earnings, and Welfare," *American Economic Journal: Applied Economics* 11, no. 3 (2019): 193–224.

9. *USA Today*, "NCAA Finances, 2016–17," https://sports.usatoday.com/ncaa/finances.

10. Here are the mathematics: $42,000,000 ÷ 19,241 undergraduates = $2,182.

11. We are not the first to find such results. Douglas Webber is one of the few other researchers to use rigorous techniques to examine the impact of state funding cuts on public college and university tuition and fees. Webber relied on a twenty-eight-year pooled cross-sectional sample of the annual tuition and fee behavior and state appropriations of 479 four-year public institutions and estimated that every $1,000 decline in state funding support led to a $257 average increase in tuition and fees. There are two potential problems with Webber's approach. First, the relationships between state funding and tuition and fees often cross fiscal years; lags exist. Individual-year observations may confuse these lags. Second, a tuition and fee increase of $1,000 in 1995 is not equivalent to a $1,000 increase in 2010. It is unclear whether Webber takes this into account. Douglas A. Webber, "State Divestment and Tuition at Public Institutions," *Economics of Education Review* 60 (October 2017): 1–4.

12. Paul Fain, "College Enrollment Declines Continue," *Inside Higher Education*, May 30, 2019, www.insidehighered.com/quicktakes/2019/05/30/college-enrollment-declines-continue.

13. The institutional net revenue numbers reported in table 4.3 are larger than those reported for the states in table 4.1 because table 4.1 includes all public higher education including community colleges and technical institutes.

14. Throughout, we use the heteroskedasticity-consistent covariance matrix correction developed by White and others. Halbert White, "A Heteroskedasticity-Consistent Covariance Matrix and a Direct Test for Heteroskedasticity," *Econometrica* 48 (May 1980): 817–38.

15. That is, nothing else is being considered except these two variables, and nothing is held constant.

16. Among many, Michael Mitchell et al., "Unkept Promises: State Cuts to Higher Education Threaten Access and Equity" (Washington, DC: Center on Budget and Policy Priorities, 2018), https://www.cbpp.org/research/state-budget-and-tax/unkept-promises-state-cuts-to-higher-education-threaten-access-and. This report concludes that "tuition increases have compensated for only part of the revenue loss resulting from state funding cuts." The evidence we present in this chapter directly contradicts this assertion.

17. We experimented first with a variable that recorded the presence of either a coordinating board or a governing board, and second with an interaction term between the two. Neither specification performed well.

18. *Chronicle of Higher Education*, "Tuition and Fees, 1998–99 through 2018–19," www.chronicle.com/interactives/tuition-and-fees?cid=wcontentgrid.

19. Education Commission of the States, "50-State Comparison: State Postsecondary Governance Structures," www.ecs.org/50-state-comparison-postsecondary-governance-structures.

20. These hypotheses are explored in Robert C. Lowry, "Governmental Structure, Trustee Selection, and Public University Prices and Spending: Multiple Means to Similar Ends," *American Journal of Political Science* 45, no. 4 (October 2001): 845–61; Michael K. McLendon, James C. Hearn, and Christine Mokher, "Partisans, Professionals, and Power: The Role of Political Factors in State Higher Education Funding," *Journal of Higher Education* 80, no. 6 (November/December 2009): 686–713; and David Tandberg, Jacob T. Fowles, and Michael K. McLendon, "The Governor and State Higher Education Executive Officer: How the Relationship Shapes Support for Higher Education," *Journal of Higher Education* 88, no. 1 (2017): 110–34.

21. Peter D. Eckel and Cathy A. Trower, *Practical Wisdom: Thinking Differently about College and University Governance* (Sterling, VA: Stylus, 2019), 12.

22. The potential relevance of such factors is demonstrated in Fabrizio Rossi, Richard J. Cebula, and James R. Barth, "Female Representation in the Boardroom and Firm Debt: Empirical Evidence from Italy," *Journal of Economics and Finance* 42, no. 2 (April 2018): 315–38.

23. National Center for Education Statistics, College Navigator, https://nces.ed.gov/collegenavigator.

24. College Navigator.

25. Harvard University Opportunity Insights, https://opportunityinsights.org.

26. Harvard University Opportunity Insights.

27. Integrated Postsecondary Education Data System (IPEDS), https://nces.ed.gov/IPEDS

28. IPEDS; American Council of Trustees and Alumni (ACTA), "How Colleges Spend Money," www.howcollegesspendmoney.com.

29. Jonathan Rothwell and Siddharth Kulkarni, *Beyond College Rankings: A Value-Added Approach to Assessing Two- and Four-Year Schools* (Washington, DC: Brookings Institution, 2015), https://www.brookings.edu/wp-content/uploads/2015/04/BMPP_CollegeValueAdded.pdf.

30. All graduation rate data were taken from the College Navigator for 2017.

31. Mark Perry, "The University of Michigan Has At Least 82 Full-Time Diversity Officers at a Total Annual Payroll Cost of $10.6M. That Would Support Full In-State Tuition for 708 Students," Twitter, December 30, 2018, https://twitter.com/mark_j_perry/status/1079564863435870208?lang=en.

32. Kevin R. McClure and Marvin A. Titus, “Spending up the Ranks? The Relationship between Striving for Prestige and Administrative Expenditures at U.S. Public Research Universities,” *Journal of Higher Education* 89, no. 6 (2018): 961–87.

33. Donna M. Desrochers and Rita Kirshstein, *Labor Intensive or Labor Expensive?* Delta Cost Project Issue Brief (Washington, DC: American Institutes for Research, 2014), https://deltacostproject.org/sites/default/files/products/DeltaCostAIR_Staffing_Brief_2_3_14.pdf.

34. Authors’ calculations from IPEDS data.

35. This category of students includes those from other countries.

36. College Navigator.

37. College Navigator.

38. College Navigator.

39. Dawn Rhodes, “Illinois Losing Even More High School Graduates to Out-of-State Colleges,” *Chicago Tribune,* March 12, 2019, www.chicagotribune.com/news/breaking/ct-met-illinois-students-college-enrollment-out-of-state-20190312-story.html.

40. The College Navigator reports that 49 percent (or 14,612) of UM’s 29,821 undergraduates in 2018–19 were non-residents. Each paid a non-resident tuition and fee premium of $34,088 annually. 14,612 × $34,088 = $498,093,856. No doubt there were financial aid and recruitment costs associated with the generation of this sum, but it is difficult not to conclude that a very large of sum of money remains after those costs have been deducted.

41. Harvard University Opportunity Insights.

42. In any case, more than 37 percent of undergraduate students who started college in 2008 transferred at least once within six years of enrolling. Paul Fain, “More Than a Third of College Students Transfer,” *Inside Higher Education,* July 8, 2015, www.insidehighered.com/quicktakes/2015/07/08/more-third-college-students-transfer.

Chapter 5. We Can Do Better I

1. Clark Kerr served as chancellor of the University of California, Berkeley, from 1952 to 1958 and president of the University of California from 1958 to 1967, when he was fired by Governor Ronald Reagan. In *The Uses of the University* (1963), Kerr coined the term “multiversity” to capture the complex expansion and evolution that was occurring in flagship state universities. Kerr warned against neglecting undergraduate students in what had become a research-heavy atmosphere. Clark Kerr, *The Uses of the University* (Cambridge, MA: Harvard University Press, 1963).

2. From Harriet Beecher Stowe, *Uncle Tom’s Cabin* (London: Low and Company, 1853).

3. *Black’s Law Dictionary*, 7th ed., ed. Bryan Garner (St. Paul, MN: West Group, 1999), 640.

4. Brett G. Scharffs and John W. Welch, “An Analytic Framework for Understanding and Evaluating the Fiduciary Duties of Educators,” *Brigham Young University Education and Law Journal,* no. 2 (2005): 158.

5. Securities and Exchange Commission v. Chenery Corp., 318 U.S. 80, 85–86 (1943).

6. Scharffs and Welch, “An Analytic Framework.”

7. Scharffs and Welch, “An Analytic Framework,” 211.

8. For discussion and analysis, see Sharffs and Welch, “An Analytic Framework,” and Kent Weeks and Rich Haglund, “Fiduciary Duties of College and University Faculty and Administrators,” *Journal of College and University Law* 29, no. 1 (2002): 53–87.

9. Dennis L. Payette, “Fiduciary Responsibility of Board Trustees and Officers in Universities and Colleges,” *Corporate Governance* 1, no. 4 (2001): 12–19.

10. Steve Dunham, “Fiduciary Duty Is the Law,” *Trusteeship* 25, no. 6 (November/December 2017), https://agb.org/trusteeship-article/fiduciary-duty-is-the-law.

11. Constitution of Virginia, art. VIII, § 9, https://law.lis.virginia.gov/constitutionexpand/article8.

12. Charles T. Clotfelter, *Big-Time Sports in American Universities,* 2nd ed. (New York: Cambridge University Press, 2019).

13. Will Jarvis, “LSU Just Unveiled a $28-Million Football Facility. The Flood-Damaged Library Is Still ‘Decrepit,’” *Chronicle of Higher Education,* July 22, 2019, www.chronicle.com/article/LSU-Just-Unveiled-a/246750.

14. *USA Today,* “NCAA Finances, 2016–17,” https://sports.usatoday.com/ncaa/finances.

15. ESPN, “LSU Athletics Donating to Academics,” September 7, 2012, www.espn.com/college-sports/story/_/id/8349529/lsu-tigers-athletics-department-donate-36m-academics. However, this was being reevaluated in 2019. Josh Auzenne, “LSU Reevaluating Fund-Transfer Policy in Which Athletics Contributes Money to Academics,” WAFB9, July 29, 2019, www.wafb.com/2019/07/29/lsu-reevaluating-fund-transfer-policy-which-athletics-contributes-money-academics.

16. *U.S. News and World Report,* “National University Rankings,” www.usnews.com/best-colleges/rankings/national-universities?schoolName=louisiana+state.

17. Jean Graves McDonald, *Changing State Policies to Strengthen Public University and College Trustee Selection and Education,* AGB Public Policy Paper 95-2 (Washington, DC: Association of Governing Boards of Universities and Colleges, 1995).

18. See, for example, William F. Blankenau, “Public Schooling, College Subsidies and Growth,” *Journal of Economic Dynamics and Control* 29, no. 3 (March 2005): 487–507.

19. Reade Pickert, "How Board of Visitors Members Get Their Seats," *Cavalier Daily,* October 19, 2017, www.cavalierdaily.com/article/2017/10/how-board-of-visitors-members-get-their-seats.

20. Politicizing a campus here means using the campus to advocate for one political party, political issue, or candidate rather than another; it is not equivalent to the holding or advocating of personal, nonviolent political positions by individual members of the campus community. Individual advocacy is permissible, if not encouraged, but in the process faculty members must take care that they do not use their classrooms for activities (political or otherwise) that are not appropriate parts of the courses they are teaching.

21. Richard Novak, "State Policies and Practices to Improve Board Governance," *Trusteeship Magazine,* September/October 2012.

22. Kellie Woodhouse, "New Push for Trustee Training," *Inside Higher Education,* July 7, 2015, www.insidehighered.com/news/2015/07/07/states-explore-required-training-university-board-members.

23. Susan D. Phillips and Kevin Kinser, *Accreditation on the Edge* (Baltimore, MD: Johns Hopkins University Press, 2018).

24. Gitta Sereny, *Albert Speer: His Battle with Truth* (New York: Knopf, 1995), 14.

25. Related to herding behavior, see Joel S. Demski, "Corporate Conflicts of Interest," *Journal of Economic Perspectives,* 17, no. 2 (Spring 2003): 51–72; and Stephen M. Renas and Richard J. Cebula, "Enron, Herding, and the Deterrent Effect of Disclosure of Improprieties," *American Journal of Economics and Sociology* 64, no. 3 (July 2005): 743–56.

26. A modern distillation of Weber's *Economy and Society* is Charles Camic, Philip S. Gorski, and David M. Trubek, eds., *Max Weber's Economy and Society: A Critical Comparison* (Stanford, CA: Stanford University Press, 2005).

27. None other than Joe Biden uttered these words. Anne Hendershott, "The Problematic Legacy of Fr. Hesburgh," *Catholic World Report,* July 2, 2013. Hendershott is one of Father Hesburgh's few critics.

28. William G. Bowen, *Boardroom: Governance by Directors and Trustees* (New York: Wiley and Sons, 1994).

29. Alice Brown, "Saving Struggling Colleges: The Role of the Board," *The EvoLLLution,* November 7, 2017, https://evolllution.com/managing-institution/higher_ed_business/saving-struggling-colleges-the-role-of-the-board/.

30. Peter D. Eckel and Cathy A. Trower, "What Boards Are Missing: Curiosity," *Inside Higher Education,* May 15, 2017, www.insidehighered.com/views/2017/05/15/boards-need-be-more-curious-be-effective-essay. For these and other of their views, see *Practical Wisdom: Thinking Differently about College and University Governance* (Sterling, VA: Stylus Publishing, 2018).

31. Eckel and Trower, "What Boards Are Missing: Curiosity."

32. Mark Bailey, *The Troublesome Board Member* (Washington, DC: National Center for Nonprofit Boards, 1996).

33. James L. Fisher and James V. Koch, *Presidential Leadership: Making a Difference* (Phoenix, AZ: American Council on Education/Oryx, 1996).

34. Paul S. Levy, "University Boardrooms Need Reform," *Wall Street Journal,* June 10, 2018, www.wsj.com/articles/university-boardrooms-need-reform-1528652211. The precipitating issue leading to Mr. Levy's resignation was his objection to the way the University of Pennsylvania treated law professor Amy Wax, whose penchant for making controversial statements relating to race has drawn strong criticism.

35. Tyler Cowen and Alex Tabarrok, *Modern Principles of Economics,* 3rd ed. (New York: Worth, 2015), 2.

36. Donald T. Campbell "Assessing the Impact of Planned Social Change," *Evaluation and Program Planning* 2, no. 1 (1979): 67–90.

37. A 2011 National Research Council study encapsulated the incentive challenge confronting governing boards when it noted that problems arise "when incentives are used with performance measures that do not adequately reflect the true value of the work that is being done." National Research Council, *Incentives and Test-Based Accountability in Education* (Washington, DC: National Academies Press, 2011), 5.

38. Richard Vedder, "Would You Buy a Used Car from a College President?" *Forbes,* July 15, 2019, www.forbes.com/sites/richardvedder/2019/07/15/would-you-buy-a-used-car-from-a-college-president/#2d6b3cd952ac.

39. William G. Bowen and Eugene M. Tobin, *Locus of Authority* (Princeton, NJ: Princeton University Press, 2015).

40. Bernard de Mandeville, *The Fable of the Bees* (1732; repr., Carmel, IN: Liberty Fund, 1988); Adam Smith, *An Inquiry into the Nature and Causes of the Wealth of Nations* (1776; repr., Chicago: University of Chicago Press, 1997).

41. For a litany of potential horrors associated with statewide governance, see Stephen Joel Trachtenberg, Gerald B. Kauvar, and E. Gordon Gee, eds., *Leading Colleges and Universities: Lessons from Higher Education Leaders* (Baltimore, MD: Johns Hopkins University Press, 2018).

42. George J. Stigler, "The Economics of Information," *Journal of Political Economy* 69, no. 3 (1961): 213–25.

43. Mark P. Keightley, *An Economic Perspective of Income Share Agreements* (Washington, DC: Congressional Research Service, July 15, 2019), https://crsreports.congress.gov/product/pdf/IF/IF11269.

44. Purdue Research Foundation, "Back a Boiler—ISA Fund," accessed January 22, 2020, www.purdue.edu/backaboiler.

45. Jason Delisle, *How to Make Student Debt Affordable and Equitable* (Washington, DC: American Enterprise Institute, 2019), https://media4.manhattan-institute.org/sites/default/files/R-0719-JD2.pdf.

46. Gottfried Wilhelm Leibniz, *Theodicy* (1710; repr., New York: Cosimo Books, 2010). Voltaire later satirized the notion of the "best of all possible worlds" in *Candide* (1759; repr., New York: Modern Library, 1959).

47. It is easy to propose that state legislatures spend more money, and we do so here. The data we believe would benefit consumers already exist on most campuses and hence would not be expensive to produce. Rather, the challenge is to determine how best to post these data in a timely fashion on websites. It would be in the best interests of state governments to ease the path toward transparency by earmarking some funding to require and support such transparency activities.

48. Adam Looney and Vivien Lee, "Parents Are Borrowing More and More to Send Their Kids to College—and Many Are Struggling to Repay," Brookings Institution, November 27, 2018, www.brookings.edu/research/parents-are-borrowing-more-and-more-to-send-their-kids-to-college-and-many-are-struggling-to-repay.

49. Institute for Women's Policy Research, "Most College Students Are Financially Independent, with Many Working and Raising Children While in School," press release, February 20, 2018, https://iwpr.org/independent-students-new-college-majority-press-release.

50. Geography Realm, "Map and List of Fortune 1000 Companies for 2018," November 13, 2018, www.geolounge.com/map-and-list-of-fortune-1000-companies-for-2018.

51. Joint Legislative Audit and Review Commission, *Addressing the Cost of Higher Education in Virginia* (Richmond, VA: JLARC, 2016), http://jlarc.virginia.gov/pdfs/reports/Rpt461.pdf, ii.

52. Joint Legislative Audit and Review Commission, *Addressing the Cost*, ii.

53. Winston Churchill in the House of Commons, June 23, 1945. Cited in Richard Langworth, *Churchill by Himself: The Definitive Collection of Quotations* (London: Ebury Press, 2008).

Chapter 6. We Can Do Better II

1. A 2018 Pew Research Center survey revealed that 61 percent of Americans believe higher education is going in the wrong direction but are far from agreement about what its direction is or should be. Scott Jaschik, "Poll: Most Americans See Higher Ed Headed in Wrong Direction," *Inside Higher Education,* July 27, 2018, www.insidehighered.com/news/2018/07/27/survey-most-americans-think-higher-ed-headed-wrong-direction; Eric Kelderman, "'Higher Education' Isn't So Popular, Poll Finds, But Local Colleges Get Lots of Love," *Chronicle of Higher Education,* May 21, 2018, www.chronicle.com/article/Higher-Education-Isn-t/243468; Karin Fischer, "Crisis of Confidence Threatens Colleges," *Chronicle of Higher Education,* May 15, 2011, https://www.chronicle.com/article/Higher-Education-in-America-a/127530?cid=rclink.

2. Jaschik, "Poll: Most Americans"; Kelderman, "'Higher Education' Isn't So Popular"; Fischer, "Crisis of Confidence."

3. Nick Anderson, "University of Alaska Crisis Eases as Governor Backs a Smaller Funding Cut," *Washington Post,* August 13, 2019, www.washingtonpost

.com/education/2019/08/13/university-alaska-crisis-eases-governor-backs-smaller-funding-cut.

4. *The Poetry of Robert Frost*, E. C. Lathem, ed. (New York: Holt Rinehart and Winston, 1936).

5. Willard Dix, "How to Rank College Ranking Sites," *Forbes,* August 29, 2018, www.forbes.com/sites/willarddix/2018/08/29/how-to-rank-college-ranking-sites/#65412c811e82.

6. James Monks and Ronald G. Ehrenberg, "The Impact of *U.S. News & World Report* College Rankings on Admissions Outcomes and Pricing Policies at Selective Private Institutions," NBER Working Paper 7227 (Cambridge, MA: National Bureau of Economic Research, 1999).

7. An excellent summary can be found in Richard V. Reeves and Eleanor Krause, "Raj Chetty in 14 Charts: Big Findings on Opportunity and Mobility We Should All Know," Brookings Institution, January 1, 2018, www.brookings.edu/blog/social-mobility-memos/2018/01/11/raj-chetty-in-14-charts-big-findings-on-opportunity-and-mobility-we-should-know.

8. The income Gini coefficient for households in the United States rose from .403 in 1980 to .486 in 2018. Federal Reserve Bank of St. Louis, "Income Gini Ratio for Households by Race of Householder, All Races," https://fred.stlouisfed.org/series/GINIALLRH.

9. Richard J. Cebula and Jerry Lopes, "Determinants of Student Choice of Undergraduate Major Field," *American Educational Research Journal* 19, no. 2 (Summer 1982): 303–12.

10. Robert E. Martin and R. Carter Hill, "Baumol and Bowen Cost Effects in Research Universities," Social Science Research Network (SSRN), March 2014, https://papers.ssrn.com/sol3/papers.cfm?abstract_id=2153122.

11. Robert Kelchen, "An Analysis of Student Fees: The Roles of States and Institutions," *Review of Higher Education* 39, no. 4 (2016): 597–619.

12. *U.S. News and World Report*, "University of Nebraska-Lincoln," https://premium.usnews.com/best-colleges/university-of-nebraska-2565.

13. University of Nebraska-Lincoln Undergraduate Catalog, 2019–2020, "French," https://catalog.unl.edu/undergraduate/courses/fren.

14. Jonathan Kramnick, "What We Hire in Now: English by the Grim Numbers," *Chronicle of Higher Education,* December 9, 2018, www.chronicle.com/article/What-We-Hire-in-Now-English/245255. See also Scott Jaschik, "The Shrinking Humanities Job Market," *Inside Higher Education,* August 28, 2017, www.insidehighered.com/news/2017/08/28/more-humanities-phds-are-awarded-job-openings-are-disappearing.

15. Emma Pettit, "Columbia Had Little Success Placing English Ph.D.'s on the Tenure Track. 'Alarm' Followed, and the University Responded," *Chronicle of Higher Education,* August 21, 2019, www.chronicle.com/article/Columbia-Had-Little-Success/246989.

16. However, a 2019 report was highly critical of many of the agreements that institutions of higher education made with off-campus distance-learning companies. Put simply, too many institutions ceded too much control and made excessive payments to off-campus providers.

17. Jeffrey R. Young, "When Colleges Consider Outsourcing Online Programs, Calculations Can Get Complicated," *EdSurge,* April 4, 2019, www.edsurge.com/news/2019-04-04-when-colleges-consider-outsourcing-online-programs-calculations-can-get-complicated.

Chapter 7. A Proposed Action Agenda for Governing Boards

1. National Center for Education Statistics, *Digest of Education Statistics,* Table 105.30, March 2018, https://nces.ed.gov/programs/digest/d17/tables/dt17_105.30.asp.

2. Federal Reserve Bank of New York, Center for Microeconomic Data, "Student Loan Debt Reaches $1.49 Trillion in the First Quarter of 2019," www.newyorkfed.org/microeconomics/topics/student-debt.

3. Annie Nova, "More Than 1 Million People Default on Their Student Loans Each Year," CNBC, August 1, 2018, www.cnbc.com/2018/08/13/twenty-two-percent-of-student-loan-borrowers-fall-into-default.html.

4. Virginia Van Natta and Alexandre Tanzi, "Paying Off Student Loans Is Taking Much Longer Than Expected," *Bloomberg,* October 12, 2019, www.bloomberg.com/news/articles/2019-10-12/paying-off-student-loans-is-taking-much-longer-than-expected.

5. College Board, *Trends in College Pricing 2018* (New York: College Board, 2018), Figure 9, https://research.collegeboard.org/pdf/trends-college-pricing-2018-full-report.pdf.

6. Robert B. Archibald and David H. Feldman have authored several articulate publications that expound this thesis, but the most complete vehicle for their views is *Why Does College Cost So Much?* (Oxford: Oxford University Press, 2011).

7. For example, see Thomas L. Russell, *The No Significant Difference Phenomenon,* 5th ed. (Chicago: International Distance Education Certification Center, 2001).

8. See James V. Koch, *The Impoverishment of the American Student* (Washington, DC: Brookings Institution Press, 2019), 186–88, for a brief discussion of this evidence, or Bryan Caplan, *The Case against Education* (Princeton, NJ: Princeton University Press, 2018).

9. Rick W. Burkett, "2018 Babson Report: Tracking Distance Education in the United States," Virtual Chalk Dust, January 6, 2018, https://virtualchalkdust.com/2018-babson-report-grade-increase-tracking-distance-education-united-states/.

10. Howard R. Bowen, *The Costs of Higher Education: How Much Do Colleges and Universities Spend per Student and How Much Should They Spend?* (San Francisco: Jossey-Bass, 1980), 20–21.

11. Koch, *The Impoverishment of the American Student,* 196.

12. Ronald G. Ehrenberg, *Tuition Rising* (Cambridge: Harvard University Press, 2000), 11.

13. Mancur Olson, *The Logic of Collective Action: Public Goods and the Theory of Groups* (Cambridge: Harvard University Press, 1965); William A. Niskanen, Jr., *Bureaucracy and Representative Government* (Chicago: Aldine, Atherton, 1971).

14. Robert E. Martin and R. Carter Hill, "Baumol and Bowen Cost Effects in Research Universities," March 2014, https://ssrn.com/abstract=2153122. For a less technical exposition, see Robert Martin and Andrew Gillen, "Breaking the Cost Spiral," *Inside Higher Education,* August 7, 2009, www.insidehighered.com /views/2009/08/07/breaking-cost-spiral.

15. *Chronicle of Higher Education,* "Tuition and Fees, 1998–99 through 2018–19," www.chronicle.com/interactives/tuition-and-fees?cid=wcontentgrid.

16. Integrated Postsecondary Education Data System (IPEDS), https://nces.ed .gov/IPEDS; Illinois State University's Grapevine, https://education.illinoisstate .edu/grapevine/.

17. David O. Lucca, Taylor Nadauld, and Karen Shen, "Credit Supply and the Rise in College Tuition: Evidence from the Expansion in Federal Student Aid Programs," Federal Reserve Bank of New York, revised February 2017, www .newyorkfed.org/research/staff_reports/sr733.html.

18. Providing compensation may require changes in state statutes.

19. Koch, *The Impoverishment of the American Student,* 235.

20. See, for example, Stephen M. Renas and Richard J. Cebula, "Investment in Human Capital and the Appropriate Discount Rate," *Social and Economic Studies* 21, no. 1 (March 1972): 61–71.

21. Patrick Callan, "Five Ways Trustees Can Help Make College Affordable," *Real Clear Education,* May 2, 2018, www.realcleareducation.com/articles/2018/05 /22/5_ways_trustees_can_help_make_college_affordable_110278.html.

22. Dave Merrill, Blacki Migliozzi, and Susan Decker, "Billions at Stake in University Patent Fights," *Bloomberg,* May 24, 2016, www.bloomberg.com /graphics/2016-university-patents.

23. Merrill et al., "Billions at Stake."

24. "Facts about Adjuncts," New Faculty Majority, www.newfacultymajority .info/facts-about-adjuncts.

25. For example, Audrey Jaeger, "Closing the Gate: Part-Time Faculty Instruction in Gatekeeper Courses and First-Year Persistence," *New Directions for Teaching and Learning,* no. 115 (Fall 2008), 39–53.

26. The "positive effects" study is David N. Figlio, Morton O. Schapiro, and Kevin B. Soter, "Are Tenure Track Professors Better Teachers?" NBER Working Paper 19406 (Cambridge, MA: National Bureau of Economic Research, 2013), www .nber.org/papers/w19406?utm_campaign=ntw&utm_medium=email&utm_source =ntw. This paper also contains a useful review of the literature on the issue.

27. Stephen Hurlburt and Michael McGarrah, *Cost Savings or Cost Shifting? The Relationship between Part-Time Contingent Faculty and Institutional Spending* (New York: TIAA Institute; Washington, DC: Delta Cost Project at American Institutes for Research, 2016), www.air.org/sites/default/files/downloads/report/Cost-Savings-or-Cost-Shifting-Contingent-Faculty-November-2016.pdf.

28. Some readers may say, "No, you can't do that." Because dollars are fungible, however, incremental funds in one area allow administrators to transfer dollars from that account to another.

29. "The College Faculty Crisis," *New York Times*, editorial, April 13, 2014, www.nytimes.com/2014/04/14/opinion/the-college-faculty-crisis.html?module=inline.

30. College Board, *Trends in College Pricing 2018*, Table 3 and Figure 10.

31. The food and beverage sub-index inside the Consumer Price Index rose an average of 0.09 percent more slowly on an annual basis between July 1990 and July 2017 than the entire Index, while the "rent of shelter" sub-index rose 0.32 percent faster. By comparison, campus room and board charges rose 2.25 percent more rapidly on an annual basis than the Consumer Price Index. Federal Reserve Bank of St. Louis, "Consumer Price Index for All Urban Consumers: Rent of Shelter in U.S. City Average," https://fred.stlouisfed.org/series/CUSR0000SAS2RS, and "Consumer Price Index for All Urban Consumers: Food and Beverages in U.S. City Average," https://fred.stlouisfed.org/series/CPIFABSL.

32. Rajashri Chakrabarti et al., "Who Is Most Likely to Default on Student Debt?" *Liberty Street Economics*, November 20, 2017, https://libertystreeteconomics.newyorkfed.org/2017/11/who-is-more-likely-to-default-on-student-loans.html?cid=6a01348793456c970c01bb09d9b1ec970d.

33. College Board, *Trends in College Pricing 2018*, Table 2, for net prices; Federal Reserve Bank of St. Louis, "Real Median Household Income," https://fred.stlouisfed.org/series/MEHOINUSA672N.

34. David Kirp, "The College Dropout Scandal," *Chronicle Review*, July 26, 2019, www.chronicle.com/blogs/letters/a-broader-picture-of-the-dropout-scandal.

35. Beth McMurtrie, "Georgia State U. Made Its Graduation Rate Jump. How?" *Chronicle of Higher Education*, May 25, 2018, www.chronicle.com/article/Georgia-State-U-Made-Its/243514.

36. For example, David Leonhardt and Sahil Chinoy, "The College Dropout Crisis," *New York Times*, May 23, 2019, www.nytimes.com/interactive/2019/05/23/opinion/sunday/college-graduation-rates-ranking.html.

37. The Opportunity Insights project at Harvard University, https://opportunityinsights.org/education, is a gold mine of data and analysis in this regard.

38. Harvard University Opportunity Insights, https://opportunityinsights.org.

Index

Page citations that end with *f* indicate a figure; with *t* indicate a table.